8045-Veterans of Gettysburg

"Isn't This Glorious!"

"Isn't This Glorious!"

THE 15TH, 19TH, AND 20TH MASSACHUSETTS
VOLUNTEER INFANTRY REGIMENTS AT
GETTYSBURG'S COPSE OF TREES

Edwin R. Root *and* Jeffrey D. Stocker

with original maps by
Richard W. Jacoby

Foreword by D. Scott Hartwig

· MOON · TRAIL · BOOKS ·

ISBN 0-9773140-0-6

Manufactured in the United States of America

Moon Trail Books, LLC
24 West Fourth Street
Bethlehem, Pennsylvania 18015

Endpapers —
15th Massachusetts veterans at the Copse of Trees during the 1898 reunion.
(From the Collections of Worcester Historical Museum)

CONTENTS

ACKNOWLEDGMENTS

Our greatest thanks is owed to the men of the 15th, 19th and 20th Massachusetts and their families, whose personal accounts echo throughout the pages of this book. Their voices have long been silent, and it is our hope that by the publishing of this work, this oversight will have at least partially been corrected.

For instilling in us our love of history, we would like to thank our parents, Edwin and Bette Root and Donald and Louise Stocker, all members of the "Greatest Generation." By their words and actions, our parents have helped us try to part the mists of the past and interpret the deeds of a more distant generation facing the greatest challenges of their lives.

A book such as this could never have been completed without the valuable help and assistance of many benevolent people and the resources of many fine institutions. A number of our friends in the Civil War Round Table of Eastern Pennsylvania, Inc., deserve special thanks. Richard Jacoby, Bonnie Fleming, Jack Minnich, Kathy Minnich and Michael Snyder spent countless hours with us combing through the pension and compiled service records of soldiers from the three Massachusetts regiments held in the National Archives. Without their efforts, many fine sources of information would have never been unearthed. In addition, fellow Round Table members Michael Cavanaugh, Jeffrey Gates, Liz Gates, Susan Kovacs, Joseph Riggs and Stephen Wright also contributed to the research process and helped locate exactly where some of the photos found in this book were taken.

We have also been blessed by the assistance of many friends who are employed by the National Park Service. These historians took valuable time away from their own projects to help answer our many inquiries, and led us to many sources that we would have never discovered without their aid. We would especially like to thank D. Scott Hartwig, supervisory park historian for Gettysburg National Military Park, for reading a draft of the manuscript and making many valuable suggestions that greatly contributed to the finished product, as well as writing the fine Foreword to this work.

Our friends Eric Campbell of Gettysburg National Military Park and Robert E. L. Krick of Richmond National Military Park also spent countless hours reading drafts of this book. Without their incisive comments and suggestions, the completed work that you see before you would have been that much the poorer.

In addition to Scott, Eric and Bobby, the following highly learned historians provided us with invaluable source material: Kathleen Georg Harrison, Greg Goodell, John Heiser, Beth Trescott and Emma Young of Gettysburg National Military Park and Donald Pfanz of Fredericksburg and Spotsylvania National Military Park. A special note of thanks is given to Greg Goodell, curator of the archives at Gettysburg. Greg uncovered many fine early photographs of the post-war monuments of the three Bay State regiments. Anyone desiring to do research involving photographs of the field of Gettysburg is doing a great disservice by not calling on Greg, who has been both pleasant and accommodating in filling our many requests.

A must in the course of any Civil War research is a trip, or several trips, to the United States Military History Institute in Carlisle, Pennsylvania. Dr. Richard Sommers and his fine staff, including Louise Arnold-Friend, Pamela Cheney and Jay Graybeal, always put the many resources of the institute at our disposal. Dr. Sommers never fails to amaze researchers with his knowledge of the Civil War and his photographic memory of where even the most obscure, but invaluable, sources are located. For their assistance, we are most grateful.

Special thanks also goes to Michael Musick, now retired, and the staff of the National Archives in Washington, D.C. Without their help, the process of navigating the potential minefield of research in the pension, compiled service, company and regimental records of the three Massachusetts regiments would have taken infinitely longer.

No author can do any kind of meaningful research without the aid of the legions of dedicated professionals who run libraries and archival repositories across the country, whose knowledge of their collections made our efforts so much easier. We wish in particular to thank the following people: Molly Cahill, Commonwealth of Massachusetts Executive Office of Health and Human Services Soldiers' Home, Chelsea, Massachusetts; Doris Chickering and Timothy Smith, Adams County Historical Society, Gettysburg, Pennsylvania; Martha Clark and Michael Comeau, Commonwealth of Massachusetts Archives, Boston, Massachusetts; Sylvia Coast, Pennsylvania Room, Franklin County, Pennsylvania, Public Library; Karen Drickamer, Penny Sites and Janelle Wertzberger, Musselman Library, Gettysburg College, Gettysburg, Pennsylvania; Kate DuVose, Massachusetts Historical Society, Boston, Massachusetts; Elisabeth Falsey, Houghton Library, Harvard University, Cambridge, Massachusetts; William Faucon, Boston Public Library, Boston, Massachusetts; Dot Griebel, Lynnfield Public Library, Lynnfield, Massachusetts; Sally Hild, Cambridge Historical Society,

Cambridge, Massachusetts; Brian Kennell, Evergreen Cemetery, Gettysburg, Pennsylvania; Gregory Laing, Haverhill Public Library, Haverhill, Massachusetts; Bob Matthias, Lynn G. A. R. Museum, Lynn, Massachusetts; Philip Metzger, Linderman Library, Lehigh University, Bethlehem, Pennsylvania; Andrew Moran and Kelly Nolin, Norwich University, Northfield, Vermont; Beverly Pelletier, Evergreen Cemetery, Portland, Maine; Jonathon Randolph, Abbot Public Library, Marblehead, Massachusetts; Alex Rankin, Howard Gotlieb Archival Research Center, Boston University, Boston, Massachusetts; Paul Sledzik, National Museum of Health and Medicine, Washington, D.C.; Tom Spitalere, Haverhill Historical Society, Haverhill, Massachusetts; and Nina Zannieri, Paul Revere House, Boston, Massachusetts.

Special thanks to Robyn Christensen for guiding us through the treasures of the Worcester Historical Museum, Worcester, Massachusetts. We would also like to express our gratitiude to Ted O'Reilly, of the New-York Historical Society, for his help and patience in providing information regarding citations from the Abner Doubleday Papers.

The following people whom we were fortunate to run across in the course of over five years of research also kept a steady stream of source material flowing to our mailboxes: Leon Basile; Bob Ducharme; Susan Harnwell; Steven Hill; Bud Livingston; Dr. Thomas and Beverly Lowry; Bob Marston; Richard Miller; Robert Mooney; Nicole Rosner; David Ward; and Steve Zerbe. Their efforts on behalf of the gallant Bay Staters have added greatly to the completed work, as did those of Michael Snyder, mentioned above, and Sally Hilgendorf List, both of whom proofread drafts of the manuscript, and by their pointed comments, saved us from much pain and embarrassment. Special thanks should also go to long-time friend David Guest and his son, Daniel, who came from their home in Hoover, Alabama, to walk the area around the Copse of Trees with us. For guiding us through a maze of computer issues, we are indebted to Emily Root and Derek Root.

At Gettysburg, just as our book was ready to go to press, we were lucky enough to meet Steven Meadow, who generously shared with us some of his photographs of members of the 20th Massachusetts Regiment.

The high-quality maps and many of the photographs found in this book are the product of many painstaking hours of work by Richard Jacoby. This publication has always been designed to put human faces on the drama which occurred on the afternoon of July 3, 1863. Dick's fine efforts have contributed mightily toward accomplishing this goal, and we are deeply grateful.

We would also like to thank Patricia N. McAndrew, principal of our publisher, Moon Trail Books, both for her expert assistance in editing the final manuscript and, most importantly, taking on this project and bringing our work to publication. Special thanks also go to Kenneth F. Raniere, for his care in designing this work.

Finally, we would like to thank our wives, Nancy Root and Marliese Walter. Not only did they endure our obsession with what happened around a small group of oak trees many years ago, they also aided us in the research process, identifying sources in many libraries and archives all around the northeastern United States. (Nancy's discovery of the unpublished John Codman Ropes map was a never-to-be-forgotten moment). Without their love, support, understanding and, finally, patience, this project never would have reached fruition.

Edwin R. Root
Jeffrey D. Stocker
"The Angle"
Gettysburg National Military Park
July, 2005

LIST OF ILLUSTRATIONS AND MAPS

MAPS

(Illustrated in 2004 by Richard W. Jacoby)

Following page 44

(53-55 From the Collections of the Worcester Historical Museum, Worcester, MA)

54. 15th Massachusetts veterans, families and friends at dedication of monument to
Colonel George Ward, June 2, 1886.

55. 15th Massachusetts veterans at Washington Street train station, Gettysburg,
Pennsylvania, June 3, 1886.

56. "High Water Mark" showing the monuments of the 15th, 19th and 20th
Massachusetts, ca. 1886. (Note: The 19th Massachusetts monument is in
its original position.)
(Gettysburg National Military Park reference #2b-123)

57. "High Water Mark" showing the monuments of the 15th, 19th and 20th
Massachusetts, ca. July, 1887. (Note: The monument to the 19th is in its
second and "correct" position.)
(57-58 Edwin R. Root Collection)

58. 15th Massachusetts monument in first position by the Copse of Trees by
Charles Tipton, ca. June, 1886. (Note: White marble bas-relief of soldier.)

59. 15th Massachusetts monument in present position. (Note: Bronze bas-
relief of soldier.)
(Edwin R. Root, 2003)

60. Colonel George Ward monument by Charles Tipton, ca. June 1886.
(Note: White marble bas-relief of Ward.)
(Edwin R. Root Collection)

61. Colonel George Ward monument. (Note: The bronze bas-relief of Ward.)
(Edwin R. Root, 2003)

62. 19th Massachusetts monument in its original position. (Note: The Cordori
Farm is in the background.)
*(Massachusetts Commandery Military Order of the Loyal Legion and the
U. S. Army Military History Institute)*

63. 19th Massachusetts in third and present position.
(Richard W. Jacoby, 2004)

64. 20th Massachusetts in present position.
(Edwin R. Root, 2003)

65. "High Water Mark" ca. 1892.
(Gettysburg National Military Park reference #3191)

66. 15th Massachusetts veterans at the Copse of Trees during the 1898 reunion.
From the Collections of the Worcester Historical Museum, Worcester, MA)

67. Plaques to the 15th, 19th and 20th Massachusetts at the Copse of Trees.
(Note: Although the order of the plaques is correct, they do not accurately
mark where the regimental monuments of the 15th and 19th regiments
originally stood.)
(Edwin R. Root, 2003)

FOREWORD

Edward Chapin, Henry Ropes, Edmund Rice, Henry Abbott, Moses Shackley . . . names that to most of us are simply names. Yet they and other men of their kind helped transform our nation, for without them the Union surely would not have been preserved and slavery destroyed in our Civil War. The men of this story represent only a tiny fraction of the mass of men the North sent to war between 1861-1865, but they are representative in many ways. They were not giants or heroes, just men who volunteered because their country called and who hoped to do their duty and return home. Some were Harvard students, others were fishermen, bookkeepers, farmers, machinists, lawyers, shoemakers, immigrants . . . they were a spectrum of the young men that the state of Massachusetts sent to war in 1861. Some 3,000 of them enlisted in what became the 15th, 19th, and 20th Massachusetts Infantry. Over the next two years the men who served in these regiments learned the cruel realities of war on the battlefields of Virginia and Maryland. Places called Seven Pines, Savage Station, Glendale, Antietam, Fredericksburg, Chancellorsville, entered the lexicon of those at home as terrible and tragic places where many of their sons and brothers, fathers and husbands, lost their lives or were crippled by wounds. Battles explained only part of the loss. Active soldiering is hard physical work. Constant exposure to the elements, poor food, or not enough food, bad water, disease, exacted a more severe toll from the ranks than did battle.

By the time these three regiments reached the small Pennsylvania town called Gettysburg in July 1863, with the rest of the Army of the Potomac, each of them was a mere shadow of what it had been in 1861. The 15th counted less than 300 men, the 19th, 160, and the 20th, 243 officers and men. Those that were left well understood the chances they ran each time they went under fire. "We have not seen the worst of this rebellion yet," wrote one of their officers only four days before the great battle of Gettysburg began. All understood that the stakes this time were enormously high. The Confederate Army of Northern Virginia had invaded the north, crossing through Maryland into Pennsylvania. If they prevailed in this showdown battle with the Army of the Potomac, no one could predict the consequences but they would be dire.

All three of these regiments served in Brigadier General John Gibbon's 2nd Division, 2nd Army Corps. They were posted on a gentle ridge that ran south from the hill that held the town cemetery. Later, someone would name it Cemetery Ridge. In the formation of the Union lines, Gibbon's men found themselves in the very center of the Federal position.

On July 2 they faced the onslaught of a Confederate offensive and held their own, although many, particularly in the 15th Massachusetts, would be counted among the army's casualties of killed, wounded and captured. But it would be on July 3 that each of these regiments would make its mark in the history of this terrible war. In a gamble for victory, Robert E. Lee launched a massive frontal assault against Cemetery Ridge to shatter the Union line asunder. The infantry assault was preceded by a two-hour bombardment. Then, nearly 13,000 infantry advanced across a mile of open ground to storm the Union defenses.

These men of Massachusetts stood tall that terrible day. This book is their story, not just of what they did to help turn back Lee's grand assault, but of what it cost them and why they never wanted subsequent generations to forget that cost. We learn something of what it meant to be a casualty in the stories of men like 19-year-old Private William Parker of the 20th Massachusetts, whose shoulder was fractured by a Confederate bullet on July 3. Parker lost his arm to amputation, and his wound took nine months to close. By the time he was discharged, Parker was a mere skeleton of a man. The army discharged him and gave him a pension of $8.00 a month. At age 26 he died, forgotten by all, save his father—a widower—and perhaps some former comrades. Now, we can happily add, the authors of this book have rescued his story and those of his comrades from the dustbins of history. In doing so, they honor Parker's memory and all of his fellow soldiers who gave so much to save their nation.

D. Scott Hartwig,
Gettysburg, Pennsylvania

PREFACE

THEY WERE VETERANS now, the men of the 15th, 19th and 20th Massachusetts Volunteer Infantry Regiments of the Army of the Potomac's illustrious II Corps, the naive days of 1861 long past. Ball's Bluff, the Peninsula Campaign, Antietam and Fredericksburg had taught these men the hard lessons of war. They had seen much and suffered greatly by the time of the Battle of Gettysburg. When the Civil War had ended and the multitude of histories about this conflict were written, all three units would be recognized for their accomplishments on the battlefield. Nineteenth-century historian William Fox, in his classic work *Regimental Losses In The American Civil War 1861 – 1865,* included the three units in the chapter, "Three Hundred Fighting Regiments"; this denoted every regiment in the Union Armies which "lost over 130 in killed and died of wounds during the war." An astounding total of more than one thousand men in these three organizations died as a result of combat or disease during the course of the armed struggle. [1]

The story of Pickett's Charge is a familiar one in American history. With hindsight and the passage of time, this event is seen by many as a gallant hope doomed to failure. However, in reality, during those tense few minutes when the Rebel tide crested on July 3, 1863, the outcome still hung in the balance. The soldiers of these three Massachusetts regiments, as well as the rest of their comrades in the Army of the Potomac, hardly thought of the assault as a forlorn hope. To them, the repulse of the Confederate attack was a close-run affair, and afterward they felt honored to have played what they believed was an important role in the climactic Federal victory.

The record forged at Gettysburg by the Massachusetts soldiers has been recounted many times since that summer day; however, it has almost always been considered as one part of a general account of the battle's climax. By the late nineteenth century, many veterans of the 15th, 19th and 20th Massachusetts did not feel that their valor and sacrifice were being properly recognized; today their individual stories are little more than footnotes to the larger-than-life image of Pickett's Charge. One historian has concluded, "A certain irony attends the fact that, in a nation that loves a winner, we remember the élan of the defeated Southerners before we recall the gallantry of the victorious Union defenders." [2]

To explain the Battle of Gettysburg fully in a tactical study is a daunting task. To tell completely the stories of all who participated would be impossible. At some point early in the battle's historiography, the role of Union troops defending the Federal center on Cemetery Ridge late in the afternoon of July 3, 1863, was consolidated into a concise account of a general overwhelming movement leading to an almost anti-climactic end. While such telescoping of action is understandable in any big-picture analysis of this event, the individual accounts of soldiers and their sacrifices made in repelling Pickett's Charge have been overshadowed by tales of the bravery of the Confederate attack.

Some examples will serve to illustrate this point. In 1897, John Vanderslice, a Union veteran and board member of the first Gettysburg battlefield preservation group, the Gettysburg Battlefield Memorial Association, published the book *Gettysburg, Then and Now*. Vanderslice described the final moments at the Copse of Trees in only two sentences. By the 1950s, Glenn Tucker's work, *High Tide At Gettysburg,* covered this action in only two short paragraphs. Edwin Coddington's masterful study, *The Gettysburg Campaign*, published in 1968, devoted a scant page out of almost 600 pages of text to the final repulse of the Confederates at the Copse of Trees. On that one page, 13 Union regiments were cited by unit, yet only two individual soldiers were named specifically. In the twenty-first century, this manner of telling the story of the climax of the Battle of Gettysburg has continued. Noah Trudeau's 2002 work, *Gettysburg: A Testing of Courage*, gives only one paragraph to the movement of the 15th, 19th and 20th Massachusetts Volunteer Infantry Regiments, as they, together with many of their Federal comrades, rushed to halt the Confederate breakthrough. [3]

History, too, as seen through the lens of memory by both veterans and historians, has tended to overlook the actions of the stalwart men from Massachusetts. Carol Reardon, in her thought-provoking study, *Pickett's Charge In History and Memory*, addressed the way in which the soldiers of various Federal units looked at their places in the legendary attack as either participants or observers. Many of the men who fought on the first two days of the battle resented that Pickett's Charge came to be the focal point of the titanic struggle; indeed, some Union veterans attempted to increase their standing in posterity at the expense of their comrades' records. In a chapter titled "Monuments to Memory," Reardon recorded and commented upon the opinions of some three dozen Federal soldiers who took part in the battle. The only reference to the 19th Massachusetts is the unfair accusation that these men "bragged" that they had been the "keystone of the Union" on July 3. No mention is even made of either the 15th or 20th Massachusetts and their roles in the contest. [4]

The cost of winning the Battle of Gettysburg should be tabulated not only in a recitation of the number of casualties, but in the price paid by the individual victors, those who were slain as well as those who suffered mutilations of the body and the mind, injuries which in many cases never healed. The following work is an attempt to add a human dimension to the action of these Massachusetts soldiers involved in countering Pickett's Charge, and to tell of the Bay State veterans' prolonged and frustrating struggle to be recognized by posterity long after the guns fell silent. It is designed to introduce the reader to private soldiers whose courageous deeds have disappeared, up until now, in the mists of the past—people such as William Moore, Benjamin Jellison and Elisha Smith. Their stories, as well as those of dozens of their comrades interspersed throughout the narrative, bring to life the Federal enlisted man's view of the desperate fighting at the Copse of Trees. This work is also intended to show what the "real" cost of winning the great battle was, when viewed in the context of the lives of the soldiers and their families at home.

One of the challenges of writing a history of events long after all the participants and their immediate descendants are dead is the necessity of relying on the words of those who were there and of having to make judgments when accounts conflict. When quoting from original source material, the authors have allowed the grammar and spelling used by the soldiers to stand unedited in order not to break the flow of the narrative.

Like all history, that of the American Civil War, when viewed as the recounting of events by fallible human beings, is not necessarily fair. Credit for success and blame for failure almost never accord with the reality of what happened on a battlefield. For some, deeds of bravery that were never witnessed or properly recorded remain shrouded in silence.

As difficult as the interpretation process may be for present-day historians, perception and reality often became blurred in recorded history, even when the Gettysburg veterans were still alive. John Bachelder, who became the battle's first historian, interviewed many of its participants within months of the event; over the succeeding years, he became more familiar with the battle and its landscape than perhaps any of the men who fought there.

Even someone with his experience realized that he did not hold all the answers to Gettysburg's puzzles. Bachelder explained his philosophy in an 1885 letter to Union Major General Winfield Scott Hancock: "It must always be borne in mind that I have no personal knowledge of events – that everything comes to me second hand, hence I must never become so fixed in an opinion that it cannot be changed where good and sufficient reasons appear to do so." [5] However, some people, past and present, have felt that John Bachelder, in his zeal to present the battlefield to visitors in an "organized" fashion, did not exactly live up to his creed in all cases. He was accused of being arrogant and intractable in his battlefield preservation philosophy, traits that ultimately had a negative impact on the men of the three Massachusetts regiments. [6]

When the veterans returned to the fields of Gettysburg, they found the landscape altered. In 1885, General Hancock recalled his impressions of the battlefield during a visit he made shortly after the conflict had ended: "The 'avenue' passing through the right of the Vermont position and leading up towards the position pointed out as that occupied by the 19th Mass. and 42nd New York, has evidently cut off and disposed of some timber and underbrush there, running along the eastern side of the 'avenue.' In 1866 and especially on the day of the battle, there was a fringe of sparse undergrowth with occasional individual trees leading up towards the position of the 19th Mass., and heading about that point. That undergrowth and some of the trees are now missing, although some isolated trees are still standing." [7]

Obviously, as the years rolled by and the landscape continued to change, it became more difficult for most of the surviving veterans to remember exactly what had occurred during the battle and where events had taken place. The resulting errors of memory, in some cases, drastically affected the placement of their regimental monuments on the field. (In response to a question one of the authors addressed to his own father, concerning his memory of places encountered during his war service, this World War II veteran replied that he "wasn't there as a tourist.") The men who fought at Gettysburg had more important things on their minds than remembering the exact location of every rock and tree.

The story we are about to tell is deliberately narrow in scope; it chronicles the activities of only a small percentage of the gallant and determined men who fought during those three deadly days in July 1863. It is not intended to be a regimental history of the 15th, 19th and 20th Massachusetts; nor is it designed to be yet another narrative of the entire story of Pickett's Charge. However, this work has a larger significance when the human element is considered, both in the desperate fighting itself and in the post-war monumentation process.

The desire to see one's service recognized and the sacrifice of one's comrades remembered by future generations is a feeling shared by almost all veterans, no matter what the era. The reader should bear in mind that the men from the Bay State had experiences in common with their comrades in the Army of the Potomac. As the years passed, veterans from most Union units who fought at Gettysburg returned to the battlefield to commemorate the service of all and the sacrifice of many.

This book had its genesis in 1993. Members of the Civil War Round Table of Eastern Pennsylvania, Inc., based in Allentown, Pennsylvania, worked through the National Park Service and funded the re-installation of iron battlefield markers to the 15th, 19th and 20th Massachusetts Regiments near Gettysburg's Copse of Trees, where the monuments once stood. In June 2000, the authors conducted a Round Table-sponsored tour for the organization's members, so that they could see the results of their preservation effort. The research involved in preparation for this visit led us to many little-known or seldom-used sources, including dozens of participants' accounts found in hundreds of pension records at the National Archives. Our journey of discovery has evolved into the volume you see before you. In many aspects, this compelling story has never been told before.

In identifying the errors (as the Massachusetts veterans, at least, considered them) made in the post-war memorialization process, it is not the the authors' purpose to have the three Massachusetts regimental monuments moved back to their original 1885-1886 locations near the Copse of Trees. Our desire is to have the actions of the soldiers of the 15th, 19th and 20th Massachusetts in the fighting on July 3, 1863 properly interpreted, in order to do full justice to these gallant men. Their conduct on that bloody day deserves nothing less.

⊷⟐ ⎯⎯ ⟐⟞

PART ONE

THE WAR YEARS

1

From Massachusetts to the Field of Gettysburg
July 12, 1861 to the Morning of July 3, 1863

he 15th Massachusetts Volunteer Infantry Regiment was formally mustered into the service of the United States on July 12, 1861, at Camp Scott in Worcester, Massachusetts. With an original enrollment of 1,011 officers and men, its membership, recruited primarily from Worcester County, came from diverse walks of New England life. Farmers, factory and mill workers as well as men from a multitude of other occupations representing the full spectrum of nineteenth-century Massachusetts society rushed to join the Union army. [1]

On October 21, 1861, the regiment was first bloodied at the Battle of Ball's Bluff, Virginia, where it lost 44 members killed and mortally wounded. The unit's total loss on that dismal day was 302. During the 1862 Peninsula Campaign, another 10 men of the regiment were killed or mortally wounded. At the Battle of Antietam, fought on September 17 of that year, 318 of the 15th's 606 soldiers engaged became casualties; an appalling 98 of these were fatalities. In the December 1862 Fredericksburg Campaign, another 5 men of the regiment lost their lives. [2]

At the Battle of Gettysburg, the veteran 15th Massachusetts was part of Brigadier General William Harrow's First Brigade of Brigadier General John Gibbon's Second Division of Major General Winfield Scott Hancock's II Corps. This Corps, some 12,300 strong, had arrived on the field of Gettysburg late on the evening of July 1, 1863, after several weeks of punishing marches northward from Virginia through clouds of dust and enervating heat and humidity. They, together with the rest of their comrades in the Army of the Potomac, had followed the invading Confederate Army of Northern Virginia into Pennsylvania from the war-torn area around Fredericksburg, Virginia. Many of the men felt that the fate of the nation would be determined by the outcome of the next fight, and events proved that they fought accordingly. [3]

The II Corps's initial position was south of Big Round Top, where the men were posted to protect the left of the Union army. After "a good supper & a comfortable sleep," the II Corps was moved toward the army's right-center early on the morning of July 2. Hancock's men were massed in a reserve position behind the main Union line, facing the Federal right flank. They remained in this deployment for close to an hour, when orders were received to move to the front line. [4]

Occupying a line almost a mile in length from north to south, Hancock's troops took position on Cemetery Ridge, a southern extension of Cemetery Hill. This hill, the location of the town burying ground, was the main rallying point for the battered remnants of the Union I and XI Corps, as they fell back from their tactical defeat suffered on the northern and western outskirts of Gettysburg on July 1. Two brigades of General Gibbon's division were positioned on both the north and south sides of a small clump of oak trees, forever after known as the Copse of Trees, in the left-center of the Federal army. (In October 1863, there were "50+ oaks," as counted by a visitor to the battlefield. The trees were described as generally no more than two inches wide, and covered a larger area than that surrounded by today's iron fence.) Some of Gibbon's men were deployed behind a low stone wall, which ended just south of the Copse of Trees on Cemetery Ridge. This wall had been built by the local farmers, and was used as a boundary marker between the various tracts of land. Where the stone wall ended, a wooden fence ran along the rest of Gibbon's line, providing dubious shelter to the troops. To Gibbon's right was the Third Division of the II Corps, and the corps's First Division was stationed on his left. The men spent the balance of the morning of July 2 resting, waiting for something to happen. [5]

Late that afternoon, Colonel George H. Ward led the 15th Massachusetts into battle against Brigadier General Ambrose Wright's brigade of Georgians. Wright's brigade, consisting of the 3rd, 22nd and 48th Georgia Infantry Regiments and the 2nd Georgia Infantry Battalion, was moving toward the main Union line on Cemetery Ridge. The Georgians' advance was part of the Army of Northern Virginia's famous en echelon attack, designed to roll up the Army of the Potomac's left flank upon its center. This attack had been launched by two divisions of the Confederate First Corps against the Union left, positioned near Little Round Top and Devil's Den. The onslaught then spread to the Federal left-center, where men from the Rebel Third Corps, including Wright's Georgians, pushed forward. In this assault, the Georgia brigade numbered approximately 1,450 officers and men. In contrast, almost two years of active service had greatly reduced the 15th Massachusetts' numerical strength, so only 18 officers and 221 men were present in the unit's ranks that day. [6]

A native of Worcester, where he worked as a machinist, the 37-year-old Ward had been a brigadier general in the ante-bellum Massachusetts State Militia. He had been appointed lieutenant colonel of the 15th on July 24, 1861. One of his men recalled that Ward's reputation in the unit was that of "a stern disciplinarian if not *severe* [emphasis in original]." At Ball's Bluff, he had been shot in his left leg and ankle; this caused such damage that the limb had to be amputated. On April 29, 1862, while still recovering from his wound, Ward was promoted to the rank of colonel. With the aid of a prosthesis, Ward returned to command of the 15th in the spring of 1863 after a long convalescence. On June 27, 1863, Colonel Ward told his family, "We have not seen the worst of this rebellion yet, and I almost shudder at the thought of what we are to pass through before the struggle is over, but I still trust and believe that things will come out well. . . . One thing is certain, our men will fight much better with their faces turned homeward." [7] These words would prove to be prophetic for Ward and many of his comrades.

At approximately 4:00 p.m. on July 2, just before the fighting began on the Union army's left flank, General Gibbon ordered the 15th, together with the 82nd New York Volunteer Infantry Regiment (also of General Harrow's brigade), deployed in an attempt to support Major General Daniel Sickles' III Corps. That morning, the two units, along with the rest of Harrow's brigade, had been placed in a reserve position below the crest of Cemetery Ridge. The men had stacked their muskets and were resting, when they received the command to move to the front. [8]

In a controversial maneuver hotly debated to this day, General Sickles, on the early afternoon of July 2, had moved his corps, on his own volition, to advanced positions forward of the main Union battle line on Cemetery Ridge; he felt this was better, more defensible ground. Unfortunately, the III Corps did not have a sufficient number of men to either anchor the left of its line on Little Round Top, a prominent terrain feature south of Cemetery Ridge, or to connect its right to the II Corps line. Therefore, the III Corps's position took the form of a salient, vulnerable to attacks from the south, west, and north, a situation the Confederates were quick to exploit. [9]

Sickles' rash decision precipitated the movement of the 15th Massachusetts and 82nd New York to the extreme front. In his official report, General Gibbon stated, "At 4 o'clock the Third Corps advanced, and, swinging round its left flank, took up a position along the Emmitsburg road. To give support to its right flank, I ordered forward two regiments of Harrow's brigade, to occupy a position along that road and to the right of a brick house."[10]

In compliance with these orders, the 15th Massachusetts and 82nd New York were stationed behind flimsy breastworks just north of the Nicholas Codori farm buildings along the Emmitsburg Road, the "brick house" referred to in General Gibbon's report. The breastworks, approximately two feet high, were composed of rails hurriedly torn from the post and rail fences lining both sides of the road and piled up by the New Yorkers and New Englanders. The position of the two units was roughly 340 yards west of the main II Corps line on Cemetery Ridge. It was very exposed and vulnerable on both flanks, since the closest Union unit, Major General Andrew Humphreys' division of the III Corps, was deployed several hundred yards south of the farm, and no Federal troops were in place on the road to the north. [11]

According to an officer of the 15th, the regiment was in this advanced location for only "about half an hour" before being attacked by Wright's Georgians. Six 12-pounder Napoleons of Battery "B", 1st Rhode Island Light Artillery, commanded by 20-year-old First Lieutenant T. Frederick Brown, fired at the advancing Rebels from their positions on a small rise of ground and rocky outcropping behind the infantrymen's right flank. These guns had advanced to this forward position, also on General Gibbon's orders, to attempt to give a measure of support to the 15th's right flank. (This hillock is located half-way between the Codori House and the Copse of Trees.) [12]

Men began to drop in the 15th, not only from the fire of Confederate artillery and the charging Georgians, but also from canister fired by the Federal cannon behind them. "Our artillery threw grape and canister which, no doubt, was intended to go over our heads; but a good share of it struck our regiment," a private in the 15th recalled. "One discharge of canister from our own guns wounded the captain of Company E [Albert Prince, a 23-year-old former shoemaker from Oxford, Massachusetts, wounded in the left hand], the orderly sergeant [James Mahoney, aged 21, a fireman from Westborough, Massachusetts, hit in the head and legs] and a private of my own company." [13]

Just before General Wright's Georgians struck the 15th, Colonel Ward dismounted and began walking behind the line of his men, holding a sword in his right hand and a large cane in his left. Three weeks earlier, on June 12, Ward had written home, "I shall fight if I get a chance, that is certain; nothing but my leg will stop me. I can ride anywhere anyone can, but if we are obliged to go where horses cannot, I shall be obliged to stop. I am in for it, and shall take the chances." [14]

The 15th was deployed in an untenable position, since the Emmitsburg Road was sunken below the level of the fields west of the road, thereby limiting the visibility of the men lying behind the breastworks. Almost before they knew it, the Georgians were upon them. Private Roland Bowen, Company B, a 26-year-old factory worker from Millbury, Massachusetts, described the initial contact: "They sprang forward with that demoniac yell wich is peculiar to themselves only, at the same time giving us a deadly volley. Now it was our turn. With a shout we sprang upon our knees and resting our muskets over the rails, we give them one of the most destructive volleys I ever witnessed. They hesitated, they reeled, they staggered and wavered slightly, yet there was no panic. As fast as we could get powder and lead into our guns we sent it at them. They returned the compliments pretty effectually." [15]

The Confederate assault overlapped the Union line on the Emmitsburg Road and threatened to envelop it. The Georgia brigade struck the 82nd New York first, exploiting the large gap on its left. Two of the 82nd's companies had been deployed around the Codori buildings, facing south, to try to protect the unit's flank, but they were quickly swamped. Under heavy pressure, the entire New York regiment broke. [16]

With its left flank now exposed and also under a frontal attack, the 15th Massachusetts fell back, pursued closely by Wright's men. In some places, hand-to-hand fighting occurred between the Georgians and the men from Massachusetts. The Bay State stalwarts' tenacity impressed an officer in the 15th: ". . . a score or more of the gallant men seeming to be resolved, standing as they were in battle on loyal soil, not to retreat, resolutely stood their ground along the road, loading and firing until enveloped by the enemy, and those who survived were taken prisoners." A soldier in the 15th considered it a disgrace to run. "I was very much excited and raved like a madman, and am sorry to say, took a good many oathes wich I will omit here, declareing that we would never leave the fence for any such sett of villions as these was," he later wrote. [17]

The commanders of the 82nd New York and the 15th Massachusetts both lost their lives as a result of the fighting on July 2. Lieutenant Colonel James Huston of the 82nd, 42 years of age and a native of New York City, fell mortally wounded to Rebel fire. Shot in the head and leg, Huston was taken to a Federal field hospital where he died later that day. [18]

Realizing that the 15th Massachusetts was being overwhelmed, Colonel Ward gave an order for the regiment to retire. No sooner had he done this than he was shot in the back of his right leg. Ward could stand, but was unable to walk. Helpless, he was carried by two of his men to a field hospital in the rear, where he was made as comfortable as possible. George Ward died at 4:30 a.m. on July 3. He left behind his widow, Emily, and six-year-old and two-year-old sons, George and Robert. The family received a pension of $34.00 per month from the Federal government. George Ward was buried in Worcester on July 8, 1863. [19]

Another officer noted that the withdrawal also caused "some disorder" in the ranks. At least 28 enlisted men from Ward's regiment were classified as missing; most of them were actually captured. According to the 15th's official report, the unit also "lost a large number, killed and wounded," including several men shot down as they fled across the open field back to the main Union line on Cemetery Ridge. [20]

One of those hit in the chaotic retreat was Sergeant Edward F. Chapin of Company H, a 23-year-old student from Whitinsville. He had enlisted in the 15th Massachusetts from Harvard University in August 1862. In a letter to his mother on July 8, 1863, Chapin recalled, "The [82nd] New York Regiment, on our left, was flanked by the Rebels, and fell back. The Fifteenth followed them, and then the men began to fall. We had to cross an open, level plain about three hundred yards wide before reaching any place of shelter. While crossing this the enemy were advancing and pouring into us a heavy fire. I fell just about ten yards from the wall, on the back of the field. . . . The first ball struck me in the right knee and brought me to the ground. As I lay there, another struck me again in the right knee and passed out at the same place as the first one. A spherical-case shot entered my left thigh and hip about an inch and a half from the joint. . . ." Despite the amputation of his right leg, Chapin died in a Baltimore hospital on August 1. [21]

The 82nd New York, which entered the fighting 394 officers and men strong, suffered 153 casualties in this action. In addition, four of Brown's six guns were temporarily captured, and the battery lost 22 men killed, wounded and missing, including Lieutenant Brown; he himself was shot in the neck and severely wounded. [22]

As darkness began to fall, the Confederates were finally repulsed by Federal counterattacks. The 15th initially reformed behind the Union artillery line on the crest of Cemetery Ridge, and later that night was moved forward into the front line. The morning of July 3 found the depleted regiment, together with the rest of Harrow's units, in position along Cemetery Ridge, some distance southwest of the Copse of Trees. [23]

After Colonel Ward had been mortally wounded, Lieutenant Colonel

George Joslin took command of the battered regiment. Born in 1839, Joslin had worked in a dry goods store in Worcester before the war and served as a lieutenant in the state militia. On August 5, 1861, he was mustered into the 15th as the original captain of Company I. On September 17, 1862, Joslin had been wounded in his right wrist at the Battle of Antietam. After his recovery, he was promoted to the rank of major on November 13, 1862, and then to lieutenant colonel on April 17, 1863. [24]

As a result of the unit's participation in the July 2 fighting, probably no more than 160 officers and men were present in position on the left of Harrow's brigade. Several of those remaining in the ranks of the 15th had been wounded in the day's action, but stayed with the colors, determined to see the battle to its conclusion. [25]

The first volunteers of the 19th Regiment of Massachusetts Volunteer Infantry arrived at Camp Schouler in Lynnfield, Massachusetts, on July 23, 1861. Over one-half of the unit's ten companies had been recruited from the city of Boston and its environs. With 1,090 officers and men in its ranks, the 19th received its state flag on August 28, 1861, and departed from Boston Common amid great pomp and circumstance for the grand adventure that lay ahead. Many campaigns and battles followed; these transformed the regiment into a highly respected, but greatly diminished, fighting force. During the Peninsula Campaign, at the Battle of Glendale, fought on June 30, 1862, 33 men in the unit were killed or mortally wounded. The fighting in the West Woods at Antietam on September 17, 1862, added 25 more to that Roll of Honor. Less than three months later, on December 11, the 19th, together with the 7th Michigan Volunteer Infantry Regiment, forged across the Rappahannock River in pontoon boats in the van of the Army of the Potomac's assault on the town of Fredericksburg. By the time that horrific campaign ended, another 29 comrades had "crossed over the river" in the mortal sense.[26]

Colonel Arthur F. Devereux commanded the 160 officers and men of the 19th Massachusetts during the Battle of Gettysburg. Devereux had been with the regiment since its inception; he had been mustered in with the rank of lieutenant colonel on August 1, 1861. The unit belonged to Colonel Norman Hall's Third Brigade of General Gibbon's division of the II Corps. [27] As previously stated, the II Corps had reached the battlefield late on the evening of July 1, and took position on Cemetery Ridge before the fighting began on July 2.

Born in 1836, the 5'8" tall Devereux was a native of Salem, Massachusetts. In his youth, he had attended the United States Military Academy at West Point, the Lawrence Scientific School, and Harvard University. Prior to the outbreak of hostilities, he worked as a civil engineer, manufacturer and bookkeeper. In the late 1850s, Devereux lived for a time in Illinois, where he served as an adjutant in a state National Guard unit and developed a proficiency in drill. When he moved back to Salem in 1860, he was given command of the Salem Light Infantry, a Massachusetts militia unit. Devereux's skill on the drill field and his strict standards of discipline stood him in good stead; he made the 19th Massachusetts "always noted for its drill and precision of movement." In recognition of his leadership abilities, in the fall of 1862, Arthur Devereux had been promoted to the rank of colonel, dating to November 29 of that year. However, Colonel Devereux had contracted "swamp fever" in the 1862 Peninsula Campaign; this plagued him periodically and sometimes made it necessary for him to resort to crutches and even be conveyed in an ambulance in order to remain with his troops. In addition, at the Battle of Antietam, Devereux was struck on his right wrist by a spent ball, which caused a severe contusion, but did not affect his ability to command. [28]

Sometime after 5:00 p.m. on July 2, on General Gibbon's orders, Colonel Hall sent the 19th Massachusetts and 42nd New York, both under Colonel Devereux's command, about 200 yards to the southwest of their initial position near the clump of small oak trees on Cemetery Ridge. Their mission was to help stem the Confederate tide overwhelming Major General Humphreys' division of the III Corps positioned along the Emmitsburg Road south of the Codori farm buildings. (The movement of these two veteran II Corps regiments to an ultimately untenable location was yet another consequence of General Sickles' ill-advised advance earlier that afternoon.) The New Yorkers and Bay Staters were accompanied by a III Corps staff officer, also sent by Colonel Hall. As Humphreys' men began to give way, Devereux asked the aide to explain the mission and to indicate where his men should form. "[The staff officer] answered, 'In support of the Humphrey's division.' I pointed out to him how useless to attempt to form a support for a division with two small regiments, numbering but 290 men together, and when that division was so much broken and fleeing in such confusion. He gave me no satisfactory answer, and at that moment galloped off." [29]

In an account written almost 15 years after the battle, Colonel Devereux remembered ". . . reaching [a] little swale, lined with willows, [where] we met the First Minnesota [Volunteer Infantry Regiment of Harrow's brigade], beaten back and badly handled by the enemy." However, in his official report dated July 7, 1863, Devereux stated that the 19th advanced "... a distance of perhaps an eighth of a mile from where we started . . ." and mentioned encountering only General Humphreys' III Corps troops. The Plum Run thicket, where the 1st Minnesota made its gallant stand, is much farther to the southwest than an eighth of a mile from the 19th's starting point on Cemetery Ridge. It is clear from an analysis of the terrain, Colonel Devereux's contemporaneous official report, and accounts from the Minnesotans themselves that the 19th Massachusetts and 42nd New York never advanced to a location where they would have encountered them. The Bay Staters and New Yorkers were in fact deployed in the field west of the present-day monuments to the Second Vermont Brigade, of the Federal I Corps, on the crest of Cemetery Ridge. [30]

In some confusion, General Humphreys' men fell back toward Cemetery Ridge, closely pursued by the Confederates. As the Federal fugitives passed through his ranks, Colonel Devereux, thinking quickly, ordered the two regiments to form behind a small knoll, with the 42nd New York on the right and the 19th Massachusetts on the left. Devereux then commanded both regiments to fire several volleys and retire almost immediately, as the Rebels had advanced some distance past both flanks. The 42nd led the retreat, with the 19th close behind, covering the withdrawal. Despite the precipitous nature of the retreat, Colonel Devereux stated that both units fell back "in good order," in marked contrast to the men of Humphreys' division.[31]

Private Charles Preston of the 19th's Company B, an 18-year-old fisherman from Salem, later described the unit's movements on the late afternoon of July 2, as well as the circumstances of his wounding: "[M]y regiment was in line of battle and we were ordered to charge and after making the charge at the 'noll' we were ordered to lay down, after which we had orders to retreat and at the time we rose up to make the retreat I was hit in the 2nd finger of my left hand. The general engagement had just commenced - the pickets having been driven in, and the shot came from the enemy in front of us, whose heads we could just see." [32]

Twenty-six-year-old Corporal Cornelius Linehan of Company F, a former painter from Charlestown, Massachusetts, writing to his father on July 17, vividly pictured the confusing and terrifying situation in which the men of the 19th found themselves: "On the right the order was given to fall back which I did not hear. I stood were I was, loading and fireing. My attention was taken up by the fellows in front of me and I never noticed the Johnnies coming down on the right of me; when I did there was the blue flag, the red cross-bars and white stars and grey coats. . . . I had to run right in front of their whole line, and such a shower of bullets as they aimed at me; I could compare it to nothing but a hail storm, and they yelling at me to halt, but . . . I escaped that shower." [33]

Private Benjamin Jellison had enlisted at age 15 in the 19th's Company C in July 1861 from his hometown of Georgetown, Massachusetts. During the 1862 Peninsula Campaign, he had suffered a gunshot wound to his chin. At Gettysburg, Jellison's company was assigned the duty of being the color company of the regiment. Private Jellison was given a battlefield promotion on the afternoon of July 2 to the rank of sergeant in recognition of his having picked up one of the regimental flags from the fallen color sergeant, Charles Rowe. A 25-year-old Boston lamp-lighter, Sergeant Rowe had dropped the banner when he was shot in the left leg. When Rowe fell, his advancing comrades of the 19th rushed over his prone figure. In the confusion, some one stomped on his right wrist and fractured it. The diminutive Jellison, who was only 5′ 3″ tall, carried the flag for the rest of the fight; he would be heard from again the next day. [34]

A pre-war civil engineer and native of Cambridge, Major Edmund Rice of the 19th, aged 20, commanded a line of about 70 men designated to act as a rear guard to cover the retreat of the Bay Staters and New Yorkers. Rice, who stood 5′ 8″ tall, had attended Norwich University in Northfield, Vermont, from 1856 to 1859, but never graduated. Major Rice was a veteran officer who had enlisted in the regiment on July 25, 1861, as captain of Company F. Renowned in the regiment for his "coolness and bravery," he had sustained a flesh wound in his right thigh from a canister round at Antietam. [35]

The close-quarter nature of the fighting is shown by the fact that while commanding the rear guard, Major Rice discharged the entire contents of his revolver, a weapon effective only at extremely short range. Somehow, the thin Federal detachment was able to hold off the Confederate onslaught long enough to enable the rest of the 19th Massachusetts and the 42nd New York to retire behind the crest of Cemetery Ridge. Other Union reinforcements subsequently were able to stem the Rebel tide and stabilize the line. [36]

Orders were later received from an officer on Colonel Hall's staff to reform on the brigade line on Cemetery Ridge, where the tired men finally arrived at 2:00 a.m. Casualties for the 19th in the fighting on July 2 were at least two men killed or mortally wounded, three officers and an unknown number of enlisted men wounded and two men taken prisoner. The 42nd New York lost 15 officers and men in this action, including three soldiers who were killed.[37]

Colonel Devereux noted that due to the 19th's having to fall back quickly to avoid being surrounded, many of the unit's casualties suffered wounds to their backs. To clear up any possible misconception, Devereux later asserted, "I consider no men could have been put to a severer test of true courage, thorough discipline and absolute confidence in themselves and their officers, and this regiment should receive the credit for it." [38]

The 20th Massachusetts Volunteer Infantry Regiment was one of the most famous of all the organizations that served in the Army of the Potomac. Many of its officers came from notable and influential New England families. In fact, the unit was popularly known as the "Harvard Regiment," as 31 men on its rolls, including many members of the officer corps, had either attended or were affiliated with that university. By the time the war was over, 18 of its officers had given their lives for the Union cause and no other Massachusetts regiment had lost more men killed in battle. [39]

Somewhat understrength for a standard Union regiment recruited at the beginning of the war, on September 4, 1861, with approximately 800 officers and men, the unit left Camp Massasoit in Readville, Massachusetts, where it had formed that July, and left by rail for the seat of war. Arriving in Washington D.C., the 20th initially encamped at Camp Kalorama on Georgetown Heights, some two miles outside the city. Action came quickly to the raw regiment; at the Battle of Ball's Bluff, 38 were killed in action or died of wounds. Total casualties for the regiment at this Federal disaster, including the many men who were captured, were 281.

The unit then accompanied the Army of the Potomac on the 1862 Peninsula Campaign, losing over 90 men killed, wounded and missing in the Seven Days' Battles. The 75th anniversary of the signing of the United States Constitution was passed while serving in Major General John Sedgwick's division at Antietam, where another 20 men died in the sanguinary fighting in the West Woods. On December 11, 1862, the 20th was part of the force that fought its way along the darkening streets of Fredericksburg to clear the town in preparation for the main Union attack two days later. The combat was street-to-street, block-to-block, and even house-to-house. The terrible fighting during the Battle of Fredericksburg proved fatal to 48 soldiers from the regiment. [40]

The 20th, now only 243 officers and men strong, arrived at Gettysburg on the morning of July 2, 1863, led by 30-year-old Colonel Paul J. Revere, a native of Boston and a grandson of the "Midnight Rider." Revere was a large man for his time, standing slightly over six feet tall. After graduating from Harvard University in 1852, he had worked as an agent in Boston. Revere had enlisted in the 20th Massachusetts with the rank of major on July 1, 1861. He was captured at the Battle of Ball's Bluff and subsequently spent several months in Rebel prisons. After his exchange, Revere served for a long time on the II Corps staff. Therefore, when he took command of the 20th in May 1863, Colonel Revere had very little combat experience, and had never led a regiment in battle. A fellow officer wrote: "[Revere is] more ignorant than any non-commissioned officer in my company of drill & the most ordinary internal arrangements of a regiment. [A]ll but the barest official intercourse will be refused him, & . . . he will be left . . . to howl & snarl out ridiculous orders until he gets publicly kicked out for shameful ignorance & inefficiency." [41]

However, by showing his fortitude in being able to endure the arduous series of marches to the battlefield of Gettysburg, Colonel Revere was able to regain the respect of his troops. Shortly after the battle, that same officer of the 20th stated: "All our pique against Revere too had long ceased, since we saw him on the march struggling so nobly with his physical weakness. . . ." [42]

Also part of Colonel Hall's brigade on July 2, the 20th Massachusetts, according to a captain in the regiment, was placed in the "second line all day, lying down . . . ," just south of the Copse of Trees. As the regiment was deployed behind other Federal units of Hall's brigade, the men were subjected to Confederate artillery overshots, while not being able to return fire. Some 30 soldiers of Companies D and G were sent forward as skirmishers, "several hundred feet in advance" of the main body of the unit. The skirmish line was stationed in the field east of the Codori house, and may even have been west of the Emmitsburg Road for a time, before being driven in by the attack of Ambrose Wright's Georgians. This detachment was commanded by Captain Henry L. Patten of Company D. Patten, aged 27, was a Harvard graduate and a former college professor from Cambridge. [43]

By late afternoon, the rest of the regiment was positioned in support of Lieutenant Brown's remaining cannon of Battery "B", 1st Rhode Island Light Artillery, along the crest of Cemetery Ridge. These pieces, along with the 15th Massachusetts and the 82nd New York, had all come tumbling back after being overwhelmed by Wright's Georgians. Brown's cannon had hurriedly withdrawn directly through the prone line of the 20th Massachusetts. Two of the guns were then stationed barely six feet in the rear of the 20th, so close that a number of Massachusetts men were burned by the muzzle blasts as the pieces fired on the Confederate advance. Despite this frightening situation, the regiment remained steady. In his official report, Colonel Hall praised the 20th for its steadfastness under these trying circumstances: "Had not this portion of the line, which was not yet joined on its left by re-enforcements, stood firm, the interval [to the south] would at least have been greatly increased and the result might have been incalculably disastrous." [44]

In war, the presence of artillery commonly draws counter-battery fire; this instance was no exception. At roughly 6:00 p.m., what was most likely Confederate case shot exploded in mid-air and struck Colonel Revere in the lung, mortally wounding him. Revere had stood up to give an order to his men, who were lying down in front of Brown's two guns, when he was hit. The colonel was taken to a temporary field hospital behind Union lines, where he was treated by the regimental surgeon. He was then transferred to the main Union supply base at Westminster, Maryland, where better medical facilities were available. Upon his arrival, Revere was able to send a short telegram to his family, which read, "Am badly wounded at Westminster, come quickly." Unfortunately, Paul Revere died on July 5, 1863, before any family members were able to reach his side. [45]

Approximately 20 men in the 20th Massachusetts, including at least 10 of the skirmishers, were killed or injured in the fierce fighting against the Georgians and from being struck by artillery fire. The casualties included Captain Patten and 26-year-old First Lieutenant Charles Cowgill of Company G, a pre-war carpenter from Dover, Delaware. Both Patten and Cowgill were wounded while serving on the skirmish line. [46]

Another man in a leadership position with the 20th wounded on the skirmish line was Sergeant Gustave Magnitzky of Company G. He was a 23-year-old immigrant from Prussia, who had worked as an iron moulder in Boston prior to his enlistment. A regimental officer described Magnitzky as being " . . . quiet and steady under fire, quiet and effective in camp, modest, distinguished in bearing and soul. . . ." While contesting the Confederate advance, Sergeant Magnitzky was shot in his left foot and fell to the ground. Caught in no man's land by the skirmishers falling back before the advancing Confederates, Magnitzky crawled to the shelter of the Codori house. When darkness fell, he was able to make his way back to the Union lines. At a field hospital the next day, the second and third toes on Gustave Magnitzky's left foot were amputated. [47]

When the day's fighting had ended and the lines were reformed, the armies paused to catch their breath and make plans for renewing the contest on the morrow. The air was still during the balance of the night, and the men of all three Massachusetts regiments slept, or at least tried to rest. Some of the men never got anything to eat and slept on empty stomachs. In the quietude, an officer of the 19th recalled easily hearing the clock of the Gettysburg courthouse, located over one mile from his position, sound three o'clock. [48]

Charles Devens

George H. Ward

15th Massachusetts Volunteer Infantry Regiment

George Joslin

David Earle

15th Massachusetts Volunteer Infantry Regiment

Hans Jorgensen   **John Murkland**

15th Massachusetts Volunteer Infantry Regiment

Edward Russell   **George Rockwood**

15th Massachusetts Volunteer Infantry Regiment

Elisha Buss   **Henry Dudley**

15th Massachusetts Volunteer Infantry Regiment

Thomas Hastings   **Amos Plaisted**

15th Massachusetts Volunteer Infantry Regiment

John Marsh, Jr.

George Boss

15th Massachusetts Volunteer Infantry Regiment

Arthur Devereux

Ansel Wass

19th Massachusetts Volunteer Infantry Regiment

Edmund Rice

Herman Donath

19th Massachusetts Volunteer Infantry Regiment

William Hill

Sherman Robinson

19th Massachusetts Volunteer Infantry Regiment

Moses Shackley   **John G. B. Adams**

19th Massachusetts Volunteer Infantry Regiment

George Patch

19th Massachusetts Volunteer Infantry Regiment

Paul Revere

George Macy

20th Massachusetts Volunteer Infantry Regiment

Henry Patten

Herbert Mason

20th Massachusetts Volunteer Infantry Regiment

Herbert Mason, Henry Patten   **Henry Abbott**

20th Massachusetts Volunteer Infantry Regiment

Henry Ropes   **Charles Cowgill**

20th Massachusetts Volunteer Infantry Regiment

William Perkins

Charles Peirson

20th Massachusetts Volunteer Infantry Regiment

Sumner Paine

John Summerhayes

20th Massachusetts Volunteer Infantry Regiment

Gustave Magnitzky

20th Massachusetts Volunteer Infantry Regiment

Nathan Haywood

20th Massachusetts Volunteer Infantry Regiment

2

To the Copse of Trees

July 3, 1863 to July 5, 1863

As dawn broke on July 3, Colonel Hall's brigade was positioned just south of the Copse of Trees. General Harrow's brigade continued the line further south. The four regiments of the last brigade of Gibbon's division, led by Brigadier General Alexander Webb, lay to Hall's north, both in front of and behind the trees. [1]

All four regiments of Harrow's brigade, their ranks reduced by the many casualties sustained the previous day, were stationed along the front line that morning. Facing the Confederate lines, from left to right, the formation was the 15th Massachusetts, 1st Minnesota, 19th Maine and the 82nd New York. The four Parrott rifles of Battery "B", 1st New York Light Artillery, commanded by 26-year-old Captain James Rorty, were in place on the crest of the ridge behind the brigade, near where Harrow's and Hall's brigades joined. The 15th was stationed approximately 235 yards southwest of the present- day High Water Mark monument, which is located just east of the Copse of Trees. [2]

The 19th was the smallest of the three Massachusetts regiments in position at the center of the II Corps line. Reduced from its original pre-battle strength of 160 officers and men by the losses of July 2 (which were not specifically delineated in the post-battle reports), the regiment held the second line of Hall's brigade just behind the crest of Cemetery Ridge; to the unit's right was the 42nd New York. The two bodies of troops, still operating in concert as a demi-brigade under the orders of Colonel Devereux, were positioned to the south of the Copse of Trees, and were posted approximately 70 yards behind Colonel Hall's front line. [3]

Twenty-three-year-old First Lieutenant Walter S. Perrin had assumed leadership of Battery "B", 1st Rhode Island Artillery from the wounded Lieutenant Brown. The battery was now reduced to four Napoleons; the fifth and sixth pieces had been sent to the rear after the fighting ended on July 2, because of the loss of so many men and horses. The remaining guns were stationed in the supporting line to the right of the 42nd New York. [4]

The 20th Massachusetts was now commanded by Lieutenant Colonel George N. Macy. The 26-year-old Macy, standing 5' 9" tall, with a sandy complexion and thinning brown hair, had been born in Nantucket and was a mortgage banker working in Boston before the war. On July 10, 1861, he had enlisted as a first lieutenant in the 20th's Company I, and had fought in most of the regiment's battles over the past two years. His latest promotion, to the rank of lieutenant colonel, had occurred on April 4, 1863. [5]

Colonel Revere's mortal wound gave Macy control of the unit's 200 or so soldiers who had survived the previous day's fighting unscathed and stayed with the colors. During the night, the men shared a single shovel with their comrades of Hall's brigade, preparing a "slight rifle pit" roughly one foot deep in preparation for whatever the next day might bring. As veteran infantrymen, the soldiers had learned the value of digging in, and they needed no orders to do so on this occasion. One of the officers of the 20th said that the men were more protected by "a little rut" they were lying in than by the excavated ground, which was piled to a height of approximately one foot in front of the rifle pit, that he called "too thin to stop anything more than a spent ball." Having been moved forward after the fighting ended on July 2, the regiment was now positioned as the left unit of Hall's front line, with the 7th Michigan to its right and the 82nd New York of Harrow's brigade to its left. Hall's last unit, the 59th New York Volunteer Infantry Regiment, was stationed to the right of the 7th Michigan. All of Hall's regiments were also reduced in numbers by the losses sustained on July 2. [6]

Although the prior day's fighting had caused a change of command in two of the three Massachusetts regiments, they were still led by battle-hardened officers. In fact, Joslin and Macy had experienced more combat in the prior two years than both Ward and Revere. All three men had been officers in their respective regiments since, at the latest, August 1861. George Joslin had commanded the 15th for several months earlier in 1863, before Colonel Ward had returned to the unit, and was deemed responsible for the regiment's "good state of discipline and feeling." In addition, Arthur Devereux had officially commanded the 19th for the past 10 months, since the previous colonel had been wounded at the Battle of Antietam, and had recently even served on the brigade staff. Also, Macy had led the 20th for various periods in the past several months in Revere's absence, including during the Battle of Fredericksburg. [7]

In addition to the numerous casualties sustained in the previous day's combat, each regiment had upwards of 50 other men not present that day.

They were absent due to illness, detached duty, or had fallen out on the arduous series of marches to the field of Gettysburg. In one of his final letters to his family, Colonel George Ward of the 15th Massachusetts described the effect that the heat and dust encountered on these marches had had on his men: "I never saw anything like it, men dropped like sheep. They would go as long as they could stand and then fall. They threw away their clothing, overcoats, blankets, undercoats." The 20th's Colonel Revere also related the trials the men in the ranks had to endure. "The whole march has been extremely severe, the heat and dust intolerable," he sympathized. "I have never seen so much unfeigned suffering during the war. In not a few cases the men fell dead by the side of the road. The conduct of the troops was beyond all praise."[8]

One of the men of the 19th Massachusetts who had given out was 27-year-old Sergeant Charles Brown of Company G, a lawyer from Cambridge and a Harvard graduate. During the Battle of Fredericksburg, Brown heroically had picked up a set of the fallen colors of the 19th under a fierce fire and planted them in advance of the regimental line, despite sustaining a wound in the head. As the Federal army marched north in June 1863, Sergeant Brown was sent to a hospital in Philadelphia, suffering from fever and rheumatism. Valiant soldiers like Charles Brown would be sorely missed in the coming battle. [9]

In the ranks of the 20th Massachusetts, 34-year-old Private Franklin B. Murphey, a pre-war sailor from Nantucket, served in Company I. Murphey had been wounded in his left knee at the Battle of Antietam. Despite not fully recovering from his wound, Murphey returned to duty in March 1863. In June, however, he was admitted to a hospital in Fairfax, Virginia, with "chronic rheumatism." Also of Company I, Private Josiah F. Murphey, 21, a Nantucket grocery clerk before the war, became ill on the march to Gettysburg and was admitted to a hospital in Alexandria, Virginia, with typhoid fever. Private Leander D. Hamblin, a 21-year-old butcher from Watertown, Massachusetts, and 25-year-old Private Andrew J. Lane, a sailor from Sandwich, both members of Company H, had deserted during the night of June 30, 1863. Two other men of the 20th, 19-year-old Private Eugene Sullivan of Company F, a Boston tailor, and Company E's Private Peter Monaghan, a 19-year-old blacksmith from the same city, fled from the ranks of the unit just prior to its going into action on July 2. Finally, Company I's Private Charles H. Raymond, 25 years of age and a Nantucket caulker by profession, had actually deserted during the fighting on that day.[10]

Fortunately, some men who had fallen out on the march to Gettysburg rejoined their units in time to participate in the battle. A soldier of the 15th Massachusetts remembered this testing of nerve: "One of the men of the regiment, about the middle of the day [July 1], seemed to have become demented. He lost all control of himself, cried like a child, and shook as if struck with death. And the captain of his company told a sergeant to take a man with him and take the poor fellow out of the ranks and a little way into the leafy woods that bordered the road and to stay with him a little while, do for him what they could and then leave him to come on when able. He was true blue. It seemed to have been a case of temporary nervous collapse. He recovered and soon joined us." The man described was Corporal John Butters, of Company H, a 22-year-old farmer from Brookfield, Massachusetts. Butters overcame his fears and fought gallantly with the 15th in all its actions until May 12, 1864, when he was mortally wounded at the Battle of Spotsylvania. [11]

Another who dropped out of the ranks of the 15th Massachusetts during the July 1 march was Private William Moore of Company G, a 22-year-old machinist from New Worcester. A veteran of almost two years' service, Moore had been plagued by chronic diarrhea since the 1862 Peninsula Campaign. The heat and overexertion on July 1 caused a severe intestinal attack and Private Moore was given permission to fall out and rest by the roadside. He caught up with the regiment on the morning of July 2 and was struck by a piece of shell in his left leg below the knee in the fighting that afternoon. Despite his illness and wound, William Moore decided to remain with his comrades, a decision that would have fateful consequences. [12]

The stone fence in front of the line occupied by portions of General Gibbon's division was generally no more than two feet high. In places rails were positioned along its top. A wooden fence began where the stone fence ended just south of the Copse of Trees. The men tore it down and made a crude breastwork with the rails. In some locations, the troops filled knapsacks with dirt and piled them up for additional protection. The ground was rough and rocky, which prevented the digging of deep entrenchments. On the morning of July 3, as they stirred and stretched their stiff limbs, one participant described the tired, campaign-worn soldiers as ". . . an army of rag-gatherers." The soldiers did their best to get comfortable. Some sheltered themselves from the sun by placing blankets or pieces of tent over muskets driven into the ground at bayonet point. Comfort did not come easy since unburied Confederates and bloating, dead horses from the previous day's fight were a constant reminder of past events and harbingers of things to come. The rising temperature added to their unease. [13]

During the early morning hours the sound of battle ebbed and flowed from behind them on Culp's Hill, on the extreme right of the Federal line. [14] Intermittent cannon fire also sounded along the Cemetery Ridge line as the Confederates tried to suppress Union skirmishers between the two armies, and Federal artillery responded. In this desultory cannonade, three limbers were hit and exploded in First Lieutenant Alonzo H. Cushing's Battery "A", 4th U.S. Artillery, stationed just north of the Copse of Trees. [15]

The struggle for control of the Bliss family's house and barn, located west of the Emmitsburg Road between the lines, also drew artillery fire from both sides. In the 20th Massachusetts, First Lieutenant Henry Ropes, a native of Boston, commanded Company K. He was an exceptional young officer, capable of leading his men in combat and yet caring for them before and after those horrible moments of death and destruction. Ropes had been in the vanguard of the regiment's fight in the streets of Fredericksburg. In his letters home after that dismal battle, he asked his family to look after and help those unfortunate members of his company who had fallen victim to illness or enemy fire. Ropes came from a privileged family. His brigade commander, Colonel Hall, said that Henry Ropes was the only man he knew in the army who fought for purely patriotic motives. A staff officer in the II Corps called him " . . . a most estimable gentleman and officer, intelligent, educated, refined, one of the noble souls that came to the country's defense. . . ." An officer in the 20th wrote that in the fighting on July 2, Henry was "conspicuous for his perfect courage . . . exposing himself to [the] terrible fire of shot & shell . . . in order to inspire the same confidence in the men which he himself appeared to feel." [16]

On the morning of July 3, Lieutenant Ropes was resting with his men, reading a newspaper, near the Union guns as they sparred with the gray artillery. Around 9:00 a.m., one of those especially tragic moments of war occurred. A shell from Captain Rorty's Battery "B", 1st New York Light Artillery, exploded as it left the cannon's mouth. Henry Ropes' chest was pierced by shell fragments, inflicting a mortal wound. At least one other man in his company was wounded by this "friendly" fire. Some said Henry blurted, "I am killed" as he was hit. By this point in the war, almost anyone who had seen combat had become hardened to its cruelty. However, in this instance, as men gathered around the body of Henry Ropes, some wept. An officer later wrote, "Never before has this regiment, in the death of any officer, received one-half so heavy a blow." Henry Ropes, Harvard Class of 1862, was twenty-four. He had seen more than 20 months of service since his enlistment in November 1861. [17]

After the firing ceased, men along the Union line settled in and sweltered as the temperature continued to rise. (A civilian in Gettysburg recorded it as being 87 degrees at 2:00 p.m. that day.) Throughout military history, war has always involved a great deal of waiting, and July 3, 1863, was no exception. As previously stated, some tried to erect shelters to shield them from the sun's rays. By 11:00 a.m., all became quiet as the fighting on Culp's Hill ended in favor of Union arms. [18]

Around this time, General Gibbon was ordered to dissolve his divisional Provost Guard and send the men back to their regiments. During an engagement, the Provost Guard was normally stationed behind the main line of battle, in order to prevent able-bodied men from fleeing the fighting. The guard was composed of men detached from all the regiments in Gibbon's division, and each of them was known to be reliable under all circumstances. One of these soldiers was 23-year-old Private Timothy Dugan from Company F of the 20th Massachusetts. A native of Boston, Dugan had plied his trade there as a seaman prior to the war. On receiving Gibbon's orders, the Provost Guard took their places with their original units at the front and waited expectantly for something to happen. [19]

The comparative tranquility was disturbed shortly after one o'clock by the firing of a Confederate cannon from the southwest. After a pregnant pause, another report was heard. [20]   Everyone present seemed to have his own opinion as to where the initial missiles struck and what damage had resulted from them. The regimental historian of the 19th Massachusetts indicated that the first shot ". . . came bounding diagonally over the ridge, like a rubber ball." A second lieutenant in the 19th, John G. B. Adams, a 22-year-old shoemaker from Groveland, Massachusetts, who had been wounded on the previous day, said that the first shell passed over where he lay in a field hospital in the Union rear. [21] Another former shoemaker, 20-year-old Second Lieutenant Sherman Robinson of Company A, who had enlisted from his home town of West Newbury, had been enjoying something to eat when he stood up at the sound of the Rebel artillery. While wiping his mouth, Robinson was hit below the left shoulder by the second shot and blown to pieces. [22]

These first two shots caught everyone's attention. Most men tried to make themselves as thin as possible as they hugged the ground. An officer in the 20th Massachusetts later described the feelings of the Union soldiers: "We are all of us pretty well steeled against the musketry fire, but artillery had by no means lost its terrors. . . ." An estimated 150 cannon erupted all along the Confederate artillery line west of the Emmitsburg Road; this fire was answered by Federal artillerists along Cemetery Ridge. It is worth noting that as the barrage began, a Rebel shot struck some of the stacked Enfield rifle muskets in the ranks of the 19th Massachusetts. [23]

For almost two hours, smoke and death flew between the opposing armies, as the Rebel guns tried to soften the Union infantry positions along Cemetery Ridge and drive away its supporting artillery, with the Federal cannon responding. The Confederate plan was to spread terror, confusion and destruction in the ranks of the defenders through an overwhelming artillery barrage, followed by an infantry assault on the Union left-center which would lead to a decisive breakthrough. Before the war, Federal division commander John Gibbon had commanded a battery in the United States Army. In his post-war recollections, General Gibbon, with the eye of a trained artillerist, described the cannonade: "The thunder of the guns was incessant, for all of ours had now opened fire and the whole air seemed filled with rushing, screaming and bursting shells. The larger round shells could be seen plainly . . . , but the long rifled shells came with a rush and a scream and could only be seen in their rapid flight when they 'upset' and went tumbling through the air, creating the uncomfortable impression that, no matter whether you were in front of the gun from which they came or not, you were liable to be hit." [24]

A man in the 15th Massachusetts had a similar impression of the bombardment: "We were at the front line lying upon the ground while the artillery duel was being fought and many shells were exploding near our line. . . . The shells were exploding and falling in all directions." In the ranks of the regiment, a solid bolt from a Confederate rifled piece struck the ground in front of where a soldier lay. The impact flung him skyward while passing beneath him. He landed on the other side of the unit's second line ten feet away, without a scratch but very dead. [25]

In his official report written eight days after the battle, Colonel Joslin stated that only two men in the 15th were wounded during the long barrage. However, a careful review of the available pension records at the National Archives reveals that at least four men in the regiment were wounded in the cannonade. These men were Sergeant Carlton DeLand of Company F, a 24-year-old former printer from West Brookfield, Massachusetts, 28-year-old Sergeant John Knight, a scythe-maker from Greenville, Massachusetts, Private Edwin Goulding, a 19-year-old mechanic from Worcester, and Company K's Private Thomas Brown, a 22-year-old factory operator from Blackstone, Massachusetts. Both Sergeant Knight and Private Goulding served in Company D. Sergeant DeLand was struck by shell fragments in his right hip and leg, and spent the next year in military hospitals. Pieces of an exploding shell hit Sergeant Knight in his right arm near the shoulder, rendering him unfit for further duty that day. Another shell burst over the prone figure of Private Goulding, tore off his cartridge box and most of his clothing and caused severe bruising and contusions to his back and hip; he was hospitalized until September 1863. Private Brown was struck by a solid shot in his left foot; this necessitated the amputation of his leg above the ankle at a field hospital the following day. [26]

Ten days later, Sergeant William B. Hoitt, aged 33, of Company I of the 19th Massachusetts, a Boston printer, remembered the cannonade from his vantage point: "The shot and shell, for two hours, rained over and down upon us like hail stones. In the first place, I was keeled over by a shell bursting along side of me. When I came to myself I was astonished to find that I still lived." The 19th's regimental historian described the cannonade as ". . . one grand raging clash of ceaseless sound—the most terrific cannonading of the war. The woods in front seemed lined with flame and smoke. Pandemonium broken loose was zephyr to a cyclone in comparison." One of the men wounded by the fire of the Rebel guns was Lieutenant Colonel Ansel D. Wass, who, at 5' 11", was one of the tallest men in the unit. Wass, a 30-year-old Boston bookkeeper, was described by an opinionated fellow officer as "a rowdy with a dyed mustache whose great act is to tell vulgar stories . . . " Lieutenant Colonel Wass was forced to leave the field when a Rebel shell burst just over his head, close enough to tear off his shoulder-straps and cause contusions to his neck and back. [27]

Another man wounded in the cannonade was Private Andrew Goodwin, Company B of the 19th, a 26-year-old illiterate farmer from Maine. A Rebel shell exploded over Goodwin's head. A piece of the shell went through his neck and entered his left arm above the elbow, while another fragment smashed the head of Goodwin's left shoulder and fractured his clavicle. Private Goodwin, who was also suffering from a rupture at the time, was borne from the field by Private Samuel Halliday of Company H, thereby costing the 19th the services of yet two more men at this critical time. [28]

In a letter to his father dated July 6, 1863, Captain Henry Abbott of the 20th Massachusetts' Company I, the 21-year-old Lowell native wrote that the Confederates " . . . began the most terrific cannonade, with a converging fire of 150 pieces, that I have ever heard in my life & kept it up for 2 hours, almost entirely disabling our batteries, killing & wounding over half the officers & men & silencing most of the guns. The thin line of our division against which it was directed was very well shielded by a little rut they lay in & in front of our brigade by a little pit, just one foot deep & one foot high, thrown up hastily by one shovel, but principally by the fact that it was very difficult to hit a single line of troops, so that the enemy chiefly threw over us with the intention of disabling the batteries & the reserves which they supposed to be massed in the rear of the batteries, in the depression of the hill." The regiment's official report stated "4 or 5 men" were lost by this fire. [29]

As the prime target of the cannonade, the Union II Corps artillery " . . . was almost annihilated . . . ," in the words of a man in the 20th. Describing the gallantry of the artillerymen, Colonel Hall later reported, "I cannot suffer this opportunity to pass without paying just tribute to the noble service of the officers and men of the batteries that served within my sight. Never during the war were so many batteries subjected to so terrible a test. Horses, men and carriages were piled together, but the fire scarcely slackened for an instant so long as the guns were standing." [30]

Men in both Rorty's and Perrin's batteries fell as individual cannon were disabled. According to a man from the 15th Massachusetts who had been previously detached to serve in the Rhode Island battery, "[T]he smoke was so dense around the guns that it was almost impossible to see the men working [them.]" The 19th's Colonel Devereux provides further details,: "Rorty's battery, behind which I lay, lost all its officers and many men, and for the last hour of the cannonade, I manned the battery with men from my own regiment, bringing ammunition from the caissons, and furnishing all the help possible from infantry troops." [31]

Captain John Reynolds, also of the 19th, later wrote that five horses and two drivers from Rorty's battery fell dead directly in the midst of the prone ranks of the regiment. In normal position, Union artillery pieces were placed about seventeen yards apart. Obviously, a closer alignment would have jeopardized too many guns, men and horses, especially in such heavy fire as this. [32]

As the cannonade continued, many men became accustomed to the constant noise and smoke. Some actually rested and dozed. In many cases it was more dangerous behind the front line than on it. The wounded Lieutenant Adams described the scene behind the slope of Cemetery Ridge: "When the shelling opened nearly all of the non-combatants were at the front, and they now made the best time possible to get out of danger. I lay near a gateway, where they passed. Down would come a pack mule loaded with cooking utensils sufficient to start a stove and tin-ware store; then a lot of colored servants, or a runaway horse. I would shout and kick; was sure that I should be either killed by a shell or trampled to death. Would beg some skedaddler to get another, and take me away. He would stop, look on me with pity and say he would, but before he could capture another, a shell would come along, and his place be vacant." [33]

As Rorty's cannon heated from the constant work, water to cool the barrels became a priority. A pre-war native of South Danvers, Massachusetts, 20-year-old Second Lieutenant Moses Shackley of the 19th's Company B grabbed a bucket and survived the 400-yard trek to the rear to obtain the precious liquid. Upon returning he told the men, "The water is cold enough, boys, but it's devilish hot around the spring." Jests from a man who had just had a cannon ball strike harmlessly between his feet drew cheers from his admiring comrades. [34]

With the Empire State artillerymen suffering more and more losses, men were needed to keep the guns firing. As previously stated, soldiers from Colonel Devereux's regiment either volunteered or were "volunteered" by their officers to repair broken wheels, haul ammunition to the cannon or man the pieces. A total of 26 officers and men from the unit aided Rorty's battery; six of them carried ammunition while 20 helped man the guns. Lieutenant Shackley, who apparently had not had enough excitement, told Color Sergeant Benjamin Jellison to join him at the guns as "we might as well get killed there as here." Devereux eventually ordered the sergeant to return to his flag. The courageous Shackley remained with the guns, "walking from piece to piece, encouraging and assisting the men," amid the terrible fire of the Rebel cannon. As men were disabled, those still able to walk were seen gingerly making their way to the rear. [35]

Both Perrin's Rhode Island and Rorty's New York batteries were damaged severely. Only three Napoleons remained in service in the Rhode Island battery, all the officers were down, and many cannoneers disabled. With ammunition nearly gone, the battery was withdrawn. In the New York battery, both Rorty and First Lieutenant Albert S. Sheldon, his second in command, were hit by Rebel fire. Captain James Rorty would later die of his wound. Almost nothing but short-range canister was left in the limber chests. [36]

From the time the Confederate bombardment ended to the present day, the effectiveness of the cannonade has been hotly debated. Certainly, the Union II Corps batteries positioned around the Copse of Trees sustained heavy losses in both men and equipment, and had their combat efficiency greatly reduced. It is also clear from a study of the pension and/or compiled service records of men from Hall's and Harrow's brigades that more Federal troops were lost in the artillery barrage than has been commonly cited, even in the official reports written by participants themselves shortly after the battle. Nevertheless, the Union soldiers who remained unscathed were still steady, determined to hold their positions to the last.

As the cannon fire started to slacken and the remnants of the Rhode Island battery displaced to the rear, at approximately 3:00 p.m., the nine Confederate brigades assigned to the assault prepared to move forward into legend. [37]

The units that would have a direct impact on the fate of the three Massachusetts regiments were three Virginia brigades comprising a division led by Major General George Pickett. As the Confederates advanced toward Cemetery Ridge, from the perspective of the Union defenders, Brigadier General Richard Garnett's regiments were on the right of the first line, Brigadier General James Kemper's brigade was to the left and Brigadier General Lewis Armistead's men were in the second line behind Garnett. Although Pickett's men were veterans, they had not seen action in the prior days' fighting. Since the division was fresh, it was designated as the spearhead of the attack. However, the Federal counter-battery fire during the cannonade had taken its toll on the hunkered-down Confederates. Reports of their casualties ranged between three and five hundred men, out of the total divisional strength of approximately 6,200 effectives. All of these losses occurred before the first step was taken toward Union lines. [38]

Depending on where a Federal soldier was posted, he could actually see the Rebels as they advanced from the woods on Seminary Ridge. Men shouted, "Here they come! Here they come! Here comes the infantry!" Every Union battery that still had solid shot, shell, and case shot opened as the Rebel formations came into view. As the Confederate skirmishers preceding the main lines of battle approached, Union skirmishers stationed west of the

Emmitsburg Road fired and retreated, repeating the process as they fell back toward the main line of resistance on Cemetery Ridge. [39]

Describing the remorseless Confederate tide heading toward him, Colonel Hall later wrote, "The perfect order and steady but rapid advance of the enemy called forth praise from our troops, but gave their line an appearance of being fearfully irresistible." Another officer in Hall's brigade termed the sight ". . . this never to be forgotten scene, rarely witnessed even once in a lifetime." [40]

When Pickett's Virginians reached the Emmitsburg Road, some 200 to 300 yards from General Gibbon's position, the Federal infantry line became a sheet of flame, smoke and death, and the beautiful Rebel lines began to break apart. (The fencing along both sides of the road, at least in front of most of Gibbon's line, had been torn down by the men from the 15th Massachusetts and 82nd New York the previous afternoon.) The surviving Confederates leaned into the Union fire and pressed forward while two large Vermont infantry regiments from the Federal I Corps—the 13th and the 16th—stationed to the immediate south and slightly to the west of Harrow's brigade, moved forward and pivoted north to take Kemper's brigade in flank. The added pressure encouraged the attacking force to slide to the north, closer and closer to the small clump of oak trees. Many Virginians took cover behind the rocky outcropping held by Brown's Rhode Island battery the afternoon before, and began to fire back at their Federal adversaries. [41]

An officer of the 19th Massachusetts, who was standing on a large boulder in front of the regiment, the next few moments frozen in his mind forever, later pictured this part of the Confederate assault: "By an undulation of the surface of the ground to the left of the trees the rapid advance of the dense line of Confederates is for a moment lost to view. An instant after they appear and rise out of the earth, and so near that the expression on their faces is distinctly seen. Now the men in Hall's brigade know that the time has come and can wait no longer. Aiming low they open a deadly concentrated discharge upon the moving mass in their front. Nothing human can stand it." [42]

The soldiers in the 20th Massachusetts, lying on their stomachs in two ranks behind their small breastworks, on the orders of Colonel Hall, rose up and fired "two or three volleys" at a range of less than 70 yards into Kemper's ranks. By this time, Kemper's brigade numbered less than 1,900 men. His regimental formation, from north to south, was the 24th Virginia, 11th Virginia, 1st Virginia, 7th Virginia and the 3rd Virginia. The 7th Virginia most probably was the regiment directly in front of the 20th Massachusetts. Private Daniel McAdams, a 19-year-old printer from Boston serving in the ranks of Company I, later described the initial punishment his unit inflicted on the Virginians: "We got orders to raise and fire and then order came for us to load and fire at will. Well we just chucked it into them." According to an officer in the 20th, "The men were wild with excitement shouting out Fredericksburg!" They saw revenge for that bloody December day now within their grasp. [43]

Captain Abbott of the 20th described the action his regiment took against its foe: "The moment I saw them I knew we should give them Fredericksburg. So did every body. We let the regiment in front of us get within 100 feet of us, & then bowled them over like nine pins, picking out the colors first. In two minutes there were only groups of two or three men running round wildly, like chickens with their heads cut off." On July 28, in a letter addressed to the father of a deceased officer of the regiment, Abbott referred to the 20th's fire as ". . . destroying the regiment that advanced against our immediate front. . . ." During the course of the entire assault, the 7th Virginia Infantry Regiment lost one third of its men. [44]

Though staggered, the Confederates returned fire, striking a handful of men, and moved north. (The flank attack by the 13th and 16th Vermont, together with the heavy fire from the men of Harrow's and Hall's brigades, encouraged this movement.) The Rebels discovered a weak spot in the Union line, a vacant area between the left of the 69th Pennsylvania Volunteer Infantry Regiment, deployed behind the low stone wall on the left of Webb's brigade, just in front of the Copse of Trees, and the right of the 59th New York of Hall's brigade. At least part of the latter unit fled in confusion as the Virginians approached. [45]

Captain Andrew Cowan, a 21-year-old former student from Auburn, New York, commanded the 1st New York Independent Battery of the VI Corps during the Battle of Gettysburg. His guns had been positioned several hundred yards to the south of the trees, on a line west of the Jacob Hummelbaugh farm, during the cannonade. As the enemy closed on the Union positions by the Copse of Trees, General Webb desperately called for help. Cowan promptly responded. Five of his 3-inch Ordnance rifles took the position vacated by Perrin's Rhode Island battery, to the right of the 42nd New York. The sixth gun was unable to stop in alignment with the others and took its station just north of the trees. As Pickett's infantry approached the stone wall, Cowan's pieces fired canister and then double canister. [46] Even Brigadier General Henry Hunt, commanding all the artillery of the Army of the

Potomac, who had ridden to Cowan's position, fired his pistol into the charging Rebels, despite having his horse killed beneath him. [47]

As the fighting reached its boiling point, hundreds of Confederates from Pickett's division reached the stone wall in front of Webb's brigade, and many began to advance over it in several places. At this crucial moment, in an urgent search for reinforcements, General Hancock rode up to the ranks of the 19th Massachusetts. The men had been ordered to lie down behind a line of boulders, to avoid exposing themselves unnecessarily. In spite of this, the unit had already suffered several casualties from Rebel fire. Furthermore, in the excitement, several of the prone Bay Staters were nearly trampled by the general's horse. Colonel Devereux, standing near the left of his regiment, saw the Virginians begin to swarm over the stone wall to his right front. Reacting to the emergency, Devereux hailed Hancock and exclaimed, "See, General, They have broken through! The colors are coming over the stone wall! Let me go in there!" According to Devereux, Hancock replied, "Go in there pretty God-damned quick!" Before riding further south along the Union line, searching for more support for Webb's brigade, the II Corps commander pointed to the trees and yelled, "Forward, men! Forward! Now is your chance." [48]

Although the next few moments would be remembered by many participants as being very chaotic, the veterans' training and discipline transcended the confusion. Realizing the urgency of the situation, Colonel Devereux ordered both his unit and the 42nd New York to the right on the double. The command rang out, "To our right and front." According to the adjutant of the 19th, the regiment's movement took the form of a right oblique, more complicated but also more direct than just a movement by the right flank. Since the 42nd New York was on the right of the 19th Massachusetts, in Devereux's words, the 42nd "became by this movement in echelon a little in advance," and struck Pickett's men first. [49]

How many men of the 19th participated in this climactic counter-attack? Understandably, in light of the confusion, no definite number was ever given by Colonel Devereux. This adjutant of the unit later stated, "We had present for duty, on the day, about 143 to 147 men in our Regiment." It is unclear from the context of the statement if this represented the 19th's strength on the morning of July 3, before the day's fighting began, or was intended to indicate only those men who took part in the counterattack. In either case, these numbers are definitely too high. [50]

Today, through an analysis of the sources now available, an estimate can be made. First, the losses incurred on July 2, around 25 to 30 in number, must be deducted from the original pre-battle strength of 160 officers and men. Then, the unknown amount of casualties suffered during the cannonade, which was probably very small, must also be subtracted. In addition, during the cannonade, 26 officers and men were detailed to assist Captain Rorty's New York battery. Some of these men probably stayed with the guns for the balance of the fighting, while others definitely returned to the unit in time to participate in the movement to the Copse of Trees. Therefore, the best assessment that can be made is that approximately 100 to 110 Bay Staters took part in this first crucial response to Pickett's breakthrough. Recalling the urgency felt by these few but gallant men, a soldier in the 19th later said, "The order was to go in; but we did not pay much attention to any order but went in." [51]

With a cheer, the 19th Massachusetts and the 42nd New York passed behind Cowan's guns as his cannoneers were blasting the attackers with double canister at ten yards. Men literally were torn apart by the shotgun-type blasts of those cannon. As the two Union regiments rushed in, Cowan pulled back some fifty yards east and north to save his guns, vacating his position. This gap was filled by the charging Massachusetts men. The New Yorkers formed their line to the 19th's right, with their front facing the stone wall. For the moment, the other three regiments of Hall's brigade remained in their original positions behind the stone wall, firing at the Rebels in their front. [52]

The 15th Massachusetts, along with the rest of Harrow's brigade, found themselves in a running fight, advancing to the north, as Kemper's men responded to the flanking fire of the Vermont soldiers by moving in the same direction toward the oak trees. By this time, Virginians of Garnett's and Armistead's brigades had reached the stone wall in front of the 69th Pennsylvania and had begun to climb over it. In this advance toward the Copse of Trees, Confederate rifles struck down Captain Hans P. Jorgensen of Company K, a 36-year-old resident of Leominster, Massachusetts, and the commander of Company G, Captain John Murkland, aged 27, of Lowell, Massachusetts, a pre-war machinist who had been born in Scotland. In describing Captain Murkland, one of his comrades wrote, "As a man, he was genial and kind-hearted, and beloved by all who knew him. As a soldier, he was prompt and efficient, and a thorough disciplinarian, while none braver than he ever trod the field of battle." [53]

Hans Jorgensen had been born in Copenhagen, Denmark; he served for three years in the Danish army prior to emigrating to the United States, where he became a piano maker. The 15th's regimental history referred to him as "a man of learning and cultivated taste and of social attainments." In his last letter, dated June 30, 1863, Captain Jorgensen predicted, "There is no doubt as to the result of this battle. Give my love to all my friends, and tell them the old Fifteenth is still gaining laurels, and by the time we get home we shall be completely covered with glory." [54]

The question is, who ordered the 15th Massachusetts and the rest of Harrow's brigade to the right in aid of Webb's troops? In his report to army headquarters dated July 17, 1863, Colonel Hall of the Third Brigade stated, "Going to the left, I found two regiments that could be spared from some command there, and endeavored to move them by the right flank to the break. . . ." However, Hall never identified these regiments, which may even have been from a I Corps brigade deployed south of Harrow's men. A man in the 15th later wrote: "When Webb's brigade was forced back, Harow's Brigade was ordered to his support at double quick. . . . I remember well as soon as we started, Col. Hall of the [Third] Brigade, cried out '[F]orward that Mass. color.' [emphasis in original]." From this soldier's description, it appears that the 15th was already moving to the right when Hall saw it and ordered the men to the danger spot. Another man from the 15th recalled: "I heard no orders at that time and do not think there were any given. It seemed as though every man had taken it upon himself to drive them. . . ." Lieutenant Colonel Joslin of the 15th, in his official report written eight days after the battle, was silent on the matter. [55]

First Lieutenant Frank Haskell, one of General Gibbon's aides, in a letter of July 16, 1863, described his role in the movement: ". . . I went at once further to the left, to the 1st Brigade.-Gnl. Harrow I did not see, but his fighting men would answer my purpose as well. The 19th Me., the 15th Mass., the 82nd N.Y., and the shattered old thunderbolt, the 1st Minn.-all men I could find, I took over to the right at the double quick." [56] Was it II Corps commander Hancock, division commander Gibbon, brigade commander Harrow, Colonel Hall of the Third Brigade, Joslin himself, or even Lieutenant Haskell, who gave the crucial order? Unfortunately, it appears that the ultimate answer is lost to history.

As Harrow's men moved north, a gap appeared in the Union line and Rebels from Kemper's brigade rushed through it to try to claim Rorty's guns. Only two of the four New York 10-pounder Parrotts remained firing, now under the command of First Lieutenant Robert E. Rogers. One cannon had overturned after firing a triple charge of canister directly into the faces of the on-charging Southerners; the other stood silent, as there was neither ammunition nor soldiers remaining to service it. Hand-to-hand fighting with the artillerymen wielding rammers and handspikes ended this threat to the cannon with Union victory. [57]

At this juncture, everything was near chaos. While General Armistead led 150 or so Confederates over the stone wall against Webb's position just to the north of the trees, many others remained in a disorganized mass in front of the stone wall, battling with the 69th Pennsylvania. [58] Colonel Devereux had responded with a movement to the contested area by his regiment and the 42nd New York. Hall's three other regiments were fighting Kemper's men at point blank range, and Harrow's soldiers were involved in a running battle toward the Copse of Trees.

As the pressure in his brigade front decreased, Colonel Hall reacted to the Confederates breaking Webb's front by ordering the 20th Massachusetts and 7th Michigan to their right to attempt to seal the breakthrough. Lieutenant Colonel Macy received an order from Colonel Hall to "... move the 20th in rear of the line and attack the flank of the enemy as they come in, at once." This was a difficult maneuver for a regiment engaged in a stand-up fight, so Macy yelled to Captain Abbott, commanding the right company of the 20th, to move en mass with his men toward the small oak trees. Macy intended to follow with the rest of the unit. [59]

In the tremendous noise and confusion, Abbott may not have heard or understood the colonel's orders in their entirety. In a letter home written three days after the battle, Abbott recalled, "We were cheering like mad, when Macy directed my attention to a spot 3 or 4 rods on our right where there were no pits, only a rail fence, [Webb's] Pennsylvania men had most disgracefully broken, and the rebels were within our line. The order was immediately given to fall back far enough to form another line and prevent us being flanked. Without however waiting for that, the danger was so imminent that I had rushed my company immediately up to the gap, & the regiment & the rest of the brigade, being there some before & the rest as quick as they could." [60]

With bayonets fixed, Abbott's men led the advance of the regiment to the Copse of Trees. Abbott later wrote, "I knew that one's voice could not be heard, but that an example could be seen. So I immediately rushed at the head of my company to the critical spot, and got there just in time, for there was hardly a soul there, and several Rebels were already over the fence, and their masses were thick close behind it." The 7th Michigan, to the 20th's right, got caught up in this movement; however, half of its men stayed and fought by the wall while the rest started to move to the trees. [61]

Obviously, with all the noise, smoke and confusion, the movement by the 20th was very disorganized. The commander of Company H, Captain Herbert C. Mason, a 23-year-old former clerk from Boston, described this change of position as follows: "[The enemy] attacked us in force with his infantry, nearly succeeding in breaking our line. Our regiment having got into confusion while changing front to prevent the enemy making a flank movement, I was shot in the groin while trying to rally [the men] toward the colors." [62]

Standing in the rear and to the right of his men, in rapid succession, Macy's sword was shot out of his hand and he was hit in the left shoulder; the impact tore off his left shoulder strap and knocked him to the ground. A minnie ball also struck his left hand, which later had to be amputated. With Macy's wounding, command of the regiment passed to Captain Abbott, the senior officer remaining. [63]

Major Edmund Rice, leading the left flank of the 19th, was already at the trees and engaged with Armistead's men as they tried to force their way through. According to Rice, ". . . [T]he whole copse seemed literally crammed with men." The distance between the contending forces was no more than 15 yards. In fact, Colonel Devereux later stated, "When my men struck the enemy at the copse of trees and just beyond that, towards the angle, they met so fiercely that there was a little rebound." [64]

Men in the rear ranks pressed forward and tried to fire through the gaps in the first line. A man in the 19th in the middle of this melee later wrote, "This is one of those periods in action which are measurable by seconds. The men near seem to fire so slowly. Those in rear, though coming up at a run, seem to drag their feet . . . Seconds are ages." Part of the regiment came under fire from Confederates behind the disassembled rail fence and stone wall to their left and also from those in the trees. [65]

Undoubtedly, in the confusion, Union muskets took a toll on their own comrades. A Federal officer later described one such tragic mistake: "Many were firing through the intervals of those in front, in their eagerness to injure the enemy. This manner of firing, although efficacious, sometimes tells on friend instead of foe. A sergeant at my side received a ball in the back of his neck by this fire." [66]

Something had to be done to break the deadly stalemate. Realizing that his voice might not be heard in the din, Major Rice of the 19th raised his sword and waved it toward the enemy. He then dashed forward with the vanguard of the unit, shouting, "Follow me, boys!" Later calling himself "the bulls eye for a good many of Pickett's men [emphasis in original]," Rice had his sword shot out of his hand, his cap knocked off, and finally suffered two gunshot wounds through his right thigh and fell among the Virginians. In fact, Colonel Devereux stated that Major Rice was so close to the Rebels that he "received his wound whilst his foot was placed on a man in the enemy's front rank who had partially fallen or purposely kneeled." [67] In belated recognition of his gallantry, on October 6, 1891, Edmund Rice would be awarded a Congressional Medal of Honor. [68]

Abbott and the rest of the officers of the 20th led the "Harvard Regiment" north from their position past the 59th New York, as some of the New Yorkers maintained their place, fighting the Rebels still in their front. These confusing events later caused these Empire State men to feel abandoned by their comrades. In April 1864, Second Lieutenant Henry N. Hamilton of the 59th wrote, "Both the regiments on our right and left gave way, leaving our regiment to contend with them alone." [69]

Attempting to determine the order in which each Federal reinforcing unit reached the area around the Copse of Trees, in the midst of all the smoke and confusion, is a daunting task. Studying the participants' accounts, there is no doubt that the 19th Massachusetts and 42nd New York reached the scene first. The order after that is more speculative. However, the surviving evidence seems to indicate that these two units were then followed by Harrow's brigade, which formed on their left, and finally by the men of the 20th Massachusetts and part of the 7th Michigan, who filled in closest to the stone wall.

A native Bostonian, Sumner Paine was new to the 20th Massachusetts in April 1863, when he was appointed a second lieutenant in Company F. The young man had just turned eighteen in May of that year, and was the great-grandson of colonial patriot Robert Treat Paine. Although a brilliant student, some youthful indiscretions had caused him to be suspended twice by Harvard University. Paine had had a taste of fighting at the Second Battle of Fredericksburg in the Chancellorsville Campaign and it left him wanting more. On May 5, 1863, he told his family, "I want to see some good tough fighting and try a few bayonet charges." [70]

However, Lieutenant Paine was extremely unpopular with the 20th's rank and file. In June 1863, 210 enlisted men sent a signed petition to Massachusetts Governor John Andrew, in which they claimed that Paine had men "incarcerated in the guard house, suspended to trees, tied in the stocks or elevated on instruments of torture," in furtherance of his own ideas of discipline. Despite the men's demands, Governor Andrew did not revoke Sumner Paine's commission or remove him from the regiment. Now Paine and the others ran toward those small trees, screaming "Hurrah for the white trefoil! Clubs are trumps! Forward the white trefoil!" (The II Corps emblem was a trefoil, the color designation of the second division being white.) [71]

A few pieces of Confederate artillery had advanced to positions near the Emmitsburg Road in support of the assault. These guns indiscriminately brought down fire on foe and friend alike. A man in the 19th Massachusetts recalled that one of these cannon shots ". . . tore a horrible passage through the dense crowd of men in blue, who were gathering outside the trees; instantly another shot followed, and fairly cut a road through the mass." Another Confederate shell exploded over the head of 27-year-old Private William Bartlett of the 19th's Company H, a former shoemaker from Lynn. One fragment imbedded itself in his right side, another struck his left thigh, and the concussion knocked him unconscious and blew him over the Union breastworks. The impact with the ground caused severe bruising of Bartlett's spine and broke his right hand. [72]

As Lieutenant Paine of the 20th, pistol in hand, came within 15 yards of the trees and 15 feet of the stone wall, he shouted, "Isn't this glorious!" his face aglow with excitement. Moments later he dropped to his knees as a piece of shell tore through his ankle, almost cleaving it from his leg. Raising himself up on his left elbow, he waved his sword and yelled, "Forward, forward!" Immediately he fell, never to rise again, struck by bullets in his arm and chest. [73]

In contrast to the harsh opinions of the enlisted men of the regiment, in a letter to Paine's father dated July 28, 1863, Captain Abbott wrote, "There is one thing I can bear testimony to, and that is, your son's wonderful talent in making himself one of the most accomplished officers I know in the army, in 2 month's time. . . . His memory and application were so great that in a month's time he knew the whole book of tactics and Regulations, and commanded a division in battalion and brigade drill as well as any old officers, besides doing all his guard and police duty, with an exactness, a vigor, an enthusiasm that the comdg. of. in vain tried to stimulate in some of the older officers, sparing neither himself nor his men. . . . [H]e was seen . . . during the action, his face . . . actually glowing with pleasure as it used to in Falmouth when he had the best of an argument. . . . He used always to be asking me, how an officer should bear himself in battle, when he should be behind and when before his men. I had always rather understated than overstated the amount of danger it was necessary to incur, because I had seen at [Second Battle of] Fredericksburg that he would be rather disposed to expose himself too much than otherwise. He certainly carried out to the letter the duty as he used to describe it of an officer charging at the head of his men, and he evidently felt all the joy that he supposed he should." His naïve desire to see "some good tough fighting" had indeed been realized. Buried in Grave E-1, Massachusetts Plot, in the National Cemetery at Gettysburg, Sumner Paine would remain forever eighteen years old. [74]

Pandemonium reigned supreme throughout the entire area. Most of Colonel Hall's and all of General Harrow's men were crowded in places six deep around the trees and the wall between the positions of what remained of Hall's 59th New York and Webb's 69th Pennsylvania. In his official report, Captain Abbott stated, "[E]very man [was] fighting on his own hook, different regiments being mixed together, and half a dozen colors in a bunch, it being impossible to preserve a regimental line." A Union captain later wrote, "We [the officers] all devoted ourselves to keeping up every man without regard to regiments." As the men in the front fired, they moved to the rear and those behind stepped forward. File closers tried to keep the line stationary, as it otherwise would have had a tendency to slide backward. Some who could not find room to fire picked up rocks and threw them over the heads of their own comrades at their enemies. [75]

In the fierce fighting, the entire color guard of the 20th Massachusetts was shot down. The colors were then seized by Sergeant Charles Curtis of Company D, a 25-year-old welder from Canton, Massachusetts. While in the act of raising the colors, Curtis was shot in his left thigh and fell to the ground with the flag. The banner was then taken by 18-year-old Private Elisha Smith of Company I, a farmer from Edgartown, Massachusetts, who was almost immediately shot in the leg and knocked down. The flag was then picked up by Private William Fuchs of Company C, a 28-year-old saddler from Roxbury, who carried the colors safely through the rest of the battle. For his bravery, Fuchs was subsequently promoted to the rank of color corporal by Captain Abbott on July 29, 1863. [76]

Virginians planted several of their battle flags on two of Cushing's guns, positioned at the wall north of the trees. Commenting on what he observed before he was shot, Major Rice later wrote, "The grove was fairly jammed with Pickett's men, in all positions, lying and kneeling. Back from the edge were many standing and firing over those in front. By the side of several who were firing, lying down or kneeling, were others with their hands up, in token of surrender." [77]

Private Daniel Corrigan of the 19th's Company E, a 23-year-old flax-dresser from Ludlow, Massachusetts, remembered the confused fighting. "During 'Pickets' charge they got in on us afore we were aware of it," he later stated, "and a few of them got in behind us, it was a hand to hand fight and one of them got in behind me and struck me with the butt of his gun and broke my collar bone. Shortly after I got up I received a gunshot wound in my right leg below the knee. That was all I could do and I was carried to the rear." [78]

This gangland-type rumble was recognized as a melee by both sides. Twenty-two-year-old Captain Alphonse N. Jones of the 7th Virginia of Kemper's brigade began the assault as the commander of the regiment's Company A. As the senior officer left in the unit after the battle, Jones, in his official report dated, July 5, 1863, wrote that his regiment had lost men at every step and that they ". . . pressed forward till our flag was planted upon the breastworks of the enemy. At this critical hour of the conflict, heavy reinforcements were moved upon us by the enemy, and the sanguinary conflict was renewed with redoubled violence; and after fifteen minutes we were driven from the enemy's works; with heavy loss in men and gallant officers." [79]

Corporal Joseph H. DeCastro, aged 18, a former waiter from Boston, of the 19th Massachusetts' Company I, found himself within the lines of the 72nd Pennsylvania Volunteer Infantry Regiment, a part of General Webb's brigade, fighting some distance to the right of his unit. He seized the flag of the 14th Virginia Infantry Regiment, one of several that had been placed at Cushing's guns, handed the colors to Colonel Devereux, and returned to the fray. On July 4, 1863, DeCastro was recognized officially for his bravery in a written statement by Colonel Devereux. On December 1, 1864, the gallant corporal was awarded the Congressional Medal of Honor for this heroic deed. [80]

Also in the ranks of the 19th was Private Benjamin Falls of Company A, a 38-year-old veteran born in Portsmouth, New Hampshire. In August 1861, the 5' 7" Falls had enlisted in the regiment from his adopted home of Lynn, Massachusetts, where he had plied his trade of seaman. Due to his age, Falls was originally made a company cook. However, at the Battle of Fredericksburg, Falls said to his company commander, "Captain, if you have no use for Ben Falls, send me home. How nice it will look when I write to my wife in Lynn that the regiment fought nobly, and I carried the kettles. I either want a musket or a discharge—and prefer a musket." His gallant request was immediately granted. Now, less than eight months later, Private Falls found himself at the wall, wrestling for possession of a Rebel banner. The standard would not move because it was still firmly held by its Confederate owner. "Hut, Tut! Let alone of that or I'll run ye through," Falls exclaimed as he held his bayonetted rifle over the Southern soldier. Falls captured both the flag of the 19th Virginia Infantry Regiment of Garnett's brigade and its bearer. After the battle, in recognition of his gallantry, Private Falls was promoted to the rank of color sergeant. Killed at Spotsylvania in May 1864, Benjamin Falls would never know that he was awarded the Congressional Medal of Honor on December 1 of that year. He left behind his 25-year-old wife, Sarah, and two daughters, aged eight and four, and a legacy of valor. [81]

Belonging to Company I of the 19th Massachusetts, Private John H. Robinson, aged 21, an Irish immigrant who had worked as a rope maker in Boston prior to the Civil War, also captured a Confederate banner in the melee in and around the Copse of Trees. After the combat ended, he turned this flag over to the wounded Major Rice of his regiment; Rice utilized the flagstaff as a cane. At the Peter Frey farm on the west side of the Taneytown Road, which was being used as a field hospital, Rice presented the flag to his wounded corps commander, General Hancock. In the post-battle confusion, it disappeared and the identity of the Confederate regiment from which it was taken was never clearly established. [82] Robinson's gallantry also would be recognized by the presentation of a Congressional Medal of Honor on December 1, 1864. [83]

Together with the other units in Harrow's brigade, the 15th had advanced to the left of the 19th Massachusetts and traded fire with Confederates behind the wall and in the trees. Nineteen-year-old Private Amos C. Plaisted of the 15th's Company B, a pre-war machinist from Fitchburg, recounted that, "[W]e ran down all in a huddle . . . and opened fire as best we could, the enemy was safely layed down behind the wall, having planted their flag in the stones and poured a deadly fire into us from behind it, while our shots affected them little more than to prevent their advance further [emphasis in original]." Many men in the 15th suffered wounds to the left sides of their bodies. They were obviously shooting at the Rebels in front of them among the trees, while receiving enfilading fire from the Virginians on their left, at and beyond the stone wall, and crouching behind the rocky outcropping used by Brown's Rhode Island battery the day before. [84]

The Confederates, according to General Kemper, found themselves in a "cul-de-sac of death . . . where [they] met an overpowering fire in front, and raking fires from both the right and the left. . . ." The Rebel breakthrough was sealed, but the outcome was still in doubt. Colonel Devereux later described this climactic moment: "Just then I felt rather than saw, [Colonel] Hall, as he appeared at my side. 'We are steady now,' he said. 'Sure; but we must move,' was my reply." [85]

The color bearer of the 15th Massachusetts, 26-year-old Sergeant Patrick Murphy, a stone-cutter from Worcester, was shot down in the midst of the fray. He was hit by a minnie ball in his right shoulder that passed through his lungs and exited his left side. Both Sergeant Murphy and the colors fell to the ground. Still the men of the 15th stood, taking heavy losses, until 25-year-old Private George Cunningham of Company B, a native of Cambridge, cried out, "For God's sake let us charge, they'll kill us all if we stand here." In a mass, the 15th moved forward. [86]

Somehow in the overwhelming tumult, the men of the 19th also heard a call to charge. Their United States flag suddenly fell to the ground but was immediately scooped up by Second Lieutenant Moses Shackley. Company C's First Lieutenant Herman Donath, while carrying his state's flag, was shot dead. When found after the battle, no blood or mark could be found on his clothing. Upon opening his shirt, one small round hole in his chest was discovered to have been the cause of death. At his death, Donath, an immigrant from Westphalia in Prussia, was only 21 years old; he had worked as a painter in Roxbury before the war. [87]

Lieutenant Shackley also crumpled with a wound. The recently appointed Color Sergeant Benjamin Jellison retrieved both flags and stood firm with them only three yards from the Rebel line. Jellison later described this sequence of events: "Lieutenant Shackley was again at my side. 'Ben' he remarked this time, 'see the rebel flag? Let's get it.' He pointed to our front, and the next moment I lost him. I rushed forward and succeeded in capturing the flag, and besides assisted in taking quite a number of prisoners. With the Stars and Stripes flying over my head, and carrying the captured flag, I retreated." [88] The flag that Jellison captured, through the use of his fists and his own flagstaff as a club, was that of the 57th Virginia Infantry Regiment of Armistead's brigade. On December 1, 1864, Benjamin Jellison's valorous deeds were recognized by the presentation of a Medal of Honor. [89]

Colonel Devereux later said of this crucial struggle between his men and the Virginians: "They appeared to stand there for a few moments, firing into each other. Then, as I have always regarded this matter, from that time everything appeared to hang in the balance. It appeared to me that whichever side got a little motion in it was sure to win. . . .'' The 19th Massachusetts surged forward in a simultaneous movement as the disorganized mass of Union regiments closed in on their prey. The Confederates resisted for a few moments but the die was cast. [90]

At some places, the fighting was even hand-to-hand. Private Johnston Acheson of the 19th's Company F, a 31-year-old Irish immigrant, had a bayonet driven completely through his left wrist. Twenty-eight-year-old Private William Gibbons, a shoemaker from Hopkinton, Massachusetts, also serving in Company F, advanced all the way through the trees to Cushing's abandoned guns, where he was stabbed in the right leg by a sword-wielding Rebel officer. [91]

Arthur Devereux later stated, "[T]hen it seemed that some influence came upon our men and they bore down among the enemy and they laid down their arms in a body." Mirroring the colonel's account, 22-year-old William A. Hill, the 19th's adjutant, who had been a clerk in Marblehead before the war, agreed that the action ". . . continued desperately without any appreciable result for some minutes. At times the advantage seemed to be with the enemy. At other times it seemed to be with us—at all events, after some few minutes there seemed to be a pressure forward with our men and, all at once, with that movement, the enemy came in large numbers, into our lines. . . ." [92]

Private Plaisted of the 15th wrote, "[T]he enemy jumped up to run and several attempted to take their <u>flag</u> off the wall, but as soon as they started we stopped and gave them a volley and nearly all lay down again and cried out to us to stop firing and let them come in, which we did. . . . [emphasis in original]." [93] In the vicinity of the 19th Massachusetts, the Virginians grounded their weapons and surrendered; very few attempted to brave the Federal fire and work their way back to Confederate lines. A solemn Confederate officer noticed the captured flags held by Colonel Devereux and said as he passed, "You Yanks think you've done a great thing, now!" "It's our turn, remember Fredericksburg," was the answer. [94]

Some of the men in the 19th had worked their way completely through the Copse of Trees, at approximately the same time as the infantrymen of the 72nd Pennsylvania swept down toward the stone wall in their front from their position just below the crest of Cemetery Ridge, on the right of the trees. The Massachusetts soldiers crossed over the stone wall in front of the trees, in a short-lived pursuit of the fleeing Rebels. They were discouraged in their efforts by blasts of Southern cannon fire. Other men in the regiment found shelter behind the wall and took pot-shots at the retreating enemy. [95]

Sergeant William McGinnis of the 19th's Company K, aged 24 and a former floor-layer from Boston, was one of the last Union casualties. As he saw the attack fail, he jumped to the top of a little ridge and exclaimed, "They've broke, boys! There they go. See em run!" As he waved his arms excitedly, a Rebel bullet struck him in the left shoulder, traveled through his shoulder blade and down into his left side, knocking him to the ground. [96]

Near the 15th and 20th Massachusetts, some Confederates broke for freedom while others came forward toward the Federals to capitulate. The men surrendering were caught in the middle of a cross fire and threw themselves on the ground as the 15th opened fire on Rebels who were retreating. Private Plaisted berated one Confederate major for acting so cowardly by exhibiting fear. The Rebel replied that he did not fear the Yankees, but the sound of his own shells was not to his liking. [97]

Evidence of the validity of the major's fears was the discovery, after the fighting ended, of the mangled body of the 19th's Joseph H. Hervey in the midst of the Copse of Trees. A 5' 10" pre-war clerk from Georgetown, Massachusetts, Hervey was a 20-year-old unmarried sergeant in Company C, described as being "popular in the company and a model soldier." He had been killed by a solid shot. [98]

As the infantry fighting ended, Captain Cowan's battery resumed its previous position just south of the Copse of Trees. Using two guns, the New Yorkers shelled an enemy battery that had moved forward to cover the retreat of their infantry. When this last spasm of violence ended, silence began to descend on the scene of carnage. [99]

I t was over. It had not taken long. Some said five minutes. Some said an hour. With regard to the disparities in estimates of the length of the fighting, the adjutant of the 19th Massachusetts later said, "Well, of course, you know it is very difficult to form an idea as to the time occupied in any Battle, but I should say it was not over fifteen minutes, although I have never found any two men who will agree to the exact lapse of time on an occasion like that." [100]

The historian of the 19th Massachusetts described the reaction of the victorious Union troops: "And then the victors cheered and the cheering rang down the line. Sixth, Fifth, Third, Eleventh united with the Second Corps and rent the air with such cheers as are seldom heard. The mighty shout

swelled and rang and died away, swelled and peeled again and until even the
distant Twelfth Corps united its voice in that mighty hymn of joy. . . ." [101]

As disorganized knots of Confederates fell back to Seminary Ridge,
Union officers began the task of reorganizing their commands. Although the
main attack had ended, desultory fire from secessionist artillery and skirmishers continued to cause casualties among the decimated Federal defenders. A man in the 15th Massachusetts later wrote, "Twenty minutes after the
infantry fighting was all done and the last rebel had disappeared across the
Emmetsburg Road, a shell was sent from a rebel battery in the vicinity of the
Codori House which exploded in the line of the 15th, then near the southeastern corner of the [Copse of Trees], with dreadful results. Men were thrown
and blown in all directions, one of them George A. Fletcher, of Whitinsville,
having the top of his head taken off and his brains splattered on those around
him. [Corporal William H.] Bergen, of Company D, had to scrape them off
his face and later said it was the most horrible of all his wartime experiences
[emphasis in original]." Corporal Fletcher, a pre-war mechanic, was only 19
years old at the time of his death. [102]

Amid this continuing bloodshed, the Union lines had to be reestab-
lished, ammunition re-supplied, the wounded gathered and cared for, and
hundreds of Rebel prisoners taken to the rear. When time and the enemy
allowed, the dead had to be buried and thousands of abandoned or damaged
muskets collected and removed.

Many Federal soldiers milled around the entire area, searching among
the casualties for their relatives or friends, aiding the wounded from both
sides, or picking up souvenirs. In fact, 27-year-old Second Lieutenant John
Summerhayes of Company G of the 20th Massachusetts took possession of a
sword purported to be that of Brigadier General Richard Garnett, who had
been killed somewhere in front of the Union line. Summerhayes sent the
sword back to his home in Nantucket, Massachusetts, where he had worked
as a mechanic before the war. [103]

Time was of the essence, since there was still plenty of daylight left,
and no one knew if another Confederate attack would follow. Colonel
Devereux of the 19th was assigned the task of reforming the Union defenders
on Cemetery Ridge so as to be able to meet a possible renewed assault. He
carried out this mission by the unusual expedient of ordering the men from
the various regiments into line where they stood when the fighting at the
Copse of Trees ended. He later stated, "I did not allow them to seek their
Regiments, but obliged them to take their positions in line, side by side, with-

out any reference to what their Regiment may have been, as our sole object, at that time, was to form a line." [104]

When it became apparent that no further Rebel assaults would be forthcoming, the men were allowed to return to their regiments, and a more coherent line was formed. Twelve men from the 19th Massachusetts were detailed to help man the decimated Battery "B", 1st Rhode Island Light Artillery, and several others from the unit were ordered to the rear to collect stragglers. The remnants of the 15th Massachusetts were sent forward as skirmishers. They remained on the skirmish line until the morning of July 4, having expended all their remaining ammunition and losing two more men wounded. [105]

3

The Price of Valor
The Battle's Immediate Aftermath

he carnage in and around the Copse of Trees stunned even the most battle-hardened veteran. An artilleryman with Battery "B", 1st Rhode Island Light Artillery, described the position held by his unit during the cannonade: " [T]he ground was strewn with torn haversacks, battered canteens, broken wheels of gun carriages, and piles of knapsacks and blankets overturned, silently telling of the destruction which had visited the place." [1] Captain Abbott noted, "The rows of dead after the battle I found to be within 15 and 20 feet apart, as near to hand to hand fighting as I ever care to see." [2] A man in the II Corps confided in his diary: "The field of battle is a sight never to be forgotten, the dead and wounded lay as thick as one ever saw sheaves of wheat in a harvest field, for a distance of a hundred yards or more in front and as far to the right and left as the eye can reach." [3] An officer in the 53rd Virginia Infantry Regiment who was captured in the assault said that he never saw as many dead men in one place in all the battles of the war as he did after the fighting had ended. He later remembered, "The blue coats were lying all over so thick that you could scarcely help stepping on them." [4]

The fighting at Gettysburg took a tremendous toll on the already re-duced ranks of the 15th, 19th and 20th Massachusetts. According to the casualty figures in the *Official Records*, the 15th, which had gone into com-bat on July 2 with 18 officers and 221 men, lost three officers and 20 men killed, eight officers and 89 men wounded and 28 men missing, a total loss of 148, or 61.9 % of the number engaged. A modern study increased the num-ber of officers and men killed in the regiment to 26, with nine more being mortally wounded. This work lists four officers as being killed outright or dying of their wounds: Colonel George H. Ward, Captain Hans P. Jorgensen, Captain John Murkland, and First Lieutenant Elisha G. Buss of Company K. Buss was a 28-year-old carpenter from Clinton, Massachusetts, who was wounded in the thigh, hip and foot during the fighting on July 2 and died on July 23, 1863, at his family home, leaving his widowed mother, Elizabeth, to collect a monthly pension of $15.00 from the Federal government. [5]

When the shooting stopped and the remnants of the 19th Massachusetts were reformed, only eight officers and 39 men were left with the colors. In the words of a sergeant in Company I, "The 19th is pretty well played out. . . . I don't think my services will be required any longer, as there is no Co. I in the regiment." [6] According to the *Official Records*, in the two days of fighting, the 19th lost two officers and seven men killed, nine officers and 52 men wounded, and seven men missing, for total casualties of 77 out of the original 160, a loss of 48.1 %. [7] Modern scholarship indicates that two of the men listed as missing, 19-year-old Corporal Charles A. Johnson of Company E and 20-year-old Private Daniel F. Reardon of Company H, both unmarried and from Boston, lost their lives as a result of the battle. (After being wounded in his left shoulder, Johnson died on August 19, 1863, from the effects of pyemia and pneumonia at the West Philadelphia Hospital. Reardon was listed as missing in action until August 11, 1875, when the Adjutant General's Office of the War Department finally changed his status to killed in action.) This study also indicates that four other men from the regiment died of their wounds, for a total loss to the 19th of 15 killed or mortally wounded. [8] In addition, one man, Corporal E. Augustus Nichols of Company C, who had enlisted as a musician in August 1861 at the age of 16, fled to the rear during the fighting near the Copse of Trees. Nichols had the dubious distinction of being singled out for this ignominious act by Colonel Devereux in his official report. [9]

The 20th Massachusetts, which had 13 officers and 230 men in its ranks before the fighting began on July 2, 1863, lost, as stated in the *Official Records,* two officers and 28 men killed, eight officers and 86 men wounded and three men missing, for a total of 127, or 52.3% of its strength.[10] The post-war regimental history correctly listed three officers killed, namely Colonel Paul Revere, First Lieutenant Henry Ropes, and Second Lieutenant Sumner Paine. A modern calculation indicates the same number of 31 officers and men killed, with an additional 12 men dying of their wounds, for a total of 43 fatalities out of the original strength of 243 in the regiment. However, a careful study of several successive Quarterly Returns of Deceased Soldiers of the 20th Massachusetts, together with a comparison of available pension records at the National Archives, reveals that even this appalling figure is too low. Two additional men, 20-year-old Sergeant George F. Cate, a gas-fitter from Readville, Massachusetts, and 44-year-old Private Leonard Harrington, a mason from Boston, both serving with Company F, were either killed or mortally wounded in the fighting. Therefore, 45 is the correct number of fatalities suffered by the 20th Massachusetts at the Battle of Gettysburg. [11]

Captain Henry Abbott, Second Lieutenant John Summerhayes and 22-year-old First Lieutenant William F. Perkins of Company A, a Boston native, were the only three officers in the 20th Massachusetts left physically un-scathed at the end of two days of ferocious combat. In a letter to his father written three days after the battle, Henry Abbott eloquently expressed the feelings of many men in the Army of the Potomac, thinking of lost comrades: "When our great victory was just over the exultation of victory was so great that one didn't think of our fearful losses, but now I can't help feeling a great weight at my heart." [12]

The Battle of Gettysburg took the lives of more than 90 men from the three Massachusetts regiments. But that is a mere number, a statistic, which can be casually read and easily forgotten. Many other men's lives ended prematurely as a result of wounds received at Gettysburg. Obviously, each had been a living individual, with a personal story of how his existence had tragically been cut short, leaving loved ones to struggle on without him. Most were so-called "common soldiers," mourned and remembered only by their families, lost to the pages of history. They were men such as Private John Marsh, Jr., an unmarried 27-year-old palmleaf worker from Worcester, who had joined Company B of the 15th Massachusetts on November 25, 1861. Called "a desperate man to fight" by one of his comrades, Private Marsh was killed in action on July 3. He was survived by his father, John Marsh, Sr., aged 58, his mother, Ann Maria, and two younger sisters, aged 14 and 12. The elder Marsh had worked before the war with the New England Glass Company, but was disabled due to asthma and rheumatism and forced to rely on his son's military pay and the charity of friends and relatives to pay the family's bills. After Private Marsh's death, his family received the sum of $8.00 per month as a Federal pension. John Marsh, Jr., is buried in Grave D-2, Massachusetts Plot, in the Gettysburg National Cemetery. [13]

Buried next to Private Marsh, in Grave D-1, is Sergeant Henry C. Ball of the 15th Massachusetts' Company F, a broom maker from Amherst who had enlisted on July 12, 1861. Sergeant Ball, aged 32, was killed instantly by a musket ball in the fighting on July 3. He left behind his wife, Harriet, whom he had married in 1853, a 7-year-old daughter, Hattie, and 4-year-old Emma. They received a Federal pension of $12.00 per month until 1871, when Harriet remarried, and the family's subsidy was reduced to $4.00 per month. Unfortunately, Harriet's second husband also predeceased her, dying in an insane asylum in Northampton, Massachusetts, in 1912. Harriet finally joined both husbands in death in June 1919. [14]

Twenty-eight-year-old Alexander Lord was a private in the 15th's Company C. Before enlisting on August 12, 1862, Lord had worked as a manufacturer in Orange, Massachusetts, supporting his 24-year-old wife, Lucia, whom he had married in February 1860. Private Lord was killed on July 3. Somehow, in the fall of 1863, Lucia Lord brought her husband's body home to Orange, where it was laid to rest. Receiving a pension of $8.00 per month, the young widow moved to Minnesota in 1864, to begin a new life. She remained there until her death in 1923, at the age of 84. [15]

One of the fatalities in the ranks of the 19th Massachusetts on July 3 was Private Thomas Doyle of Company F, a 33-year-old tailor from Roxbury. Bridget Doyle, his widow, whom he had married in 1850, was illiterate, and had to support their four children, aged 9, 5, 3 and 2 on a widow's pension of $8.00 per month, plus $2.00 per month for each child. [16]

Resting in Grave C-31 of the Massachusetts Plot, Gettysburg National Cemetery, is Private Thomas Tuttle, Jr., of Company I of the 19th Massachusetts. Private Tuttle was a "mere youth" of 17 when he enlisted on July 11, 1861, from his hometown of Somerville, Massachusetts, where he worked as a machinist.   Tuttle's mother had died in June 1854, and her will left her "beloved son" the sum of $100.00, and her husband, Thomas, Sr., aged 43 in 1863, the yearly rents from her real estate holdings. Thomas Tuttle, Jr., was killed on July 3, leaving his father, now the sole survivor of his family, to collect a monthly pension of $8.00. [17]

As stated previously, the 20th Massachusetts lost "only" four or five men to the effects of the cannonade preceding Pickett's Charge. One of these unfortunate victims was 22-year-old Private August Duttling of Company D, an unmarried farmer from Dorchester. Private Duttling was the sole support of his widowed mother, Esther, to whom he sent part of his military pay. He suffered a shell wound in the bowels, and "died on the field" on July 3. Private Duttling is now buried in Grave A-17, Massachusetts Plot, incorrectly identified as "Augustus Deitling." His 56-year-old mother received the standard $8.00 per month allowance from the Federal government. [18]

The man lying in Grave A-10 of the Massachusetts Plot is denoted as being "Michael Vinnarke." Actually, this plot holds the mortal remains of Private Michael Kennarick of Company H, 20th Massachusetts, a 31-year-old Irish laborer, who had immigrated to Lynn, Massachusetts, in the late

1840s. Private Kennarick was killed instantly on July 3, leaving his wife, Bridget, aged 40, to raise their four young daughters on a pension of $16.00 a month. When Bridget Kennarick died in 1872, none of the children had reached the age of 16; all then became wards of the Commonwealth of Massachusetts. [19]

When Patrick Quinlan, aged 28, a laborer from Roxbury, enlisted as a private in Company H of the 20th Massachusetts on July 18, 1861, he left behind his wife, Susan, and three children, Annie, aged 8, Susan, 6, and Edward, 3. Tragedy struck a double blow to the Quinlan family in 1863. First, wife Susan died in April and then Patrick Quinlan was killed by a gunshot on July 3. Patrick's 21-year-old brother, Edward, who was illiterate, became the guardian of his nieces and nephew, and collected $14.00 per month from the United States government. Patrick Quinlan rests forever in Grave A-20 of the Massachusetts Section in the National Cemetery at Gettysburg. [20]

Death came to George Joeckel, who was 27 years old when he was felled by a gunshot to the head on July 3. He had enlisted as a private in Company B of the 20th Massachusetts on July 26, 1861, from his hometown of Roxbury, where he made his living as a cabinet maker. Joeckel was promoted to the rank of first sergeant of the company in December 1862, for "gallant conduct at Fredericksburg." As the oldest of five children, Joeckel helped support his widowed mother, Barbara, by sending her $10.00 per month out of his military pay. After his death, his mother received a monthly pension of $8.00 from the United States government. [21]

The plight of those wounded in the battle is almost beyond comprehension. The following few examples will speak for the suffering of thousands, including the more than 250 men who were wounded while serving in the 15th, 19th and 20th Massachusetts. Private Charles Murray of Company I of the 15th Massachusetts, who stood only 5' 2" tall, was a 21-year-old drover and horse-dealer from Webster, Massachusetts. He was shot in the head of his left humerus on July 3; this caused a fracture of the bone. His treatment consisted of having part of the humerus excised the next day at a field hospital. The young private was discharged for disability in February 1864. Although Murray survived his wound, his left arm was shortened by two inches and he lost the total use of the limb. Beginning in March 1864, he received a disability pension of $8.00 per month from the Federal government; this had increased to $12.00 by the time of his death in January 1893. [22]

David Welch was 38 years old when he enlisted in Company A, 15th Massachusetts, on July 31, 1862. He had worked as a shoemaker in Worcester prior to joining the army, supporting his wife, who was illiterate, and two young children. On July 3, a ball passed through his hand, and he was badly sunstruck, caused by "intense heat and severe fighting." Private Welch was hospitalized until November 20, 1863, and was then transferred to the Veteran Reserve Corps. The records indicate that Welch was absent, sick beginning March 10, 1864, suffering from fits. He died on July 9, 1864, while home on a sick furlough. Private Welch was delirious for five days prior to his death. The fits were medically attributed to the sunstroke he had suffered on July 3, 1863, while participating in the repulse of Pickett's men. Subsequently, his wife and children received a pension of $12.00 per month from the United States government. A final note: in the pension records, Private Welch is described as a "good soldier." [23]

Private William Moore of the 15th Massachusetts' Company G had been afflicted with diarrhea on the march to the battlefield and was struck in the left leg by a shell fragment on July 2, but still remained on duty. In the fighting on July 3, a minnie ball hit Moore in the left cheek, broke all his teeth on the left side, knocked out all the teeth in the right side of his mouth, fractured his right jaw, and blew away a piece of his face under his right eye. For the rest of his life, Moore could open his jaw only half an inch and had to subsist on soft food. Private Moore remained in a series of military hospitals until October 20, 1863, when he was transferred to the Veteran Reserve Corps. He was discharged in July 1864 and began receiving a Federal pension of $6.00 per month. After the war, William Moore was married twice and fathered a son. He found work as a cigar maker, salesman and as a janitor in a store owned by the father of one of his former regimental comrades. Moore died in April 1908 in Worcester of heart disease. [24]

Joseph Matthews, a mechanic from Leominster, was a 43-year-old private who had served in Company B of the 15th Massachusetts since enlisting on July 12, 1861. On the afternoon of July 3, Matthews was struck by a minnie ball in his right thigh near his hip. The ball exited his left thigh. Private Matthews remained in a temporary hospital outside Gettysburg until July 7, when he and ten of his regimental comrades paid a farmer $50.00 to take them to Littlestown, Pennsylvania. Once there, he was deposited on a brick sidewalk, until a local citizen took him into his home. Matthews remained in various military hospitals until his discharge in April 1864, when he began receiving a pension of $6.00 per month. For the rest of his life,

Joseph Matthews' right knee was permanently stiff. He could walk only with the aid of crutches or a cane and required the help of his family to dress and undress. By the time of his death in 1897, his monthly Federal pension had increased to $24.00. [25]

Thomas Henry was a 30-year-old shoemaker living in Webster, Massachusetts, when he enlisted as a private in the 15th Massachusetts' Company B on July 12, 1861. Sometime during the fighting on July 2, Private Henry was shot through the inside of his right arm, with the ball destroying three inches of bone. After the war, Henry moved to Thompson, Connecticut, and began receiving a pension of $8.00 per month from the United States government. However, his arm continually pained him; in fact, by 1871, his right arm had a lump on it "as big as a large walnut." On October 10, 1872, in an attempt to alleviate Henry's pain, a doctor opened his arm to drain the accumulated pus and discovered that the humerus bone was necrotic. Over the next several days, Thomas Henry fell into a state of delirium, which lasted until his death on October 14, 1872. The cause of his demise was determined to be blood poisoning resulting from his Gettysburg wound, suffered over nine years before. [26]

Second Lieutenant John G. B. Adams of Company I of the 19th Massachusetts was shot in the groin and right hip in the combat of July 2. After a cursory examination of his wounds by a doctor at a field hospital that day, Adams was told that his wounds were mortal and he would not live twenty-four hours. Therefore, in the harsh triage prevalent at the time in light of the field hospitals being overwhelmed by thousands of wounded men, Adams received no treatment and was put aside to die. After lying nearly helpless for over a week after his wounding, the young lieutenant took matters into his own hands and paid a local citizen $5.00 to take him and another wounded man from the 19th to the railroad station in Gettysburg. Two days later, Adams traveled by train to Baltimore, where pieces of bone, clothing and even maggots were washed out of his wounds. His injuries were then dressed for the first time. Amazingly, not only did Adams survive, but also he returned to duty with the regiment by early 1864. [27]

A 25-year-old shoemaker from Beverly, Massachusetts, George P. Ham enlisted as a private in Company I of the 19th Massachusetts on August 23, 1861. His wife, Martha, aged 20 in 1861, and daughter, Sarah, born in September 1859, moved in with Martha's mother after Private Ham's enlistment. On July 3, George Ham was severely wounded. When his condition seemed to stabilize, he was transferred from a field hospital in Gettysburg to McDougal

General Hospital at Fort Schuyler, New York. Unfortunately, on August 2, 1863, George Ham died there from the effects of a secondary hemorrhage, leaving his young wife and daughter to collect a pension of $10.00 per month. [28]

Sometime during the fighting on July 3, Sergeant Stephen Armitage of Company C, 19th Massachusetts, was struck in the neck and left side of his head by shell fragments. Armitage, 25 years old in 1863, was an illiterate shoemaker from Rowley, Massachusetts. The pieces of shell fractured his skull and permanently impaired the sight in his left eye. Sergeant Armitage was already in poor health at the time of his wounding, having been afflicted with chronic diarrhea since the 1862 Peninsula Campaign. Never able to return to duty with the regiment after his wounding, Armitage was discharged in August 1864. He weighed only 98 pounds at that time, and was described as being a "mere skeleton." Stephen Armitage went back to his hometown of Rowley, where he resided until his death in 1909. When he died, Armitage's monthly pension check from the United States government was in the sum of $15.00 per month. [29]

On July 3, Private William Edwards of the 19th Massachusetts' Company A was lifting his musket to fire when he was shot through his left arm by a musket ball. The round fractured the bone two inches below the elbow, cut through muscles and tendons, and exited just above the wrist, leaving Edwards' hand nearly useless. At age 52, Private Edwards was one of the oldest men in the unit. He received a pension of $5.00 per month, since he could never work again in his former occupation of painter, nor perform any other type of manual labor. William Edwards died impoverished in December 1881. [30]

Private William B. Parker of the 20th Massachusetts' Company I was a 19-year-old unmarried painter from Medford, Massachusetts. Shot under his shoulder blade in the fighting of July 3, Parker suffered a fracture of his left humerus, which necessitated the amputation of the arm at the shoulder. The open wound took nine months to close. He was discharged for disability on January 6, 1864, and was described by his sister at that time as having ". . . wasted away to a skeleton." He then began receiving a pension of $8.00 per month. Unfit for any type of manual labor, Parker's only other income came from selling vegetables raised in his garden. In June 1867, Parker enlisted in the 42nd United States Infantry Regiment, but again proved unable to withstand the physical life of a soldier. On March 31, 1869, he was again discharged for disability, and his Federal pension was increased to $15.00 per month. William Parker died in March 1870 at the age of 26 from heart disease, after suffering from constant pain in his neck and shoulder since the time of his wounding. His personal physician indicated that he believed that the heart disease had resulted from the effects of Parker's being shot at the Battle of Gettysburg almost seven years before. However, the Federal government refused to grant his widowed father a survivor's pension, as it was felt that Parker's death was non-service related. [31]

A 30-year-old Boston bootmaker, Corporal James F. Goulding, serving in the 20th Massachusetts' Company C, was hit in his right thigh by a musket ball on July 3. The damage to the limb was so extensive that regimental surgeon Nathan Hayward amputated Goulding's leg on July 4. Corporal Goulding was discharged from the service on January 28, 1864, the date of his release from a military hospital in Philadelphia, and immediately began receiving a pension of $8.00 per month. Unfortunately, Goulding's leg had been amputated so near the hip joint that no sufficient stump remained for him to use a wooden leg, and he was relegated to the full-time use of crutches. By the time of his death in June 1874, Goulding, who was unmarried, was indigent, and his pension had been raised to $18.00 per month. [32]

Twenty-year-old Corporal Lusher White, a 5' 10" farmer from Dedham, Massachusetts, was a member of Company K of the 20th Massachusetts. In the fighting of July 3, he was struck by a piece of shell in the right side of his head, which fractured his skull and, as later described by a civilian volunteer nurse, ". . . tore off part of his ear, and shattering his jaw, laid bare one side of his throat." White was unconscious until July 6, when he briefly regained his senses, and then sank into a stupor again, and, it was thought, died. He was taken on a stretcher to a temporary cemetery, which was rapidly filling up with the bodies of those who had died from their wounds. When the stretcher was roughly dropped on the ground by its bearers next to a prepared grave, White, suddenly conscious, said, "Boys, what are you doing?" Told he was about to be buried, he replied, "I don't see it boys; give me a drink of water, and carry me back. I won't be buried by this raw recruit!" The corporal survived his terrible wounds and his premature trip to his own grave. White was hospitalized at Gettysburg until September 1863, when he was transferred to Mower U.S.A. General Hospital in Chestnut Hill, Pennsylvania, where he stayed until he was discharged for disability on July 21, 1864. The whole right side of White's face was paralyzed; he had lost the sight in his right eye and the hearing in what remained of his right ear. Beginning in July 1864, White received the sum of $5.33 per month as a Federal disability pension. He became a ward of the State of New Hampshire, where he had moved after his release from the hospital. Lusher White died of consumption in June 1866. [33]

Private Patrick Manning of Company D of the 20th Massachusetts was a 26-year-old shoemaker from Royalston, Massachusetts, who was wounded in both wrists on July 3. Both of his radii were excised by the regiment's surgeon Nathan Hayward. However, Manning died of pyemia on July 12, 1863, and is now buried in Grave A-23 in the Massachusetts Plot of the Gettysburg National Cemetery. Manning left behind a wife and two-year-old daughter, who received a $10.00 per month pension from the Federal government. [34]

A roofer from Providence, Rhode Island, 28-year-old Private Thomas Tiernan had enlisted in the 20th's Company A on August 25, 1861. On July 3, 1863, Private Tiernan was shot in his right eye. The bullet completely destroyed the eyeball and fractured Tiernan's right cheekbone. That night at a field hospital, the ball was removed from the eye socket. Amazingly, Thomas Tiernan survived this terrible wound, but was subject to continual vertigo, headaches, and permanent dilation of his left eye. Upon his medical discharge in May 1864, he began receiving a Federal pension of $6.00 per month. After the war, Tiernan returned to Rhode Island, married and fathered a daughter. Unfortunately, in 1888, Tiernan began to lose the sight in his left eye. By the time of his death in 1904, Thomas Tiernan was completely blind and his pension had increased to $18.00 per month. [35]

At some point during the close-in fighting at the Copse of Trees, Private Arthur Hughes of Company F, 20th Massachusetts, was struck in his lower right leg by a ball and three buckshot. Hughes, a 24-year-old shoemaker from Georgetown, Massachusetts, had enlisted in the regiment on July 26, 1861, and survived almost two years of war unhurt; on this day, however, his luck ran out. Confederate rounds splintered his leg bone and left a gaping wound. From July 3 to July 14, 1863, Private Hughes was treated at a field hospital in Gettysburg, where bone fragments were removed from his leg. He was then transferred to McDougal General Hospital, Fort Schuyler, New York, where he remained until November 1863. After his release from the hospital, Hughes was sent back to his regiment on a light-duty basis. He served as an officers' servant until discharged from the army on July 21, 1864. Arthur Hughes tried to return to his profession of shoemaking, but he could not stand at his work bench on his damaged limb, and began receiving a Federal pension of $2.00 per month. When a government physician reexamined his right leg in 1873, Hughes' wound was still open and several small pieces of bone were removed. Arthur Hughes died of kidney disease in September 1896. By that time, his Federal pension had been increased to $12.00 per month. [36]

At age 54, Private Edward Murphy, serving with Company K of the 20th Massachusetts, was one of the oldest soldiers in the regiment. He had worked as a laborer in Boston before the war. On July 3, during the cannonade proceeding Pickett's Charge, a Rebel shell fragment struck Murphy in the left groin and exited at his right buttock. While going to the rear for aid, another Confederate shell burst over his head, wounding him in the eyes and neck and temporarily blinding him. After receiving treatment for his wounds for a period of several months, on December 28, 1863, Edward Murphy returned to duty with his unit. Unfortunately, on May 5, 1864, at the Battle of the Wilderness, Murphy was hit again, this time in his right arm. The last notation in Murphy's Federal pension file is from 1882, when he was living alone in the National Soldiers' Home in Montgomery County, Ohio, receiving a pension of $16.00 a month. [37]

Pickett's division, too, paid a terrible price for its heroism. Becoming a legend at Gettysburg cost the Virginians 499 officers and men killed, 1,473 officers and men wounded, and 681 taken prisoner, for total casualties of 2,653. [38] Neither Major General George Pickett nor any member of his staff was killed or wounded, which in itself was a source of much post-battle controversy and sullied his reputation. [39] However, Brigadier General Richard Garnett was killed, Brigadier General Lewis Armistead was mortally wounded and died in Union hands, and Brigadier General James Kemper was seriously wounded and temporarily captured. [40] Of the 40 field-grade officers in Pickett's division (colonels, lieutenant colonels and majors), 12 were killed or mortally wounded, 13 were wounded, and five were captured, including four of the wounded. [41] The unit's final destruction came in the waning days of the war in April 1865, at the Battle of Five Forks.

Battlefield statistics are clearly an impersonal abstract of the pain and death that soldiers suffer. The individual accounts of vibrant life cut short strip away the cold mathematics to reveal the face of war in all its ugliness and terror. On occasion, though, those killed in battle were deemed the fortunate ones.

In Major General Pickett's division, 210 men died while being held prisoner, almost half at Fort Delaware on Pea Patch Island, Delaware. [42] Dying from chronic diarrhea, typhoid fever and smallpox is not the death of song and epic poem, but those young men were just as dead as those killed on the battlefield. Others survived their imprisonment but carried the pain and scars, both physical and mental, for however long they walked the earth.

A review of the records for the infantrymen of the three Massachusetts regiments who were taken prisoner during the Battle of Gettysburg reveals that they were more fortunate than their Confederate counterparts. Over 30 men from the 15th, 19th and 20th Massachusetts were captured in the fighting, the majority from the ranks of the 15th when the regiment was overwhelmed by the onslaught of Wright's Georgians in the late afternoon of July 2. Only one man captured at Gettysburg from the ranks of the three units, 42-year-old Private John Doherty from Company E of the 19th Massachusetts, a pre-war laborer from Boston, died in a Confederate prison. Doherty, taken captive on July 2, perished on December 31, 1863, from "starvation and cruel treatment" (as quoted from his pension file), at Belle Isle prison camp in Richmond, Virginia. [43] This remarkable survival rate, however, does not show how many of the Union captives had their health impaired or broken by the harsh conditions that were all too common in Civil War prisons—stories that remain hidden, even to this day.

One such man was Private Charles Brown of Company H, 19th Massachusetts, an 18-year-old farmer from Salem. Brown was captured on the afternoon of July 2. With thousands of other prisoners, he was forced-marched to Staunton, Virginia, by his Confederate captors, who stole his boots from him, leaving him in his stocking feet. In Staunton, Private Brown and his unfortunate companions were put on railroad cars and sent to Richmond, where they arrived on July 21, 1863. Brown was then held at Belle Isle prison camp and was ". . . obliged to lie on wet grounds entirely without shelter from the weather." Paroled only a month later, Private Brown was deemed unfit for further active duty due to rheumatism, pleurisy and hemorrhoids contracted during his captivity and was transferred to the Veteran Reserve Corps. Upon his discharge in December 1864, Charles Brown began receiving a Federal pension of $2.00 per month. He later married and found work as a shoemaker, but was constantly plagued by rheumatism and hemorrhoids. By the time of his death on May 6, 1916, Brown's pension had increased to $25.00 per month. [44]

Finally, what of Private Timothy Dugan of the 20th Massachusetts, who had previously been detached to serve in the Provost Guard of General Gibbon's division and had been sent back to the ranks of the regiment just prior to the cannonade's onset? Dugan survived the carnage around the Copse of Trees, but deserted during the night of July 3, and disappeared from the rolls of the regiment forever. [45]

The purpose of these vignettes has been to show just a fraction of the "real" cost of helping to win the Battle of Gettysburg. No glory, no pomp, no waving flags. Just "common" Americans dealing with the loss of husbands and fathers, brothers and sons. Just men trying to struggle through life missing eyes or limbs, attempting to support their families in menial jobs, aided by a pittance of a government pension. The lives of literally thousands of Massachusetts men, women and children were permanently altered by what occurred outside a small Pennsylvania town on July 2 and 3, 1863. In that regard, these unfortunate Bay Staters shared the suffering of untold numbers of their fellow citizens, both North and South, long after the guns of Gettysburg fell silent.

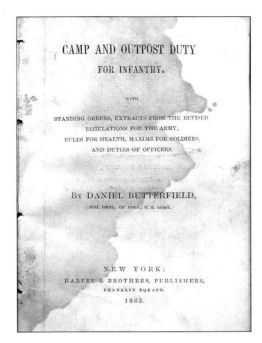

Book of camp instruction owned by Col. George Ward and found on the battlefield.

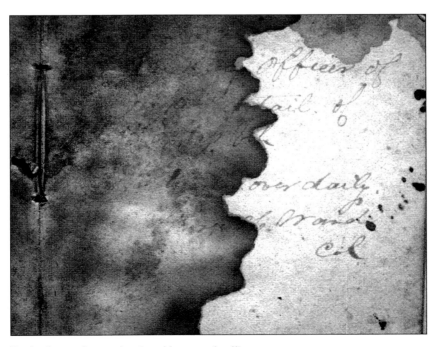

Book of camp instruction (outside cover detail).

15th Massachusetts colors. Post-war photograph.

Benjamin Falls holding colors of 19th Massachusetts.

Edmund Rice's Medal of Honor.

20th Massachusetts colors. Post-war photograph.

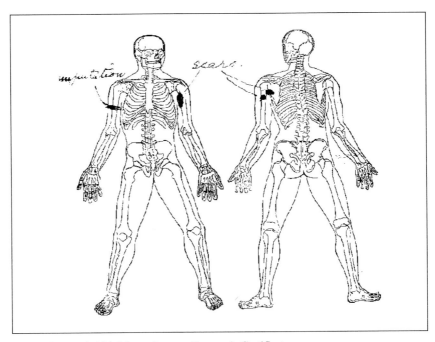

Chester Leonard, 20th Massachusetts, Surgeon's Certificate.

Spring from which Moses Shackley drew water during cannonade of July 3, 1863.

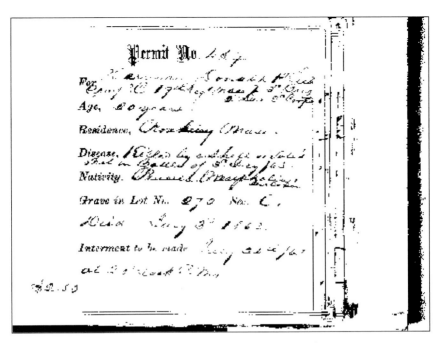

Herman Donath's grave registration, Evergreen Cemetery, Gettysburg.

Herman Donath grave, Evergreen Cemetery, Gettysburg, Pennsylvania.

Sumner Paine grave, Gettysburg National Cemetery.

Sherman Robinson grave, Gettysburg National Cemetery.

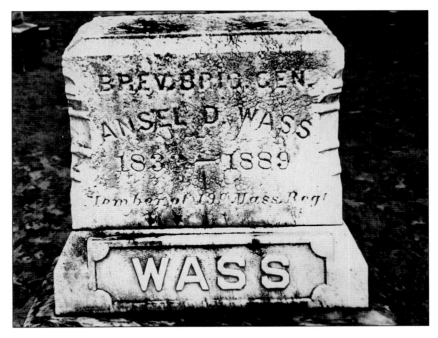

Grave of Ansel Wass, Evergreen Cemetery, Portland, Maine.

Benjamin Falls grave, Lynn, Massachusetts.

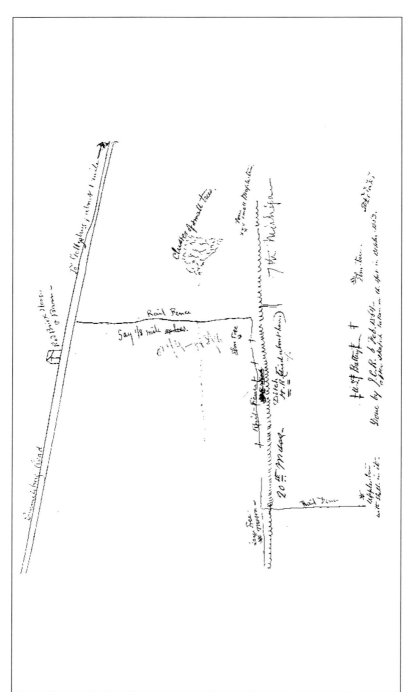

John Codman Ropes map of the position of the 20th Massachusetts on July 3, 1863, drawn after his October, 1863 visit to the battlefield.

4

The Long Road to Home
July 6, 1863, to July 3, 1865

T he battered remnants of the three Bay State regiments, in conjunction with the rest of their surviving comrades in the II Corps, left Gettysburg in pursuit of Lee's army on July 6, 1863.[1] Although hindsight has shown that Robert E. Lee's defeat at Gettysburg was the turning point of the war, at least in the Eastern Theater, it took another twenty-one months of hard fighting, with its attendant terrible casualties for both forces, before the Army of Northern Virginia was finally brought to bay and forced to surrender at Appomattox Courthouse on April 9, 1865. As part of the vaunted II Corps, the three Massachusetts regiments were destined to again pay a horrific price in the forthcoming campaigns.

Fortunately for the Massachusetts men, the next several months were relatively quiet. Several minor skirmishes and less sanguinary engagements were fought in the fall of 1863, mainly at Bristoe Station, Virginia, in October and at Mine Run, Virginia, in November. Casualties were very light for the three units in both of these encounters.

The 15th Massachusetts lost two men killed and eight wounded at Bristoe Station and had 10 wounded and five missing in the Mine Run campaign.[2] The most serious loss to the regiment was the capture of Lieutenant Colonel Joslin at Mine Run, while he was establishing the skirmish line. Joslin was held in various Confederate prisons until his exchange in August 1864.[3]

At Bristoe Station, according to the *Official Records*, the 19th Massachusetts lost four men wounded, one of whom later died. In the Mine Run campaign, the unit was engaged in the fighting near Locust Grove, Virginia, west of Chancellorsville, and lost one man killed and two wounded.[4]

The 20th was similarly fortunate in that the regiment was only lightly engaged at both Bristoe Station and Mine Run. At the former engagement, the 20th Massachusetts had one man killed and six men wounded and lost only one soldier killed and one taken prisoner at Mine Run.[5]

The men of the three regiments spent the remainder of the winter of 1863-1864 encamped around Brandy Station, Virginia. [6] During this time, these units faced a crisis that threatened the very fabric of the Union army. The three-year enlistments of many soldiers in the army were due to expire in the spring of 1864, in the middle of the prime campaigning season. Should a majority of these men not reenlist, the Army of the Potomac, together with all other Federal armies then in the field, would lose its most valuable asset - its hard core of veteran fighting men. Accordingly, the Federal government, rather than the individual states, which had initially recruited the regiments in the spring of 1861, undertook a major effort to keep these men in the ranks.

These veterans, who had faced death on many a terrible field, and had not gone home in almost three years, were offered a furlough of thirty days and a $400.00 Federal bounty to reenlist. In addition to the national bounty, most states and many local municipalities offered their own financial inducements. Three-year veterans who reenlisted also got the right to wear a special chevron on their uniform sleeves. Further, if three-quarters of the men in the regiment re-upped, their regiment would retain its numerical identity and not go out of existence when its original three-year term of service expired. In many Union regiments, this appeal to unit pride proved very effective. [7]

The Massachusetts veterans reacted very differently to this situation and the inducements to stay in the service. Only 55 of 235 men eligible to re-enlist in the ranks of the 15th Massachusetts did so, according to Captain George Brown, then commanding the regiment in February 1864. Captain Brown stated: "Of the following, a large proportion have signified their willingness to reenlist, provided the regiment be ordered to Massachusetts to reorganize and recruit. There can be no doubt that three-fourths of the remaining number would reenlist, and in my opinion a much larger proportion." [8] Army headquarters refused this request, so the 15th was to cease to exist upon the expiration of its three-year term of service in July 1864.

The opposite was true in the 19th and 20th Massachusetts. Valiant Ben Falls of the 19th was remembered as saying: "Well, if new men won't finish this job, old men must, and as long as Uncle Sam wants a man, here's Ben Falls." He reenlisted, as did 145 of the approximately 185 men in the regiment's ranks eligible to do so. In a post-war memoir, a veteran of the 19th wrote eloquently about the reenlistment of the unit's veterans during the winter of 1863-1864: "To my mind the reenlisting of the three years' men in the field was the most patriotic event of the war. They knew what war was, had seen their regiments and companies swept away until only a remnant remained. They did not have the excitement of the war meetings to urge them on, but with a full knowledge of the duties required and the possibility that many would fall before their term expired, with uncovered heads and uplifted hands they swore to stand by the flag until the last armed foe surrendered." [9]

His comments are germane, not only for the men of the 19th, but for all men who stood tall in their nation's hour of need. The records show the 20th Massachusetts had similar success in convincing the necessary amount of its veterans to remain in the service, and thus, both regiments retained their unit identity for the fateful spring of 1864. [10]

B y the start of the 1864 campaign season, the shattered ranks of all three regiments had been expanded by the receipt of new volunteers, draftees, and the return of veterans from convalescent leave. By the beginning of May, there were 287 officers and men present for duty in the 15th Massachusetts, including 48 new recruits. On May 1, 1864, the 19th Massachusetts had 362 officers and men ready to face the forthcoming test, while the 20th Massachusetts received 236 new recruits from March 1, 1864, to May 1, 1864, bolstering its ranks to 15 officers and approximately 400 men. [11]

One of the heroic figures in the 19th Massachusetts was destined not to participate in the coming battles. Second Lieutenant Moses Shackley, who had played so prominent a role in the repulse of Pickett's men, anticipated a promotion to the rank of first lieutenant after the battle of Gettysburg. When this advancement was not forthcoming, Shackley's pride was wounded and he sent in his resignation. However, the resignation was not accepted by army headquarters. As a protest, Lieutenant Shackley went absent without leave from October 17, 1863, to October 21, 1863. In consequence, on November 1, 1863, Moses Shackley was court-martialed for this offence, found guilty, and was dishonorably dismissed from the service, effective November 12, 1863. [12]

In preparation for what was to become known as the 1864 Overland Campaign, the Army of the Potomac was reorganized. The three Massachusetts regiments were now assigned to the same brigade, serving with their comrades of the 42nd, 59th, and 82nd New York, the 19th Maine, the 7th Michigan, and the Andrew (Massachusetts) Sharpshooters. Their division was still commanded by Major General John Gibbon, but the new brigade was led by Brigadier General Alexander Webb, commander of the "Philadelphia Brigade" at Gettysburg. [13]

At the regimental level, as Lieutenant Colonel Joslin was still held in a Confederate prison, the 15th Massachusetts was now commanded by Bostonian Major I. Harris Hooper, aged 24, who had joined the regiment in July 1861. The 19th was led by Edmund Rice, recovered from his Gettysburg wounds and now a lieutenant colonel; Colonel Arthur Devereux had resigned on February 27, 1864, to take care of "private affairs" at home. Promoted to the rank of colonel, effective as of July 5, 1863, George Macy, with an artificial hand replacing the one lost at Gettysburg, had returned from a long convalescence and was again in command of the 20th Massachusetts. [14] The fighting that these Massachusetts men would endure, with the rest of the Army of the Potomac, in the Overland Campaign, was even more intense and horrible than anything they had seen before in their service.

The casualties suffered by the three regiments in this campaign, which lasted less than two months, almost completely destroyed the units. The fighting began in earnest with the Battle of the Wilderness, on May 5 and 6, 1864, in the thickets and dense chapparral of the Wilderness of Spotsylvania County, Virginia. In the two days of bloodshed, the 15th Massachusetts lost four men killed, 16 wounded and three missing. The 19th lost four killed, 12 wounded and four missing. One of the regiment's wounded was Sergeant Ben Falls, now carrying the unit's colors. Falls was shot in the arm but refused to go to the rear for medical attention. He was remembered as saying, "Some fool will get hold of the color and lose it. I guess I'd better stay by [it.]" [15]

By far the most serious losses of the three regiments were suffered by the 20th Massachusetts. The post-war regimental history does not specifically enumerate the casualties suffered by the unit in the Battle of the Wilderness; it lists the losses sustained as a whole in the entire campaign. However, a modern work indicates that the 20th lost 23 men killed, 108 wounded and nine missing in the fighting. [16]

Among the wounded was Captain William F. Perkins, one of the unit's three officers to survive Gettysburg unscathed. In the fighting on May 6, Captain Perkins was shot through the throat, with the bullet passing between his jugular vein and cartoid artery and lodging in his cervical vertebrae. A fellow officer later stated that Perkins "fell as rigid as an iron bar." William Perkins received a discharge for disability on November 4, 1864, and remained paralyzed for eighteen months. [17]

Also wounded was William B. Fuchs, now with the rank of color sergeant, who had gallantly picked up the regimental flag in the advance to the Copse of Trees, for which he was subsequently promoted. In the fierce combat of May 6, Fuchs was shot and the colors fell to the ground. Two men in the 20th then grabbed the flagstaff and began arguing over who would have the honor of carrying the colors. Suddenly, a bullet cut the staff in two and ended the dispute. [18]

Among the dead was Henry Abbott, now a major. Abbott had taken command of the 20th Massachusetts during the battle when Colonel Macy was shot in both legs and forced to leave the field. Mortally wounded in the abdomen, after giving instructions that all of his money should go to the widows and orphans of the regiment, Henry L. Abbott, aged 22, died on the afternoon of May 6, 1864. General Alexander Webb, his brigade commander, wrote of him: "It will be found very difficult to replace him. No truer soldier was in my command. His reputation as an officer stood far beyond the usual eulogies pronounced on our dead officers. I feel that his merit was so peculiar and his worth so well known to all officers of the corps and to the general commanding that it is not necessary for me to attempt to do him justice. My brigade lost in him its best officer." In a letter home, a surgeon serving with the 20th Massachusetts penned this final tribute to Major Abbott: "Harry Abbott was an ideal man; an ideal officer, reverenced by his friends and deeply respected by all who knew him. What will become of the Twentieth without him I cannot imagine; for he was its life, its discipline, and its success." Abbott received a posthumous promotion to the rank of brevet brigadier general, to date from March 13, 1865, for "gallant and meritorious service" at the Battle of the Wilderness. [19]

In the Battle of Spotsylvania, the three Bay State regiments again suffered terrible losses, which, in the cases of the 15th and 20th Massachusetts, were not specifically broken down in the regimental histories. However, a post-war study of Union battle deaths lists 14 and 25 men killed or mortally wounded in the 15th and 20th, respectively, for the entire Battle of Spotsylvania, which lasted from May 8 to May 18, 1864. [20]

According to a detailed casualty listing in the 19th's regimental history, in the engagements around Spotsylvania, the regiment lost 11 killed or mortally wounded, 35 wounded and nine captured or missing. One of the dead of the unit was Ben Falls, shot in the body while carrying the unit's national colors on May 12, 1864. Barely clinging to life, Falls was taken to the rear, where he died on May 14, 1864. Lieutenant Colonel Edmund Rice, commanding the 19th, was wounded and captured on May 12, 1864. [21] Deducting the losses suffered in the battles of the Wilderness and Spotsylvania, each unit now had roughly 150 men remaining in its ranks.

As the campaign continued, with General U. S. Grant trying to draw the Confederates out of their impregnable entrenchments around Spotsylvania Courthouse and into an open fight, the losses continued to rise for the already decimated Massachusetts units. From May 22, 1864, to June 1, 1864, the 15th suffered casualties consisting of two men killed and 10 wounded, mainly in fighting at the North Anna River, leaving only 140 officers and men in the ranks. The 19th lost two killed and six wounded, and the 20th had one man killed and an unknown number of wounded. [22]

The Overland Campaign culminated in the Battle of Cold Harbor, which lasted until the middle of June 1864. The main action involved a large-scale attack on the Rebel lines early on the morning of June 3, 1864; this resulted in a disastrous Union repulse. In this assault, many units in the Federal army suffered horrific casualties. After the failure of the attacks on that day, both armies dug in and contented themselves with skirmishing and sharpshooting.

In the entire battle, the 15th lost 14 men, five of whom were fatalities. The 19th lost 29, six of whom were killed or mortally wounded. One of the casualties was Sergeant Benjamin Jellison, captor of the flag of the 57th Virginia on July 3, 1863. Jellison was shot in his left knee and severely wounded on June 3, 1864; he was not able to return to duty until September 16, 1864. [23]

The losses of the 20th Massachusetts at Cold Harbor were not specifically delineated; however, for the period from May 18, 1864, to June 15, 1864, the regiment lost 77 men, of whom 12 were killed or mortally wounded. One of the wounded was Captain John Summerhayes, who, as a second lieutenant, allegedly had picked up a sword belonging to General Garnett after the fighting had ended on July 3, 1863. Summerhayes was shot through the right wrist. After his recovery, John Summerhayes was appointed divisional inspector and served for the rest of the war in staff positions. [24]

B y this time, the three Massachusetts regiments had been bled white. The 15th was reduced to about 75 officers and men. The 19th, even with the addition of approximately 100 new recruits who had arrived on June 11, had only 140 in the ranks, and the 20th, after deducting the losses suffered at Cold Harbor, had a strength of less than 100 men, including the few officers still on their feet. [25]

The final blow fell on the afternoon of June 22, 1864, during the initial phase of the Petersburg Campaign. On that date, several Confederate brigades from General William Mahone's division fell on the left flank of the unsuspecting Union II Corps, positioned southwest of Petersburg, Virginia, near the Jerusalem Plank Road, and rolled it up like a blanket. Even though the three Massachusetts regiments, together with the rest of Gibbon's division, were stationed on the right of the II Corps line, the Rebel advance still caught them unaware and overwhelmed them. [26]

With no warning of the sudden onslaught, most of the Massachusetts men's only alternative was to surrender. The 15th Massachusetts, the first of the three units to be struck, lost all but six of its men, with the great majority, some 69 in number, being captured, along with the regimental colors. In the confusion, the color-bearer had hidden the flag in a ditch and tried to retrieve it later, but his plan was discovered and the banner seized. Ironically, one of General Mahone's units which decimated the 15th in this attack was Wright's Georgia brigade, their adversaries on July 2, 1863. [27]

The 19th Massachusetts, which was now so reduced in numbers that it had been consolidated from 10 to two companies, and formed only a single line of battle, lost all but approximately 30 soldiers. Again, most of the losses were men taken prisoner, as 153 officers and men from the regiment were captured. As was the case with the 15th Massachusetts, the 19th's set of regimental colors also fell into Rebel hands. One of the men in the unit who surrendered was John Robinson of Company I, captor of an unidentified Confederate banner on July 3, 1863. Shot in his right forearm in the fighting and then taken prisoner, Robinson was held in various Rebel prisons until his exchange on November 27, 1864. [28]

Fortunately, Major Henry Patten of the 20th Massachusetts, then commanding the regiment, which was stationed further to the right in the divisional alignment, was able to turn the unit to the left and check the enemy's advance. [29] Again, the 20th's losses in this catastrophic engagement were not specifically given in the regimental history.

Most of the men from both the 15th and 19th who were captured in this disaster ended up in the Andersonville prison camp, where at least 26 men from the 15th and 42 soldiers of the 19th died. In addition, the health of many of those who survived imprisonment was permanently damaged by the dreadful conditions all too common in Civil War prisons. [30]

In a letter written after this debacle, Major Patten clearly described the effects that more than a month of constant marching and fighting had had on the men, and himself: "[The soldiers] have been so horribly worked and badgered that they are utterly unnerved and demoralised. They are easily scared as a timid child at night. Half our brigade were taken prisoners the other day, in the middle of the day, by a line no stronger than themselves, without firing a shot. . . . We, our brigade, have made fourteen charges upon the enemy's breastworks, although at last no amount of urging, no heroic example, no threats, or anything else, could get the line to stir one peg. For my own part, I am utterly tired and disheartened and if I stay at all, it will be like a whipt dog—because I think I must." [31] Stay Henry Patten did, but to an unfortunate end. He was shot in his left leg on August 17, 1864, and died of blood poisoning in a Philadelphia hospital on September 10 the same year. [32]

The three-year term of enlistment ended for the survivors of the 15th Massachusetts on July 12, 1864. Only 85 men of the original complement of 1,011 boarded the train for the return trip to Worcester, where they arrived on July 21. (The ranks had grown to 85 due to recovered convalescents and returning detached troops. Those men who had enlisted in the unit after July 12, 1861, whose terms of service had not expired, were designated as the 15th Massachusetts Battalion, and were transferred to the ranks of the 20th Massachusetts, to serve out the balance of their time.) A reception was held in Worcester on July 28, 1864. There, John A. Andrew, governor of Massachusetts, read a proclamation honoring and thanking the men of the 15th, both living and dead, for their heroism and sacrifices. On that day, the men were formally mustered out of service, and the name "15th Massachusetts Volunteer Infantry Regiment" passed into the pages of history. [33]

The 19th and 20th Massachusetts, greatly reduced in numbers, maintained their unit identities and fought with the II Corps for the rest of the war. They were present when the Army of Northern Virginia surrendered at Appomattox on April 9, 1865, and each marched in the Grand Review of the Army of the Potomac, held on May 23, 1865, in Washington, D.C. [34]

But the men who had left Massachusetts to put down the rebellion, the famous "Boys of '61," who had played so great a role in winning the war, were mostly gone, lying in unmarked graves, or in countless hospital beds, or at home, trying to rehabilitate their broken bodies. In fact, of the 37 commissioned officers of the 19th Massachusetts who left their home state on that long-ago day of August 28, 1861, only one, Edmund Rice, now commanding the unit, returned to Readville, Massachusetts, with the regiment on July 3, 1865. [35]

The 19th Massachusetts Volunteer Infantry Regiment was officially mustered out of United States service on July 20, 1865, at Readville. The 20th
Massachusetts followed suit on July 28, 1865, also at Readville. [36] The war
had been won, but at a terrible price. Now it was time for the surviving
veterans and the widows and orphans of their fallen comrades to rebuild their
lives, in peace.

PART TWO

THE
STRUGGLE
FOR
REMEMBRANCE

5

The Veterans Return

The Quest to be Remembered

For many people, there is a special aura about the battlefield of Gettysburg. Others say it smells different. It is a sacred place for many because of what occurred there. However it impacts the senses and for whatever reasons, the battlefield began drawing many visitors shortly after the guns fell silent, and it continues to attract multitudes of tourists each year. Initially, those who came consisted of people helping to mend the physical wounds of the men who had borne the fight, along with those looking for loved ones, praying to find them alive or at least learn for certain of their fate. Many families in both the North and South never ascertained what happened to sons, brothers, husbands and fathers, forever labeled as "missing in action." In a letter to a widow dated September 26, 1863, the surgeon of the 19th Massachusetts wrote, "You may readily conceive that among the thousands of wounded and killed at that time, the fate of many will always remain a mystery." [1] The certainty that death had overtaken their kith and kin became apparent with time, but never to discover where they lay was a wound that never completely closed.

Even before President Abraham Lincoln consecrated the new National Cemetery on November 19, 1863, an event that redefined not only the Civil War but also America herself, veterans were already revisiting the scene of their mortal combat. One of those early returning soldiers was Colonel George N. Macy, commander of the 20th Massachusetts during the battle, who came back to the field on October 10, 1863, to see where his regiment had fought and also to tour the entire battlefield. (In recognition of his gallantry during the battle, Macy had been promoted to the rank of colonel, to date from July 5, 1863.) [2] Even at that early date, names like Big and Little Round Top, Cemetery Hill and Culp's Hill were already well-known to the American public. Accompanying Colonel Macy were John Codman Ropes, Robert Treat Paine and William Pratt Lyman. John Ropes was the brother of slain First Lieutenant Henry Ropes, and Robert Paine was the sibling of the fallen

Second Lieutenant Sumner Paine. Robert Paine and William Lyman were brothers-in-law. [3]

John Ropes, in addition to being a bereaved relative, became one of the premier 19th-century historians of the Civil War; so, during his visit, he viewed the battlefield from both perspectives. In a letter dated October 19, 1863, Ropes related how the four men had arrived ". . . after some difficulty, in selecting the best route" from Massachusetts. Upon reaching the town of Gettysburg, they took a carriage south along the Emmitsburg Road to the area where the 20th Massachusetts had fought. The visitors walked from the road across the open field in front of the former Union line. Macy, with little trouble, soon stood again where he had lost his hand on that bloody Friday. Although the restored fence line caused some momentary puzzlement, the Colonel ". . . soon remembered all the points in the vicinity," and was "thus able to point out to [Ropes] the very place where Henry was when he was struck by the fatal shell." Ropes wrote simply, yet eloquently: "I cannot tell you what I felt when I saw the spot." [4] Pilgrimages such as his would take place on thousands of occasions over the next several decades.

That Gettysburg and other Civil War battlefields were destined to play an important part in the lives of surviving veterans for the rest of their days became apparent almost immediately after the battle had ended. Only a month after these men consecrated the Pennsylvania fields and hills with their life blood, Gettysburg lawyer David McConaughy contacted leading residents of the town asking that they remember that "there could be no more fitting and expressive memorial of the heroic valor and signal triumphs of our Army than the Battlefield itself, with its natural and artifical defences preserved and perpetuated in the exact form and condition they presented during the Battles." [5] Over the next several months, McConaughy garnered more support for his preservation project.

Property for the development of the National Cemetery was purchased in July 1863. Areas where the visual evidence of fighting was most striking were also pursued. These initial acquisitions, paid for personally by McConaughy, included the western portions of Little Round Top, McKnight's Hill (known today as Stevens's Knoll), and later Raffensperger's Hill (today's East Cemetery Hill), and Culp's Hill, where damaged landscapes and abandoned breastworks abounded. [6]

Partly as a result of attorney McConaughy's efforts, in April 1864, the Commonwealth of Pennsylvania incorporated the Gettysburg Battlefield Memorial Association, a private organization composed of influential local citizens. [7] For the next 31 years, this group preserved, protected and organized the battlefield of Gettysburg. In February 1895, the United States Congress created a National Military Park at Gettysburg. That May, the Gettysburg Battlefield Memorial Association transferred 600 acres of battlefield land, including 17 miles of roads and 320 monuments, to the auspices of the Federal government. [8]

Shortly after the fighting ended, a watershed event in the formation of the future National Park occurred. Thirty-seven-year-old John Badger Bachelder, an artist from New Hampshire and a budding historian, arrived in Gettysburg to study the great battle. He spent most of the subsequent three months exploring the field in great detail. Over the next 30 years, during 14 of which he served as a director of the Gettysburg Battlefield Memorial Association, Bachelder played a major role in the historiography of the Civil War's bloodiest engagement. [9]

The quest of the Massachusetts veterans to properly remember and honor their comrades, both living and dead, primarily covered the years in which the Gettysburg Battlefield Memorial Association worked to save the land for posterity; however, their efforts also extended into the beginning years of the stewardship of the Federal government. The impact of decisions and events of those years can be felt even to the present day. Since events and conditions concerning the efforts of the veterans did not exist in a vacuum, a summary of the preservation activities that took place during the years leading up the placement of their monuments is necessary.

By June 1864, the Gettysburg Battlefield Memorial Association had already protected 70 acres of battlefield land. However, over the next three years, due to a lack of funds and diminished enthusiasm, the Association acquired only another 70 acres. [10] A lack of financial support would plague the organization for its entire existence. Fortunately, in 1867 and 1868, the sum of $3,000.00 was appropriated by the Pennsylvania State Legislature for land acquisition. It is believed that this $6,000.00 was utilized to purchase additional portions of Culp's Hill, East Cemetery Hill and Little Round Top. [11]

The process of placing monuments on the battlefield developed slowly in the years following the great battle. In 1867, veterans of the 1st Minnesota Volunteer Infantry Regiment placed a memorial urn in the National Cemetery, in the midst of the graves, to honor their fallen comrades. It was not until the summer of 1879 that a bronze tablet, placed in the top of a boulder by former members of the 2nd Massachusetts Volunteer Infantry Regiment, became the first unit marker on the battlefield. (The boulder is located along the edge of Spangler's Meadow, at the foot of Culp's Hill, where the regiment had made an ill-fated charge on the morning of July 3, 1863.). [12]

In 1873, John Bachelder published *What to See and Do In Gettysburg*, a tour book that not only described the entire battlefield, but also advised visitors on how to get to the field and where to stay. At this juncture in Gettysburg's history, most visitors were veterans, accompanied by families and friends. Guidebooks such as this became a staple of a tourism industry that continues to the present day. [13]

Ironically, the vicinity of the Copse of Trees was ignored by the photographers who visited the field immediately after the battle. By then, all the dead who had fallen there had been removed or were buried; furthermore, as the significance of the trees was not yet recognized, there were no other prominent landscape features to draw the attention of these early chroniclers of the battle. In fact, the earliest-known existing photograph of the Copse of Trees was taken sometime in 1876 or 1877. Although John Bachelder early on perceived the historic importance of the trees and mentioned them in his 1873 guidebook, the area remained in the backwater of visitors' minds until the 1880s. In the first part of that decade, a number of events occurred that changed the perception of tourists regarding this portion of the battlefield. For one thing, French painter Paul Philippoteaux began his work on the Gettysburg Cyclorama in 1882, using the Copse of Trees as a focal point. In addition, at that time, a battlefield avenue along Cemetery Ridge was laid out, allowing easier access to the area. Federal veterans' associations also started to erect monuments to memorialize their actions along Cemetery Ridge. [14]

An organization of immense importance to the historiography of the Civil War was the Grand Army of the Republic, a nationwide association of Northern veterans formed in 1866. It quickly became known for advancing the cause of veterans' affairs and benefits. State organizations and individual local branches called "Posts" existed not only in the North, but in the South and West as well, wherever numerous former Yankee soldiers had settled after the war. This large and powerful veterans' organization, which, at the height of its power, numbered over 400,000 members, wielded great political clout at all levels of government. [15] Beginning in 1880 and occurring every year until 1894 (except 1884 and 1891), the Grand Army of Pennsylvania camped on the battlefield during the summer. By 1883, the growth of the organization was evident; that year East Cemetery Hill was covered with about 900 tents erected to accommodate the visiting former soldiers. [16]

The summer of 1880 also marked the beginning of the Gettysburg Battlefield Memorial Association's greatest period of preservation activity.   In order to purchase land, the organization needed both a national power base and substantially more money. Changes in the organization's leadership structure brought both of these crucial ingredients. Before the Association's annual election, on June 21, 1880, the Grand Army of the Republic moved to secure a greater voice in the operation of the Gettysburg organization. This campaign for influence resulted in making it known in Gettysburg, just prior to the election, that it would be desirable to place into power a board of directors consisting largely of members of the Grand Army of the Republic. [17]

Indicative of the battlefield preservation organization's subsequent progress are the financial reports. At the annual meeting of the Gettysburg Battlefield Memorial Association in 1880, receipts of $775.00 (with a balance in hand of $515.97) were reported. Only two years later, that balance had grown to $6,922.49. [18]

As the 1880s unfolded, more monuments to individual Union soldiers and regiments began to be placed on the field. Federal legislation promulgated in early 1881 evidenced the increased interest in Gettysburg. Henry Bingham, a congressman from Philadelphia, introduced a bill before the House of Representatives that provided for the marking of regimental positions on the Gettysburg battlefield with metal signs or granite posts. Significantly, agreement by the Gettysburg Battlefield Memorial Association was necessary before the law could go into effect; only then could such unit signs be placed on land owned by the preservation organization. [19]

A battle fought over such a wide area as Gettysburg and its environs made it difficult for the average tourist to understand the scope of the struggle and the distances involved from one portion of the field to another. Consequently, in July 1881, workers began the construction of a 35-foot wooden tower at the top of Big Round Top. This structure was designed to provide a view both "far reaching and enchanting." [20]

On July 13, 1881, the *Compiler*, a Gettysburg newspaper, reported that the Gettysburg Battlefield Memorial Association had decided to open a battlefield avenue between the Taneytown Road and Little Round Top. [21] This proposed road, which, in November 1887, was named Hancock Avenue where it passed the Copse of Trees, traversed the land of seven different landowners. All of these families wanted more money for a right of way across their property than the Association was willing to pay. As a result, the organization invoked the powers of condemnation established in its charter in order to secure the land, with the cost considerations being determined by the local court system during the winter of 1881. Gettysburg newspapers proclaimed the road open to travel on July 12, 1882. [22] This important part of the battle-field, where the men from Massachusetts had fought and died, was only wide enough to encompass the road and space on either side of it to place the memorials of the Union regiments that fought in the area. [23]

The very nature of the growing importance of Gettysburg as a historic site led to the beginning of development that would eventually become, to some people, a desecration of the very thing intended to honor and preserve. The need to accommodate the growing number of visitors became increas-ingly apparent in ensuing decades. For instance, in July 1882, prior to the summer's Grand Army of the Republic encampment, 2,000 men applied for tent accommodations. This figure did not include the many people who found space in hotels and boarding houses. A local newspaper boasted, "Room can be found by all who may come. This town has learned how to feed and sleep a big crowd." [24]

G ettysburg had first attained access via railroad in 1858. Over the years, the original transportation carrier had not fared well financially. By the 1880s, its limited schedule could not meet the growing visitation needs of the town and the battlefield. Consequently, a new railroad company came on the scene; by September 1883, workmen of the Gettysburg and Harrisburg Rail-road were engaged in laying one half mile of track daily, as their line ad-vanced from Carlisle toward Gettysburg. That same month, plans were com-pleted to construct passenger and freight stations on the northwest corner of Washington and Railroad Streets in the town. In keeping with the building style of the period and to provide a welcoming atmosphere, the passenger structure was to be ornamental, with a center tower and separate spacious "retiring" rooms for men and women, complete with attached water closets. A baggage room and covered platforms were also included in these plans. Track was laid from this point toward the Gettysburg and Harrisburg line, where a junction between the two sections would occur outside of town. The local *Star and Sentinel* newspaper trumpeted the fact that "a good deal of money will be expended in putting up commodious pavilions and other build-ings for the accommodation of excursionists - the purpose being to make the grounds attractive and inviting." [25]

On February 21, 1884, the railroad tracks emanating from the town toward the north met those being laid by workmen moving south. On March 4, 1884, at this junction, located approximately one and a half miles from Gettysburg, two golden spikes, one inscribed "1863" and the other "1883" were hammered into the iron. At 11 a.m., with the firing of a ceremonial cannon, the flag-covered engine "Jay Cooke" rolled into the Gettysburg, whistle blaring, amidst cheering from the festive crowd. On that memorable day, the Gettysburg and Harrisburg Railroad Company dedicated the line from Harrisburg, which satisfied the transportation needs of those who wished to visit the battlefield. Due to this railroad line, the 49 miles between Harrisburg and Gettysburg could now be traveled in only two hours. The battlefield was now considered conveniently accessible to the average tourist; the railroad opened what had been considered "a sealed book." [26] A guidebook printed in 1885 stated: "Fifty thousand persons visited the field during the Summer of 1884," and the desire that ". . . hundreds of thousands should come." The company believed, "No American's historical education is complete until he has made a thorough study of this pivotal battle-ground." [27]

The new station on North Washington Street near Gettysburg College (then known as Pennsylvania College) welcomed tourists for the first time on April 21, 1884. A visitor could, at this juncture, hire a guide and tour the field via carriage, or purchase train passage on the Gettysburg and Harrisburg's Round Top Branch. In September 1882, a charter had been granted by the Commonwealth of Pennsylvania for a railroad line to run from the town of Gettysburg to Round Top. Completed in mid 1884, this extension terminated at the base of Little Round Top, a distance of two and a half miles from town. As the tracks left Gettysburg, they cut through fields and crossed the Emmitsburg Road near the Codori farm. Before reaching Little Round Top, the line passed directly by the spot where Major General Winfield Scott Hancock had been wounded on July 3, 1863. [28]

As the train moved down the former Union line on Cemetery Ridge, a guide book directed the attention of the visitor toward the left, where he or she would ". . . find what has been named by history the UMBRELLA CLUMP OF TREES. This was the focus and centre of PICKETT'S CELEBRATED CHARGE [emphasis in original]." However, the train did not stop near the Copse of Trees. The "High Water Mark" was not the primary stop on the excursion; at that time, it was Little Round Top. [29]

In July 1883, Massachusetts became the first state to appropriate money for the erection of individual regimental monuments on the battlefield of Gettysburg, designating a total sum of $5,000.00 for that purpose. In August 1883, Governor Benjamin Butler, a former Union general, asked for a meeting of Massachusetts veterans to help ascertain how that money should be spent. The location of each memorial—a decision to be made in conjunction with the Gettysburg Battlefield Memorial Association—was to be determined for the purpose of land acquisition, leading to the placement of regimental memorials. To fulfill that goal, representatives from various Massachusetts regimental organizations would travel to Gettysburg in late October 1883. [30]

Prior to the arrival of the Bay Staters, events had occurred that would prove to be the beginning of the 15th, 19th and 20th Massachusetts' fading from history's recollection of the climactic moments of Pickett's Charge. On April 27, 1883, representatives from the 72nd Pennsylvania located a site " . . . for a monument on the battlefield, along the new avenue, near the center of Hancock's line, which they occupied at the time of Pickett's Charge." Less than four months later, the August 22 edition of the Gettysburg *Star and Sentinel* newspaper reported that the 72nd had erected a "handsome granite memorial stone on the avenue near the point of Pickett's assault on our lines." Five days later, during a regimental reunion, a large group of the 72nd's veterans, families and friends celebrated the unveiling of their new "brigade" memorial with speeches and prayers. The keynote speaker was former General Alexander Webb, commander of the brigade under whom these men had served on that memorable day. In his speech, General Webb reviewed the history of the regiment and the important role it played in repulsing the famous assault. Little did the soon-to-arrive Massachusetts veterans realize how this ceremony would evolve to their disadvantage. [31]

On October 24, 1883, a committee from the Gettysburg Battlefield Memorial Association and members of the local Grand Army of the Republic Post Number 9 met 135 Massachusetts veterans upon their arrival. To the accompaniment of a drum corps, the veterans were escorted the short distance to their accommodations at the Eagle Hotel, at the northeast corner of Washington and Chambersburg Streets. During this visit to mark the regiment's position during the fighting, the 15th's David M. Earle, formerly of Company F, Henry T. Dudley, who had served in Company A, and Thomas J. Hastings, of Company D, officially represented the regiment. [32]

The role these men played was more personal than that of simply delegates, as all three had been present with the regiment during the battle. Dudley had been wounded in the side, but the others had passed through the fighting unscathed. Earle was the acting adjutant of the regiment on July 2, 1863; it was to him that Colonel Ward had given the order for the regiment to retire when the 82nd New York collapsed to the 15th's left in the fighting on that day. Over 22 years later, David Earle, now the warden of the Massachusetts state prison, returned to help locate the spot where Colonel Ward had received his mortal wound. The men also placed a marker along the southeastern edge of the Copse of Trees, next to the dirt road, to indicate where the regimental monument should be erected. This was where color-bearer Patrick Murphy had fallen wounded while carrying the unit's banner, as the 15th fought to help stem the tide of Pickett's men on July 3. [33]

Four additional veterans of the 15th accompanied the regimental committee. One of them was former Corporal Priestly Young of Company D. Born in Schenectady, New York, Young was a 42-year-old married merchant at the time of his enlistment in 1861. Another was Joseph Frost, a 21-year-old farmer from Belmont, Massachusetts, who had enlisted in Company C on August 14, 1862, with his 17-year-old brother Albert. Both brothers had become casualties during the battle; Albert died in a Gettysburg hospital on July 16, 1863, after being wounded in his leg. One can only imagine Joseph's emotions as he returned to the place where he had been wounded in the hand and had lost his younger brother. A third man, Edward Anderson, a native of Sutton, Massachusetts, had been a member of Company D. Anderson was a 23-year-old shoemaker when he entered the service in 1861. His visit to Gettysburg was from a different perspective, as he had been discharged for disability on December 30, 1862, and consequently was not present during the battle. [34]

The fourth veteran, Elbridge Ackers, late a private of Company D, had been born in Claremont, New York, and was a 31-year-old bachelor from Oxford, Massachusetts, when he enlisted in the regiment on August 11, 1862. The former merchant had been wounded in the foot at the Battle of Antietam. Since his three-year enlistment had not been completed when the 15th Massachusetts was mustered out in June 1864, Ackers was transferred to the 20th Massachusetts to finish his term of service. [35]

On October 25, a beautiful but muddy day, the Massachusetts veterans visited the battlefield. Later that day, they returned to the G.A.R. Post in town for an evening of speeches and song; there John Krauth, representing the Gettysburg Battlefield Memorial Association, officially greeted them. The following day, the field was again invaded by veterans representing all but two of the Massachusetts units that had fought there. Seven other organizations that were not present on the field were also represented, as well as men of six units from other states. [36]

On October 27, 1883, the contingent gathered at the railroad station for a final round of speeches filled with gratitude and comradeship. After the old soldiers had expressed their appreciation to the citizens of Gettysburg, Colonel C. H. Buehler, also a member of the Gettysburg Battlefield Memorial Association, responded with a "graceful speech," ending with "God save Massachusetts." (Both John Krauth and Charles Buehler, as directors of the Gettysburg Battlefield Memorial Association, would play important roles only a few years later in the tribulations involving the memorials to the 15th, 19th and 20th Massachusetts.) Afterwards, the *Star and Sentinel* reiterated that both veterans and local residents were pleased with the visit, and that "the work done by them in their two days stay will be of permanent and lasting value and when the tablets are prepared, every point occupied by a Massachusetts regiment, battery or company, will be enduringly marked." [37]

On November 14, 1883, the *Star and Sentinel* reprinted an article written by well-known author and correspondent Charles Coffin, who had accompanied the Massachusetts veterans to the battlefield. The writer's commentary outlining the movements of the Massachusetts troops during the battle originally had been published in a Boston newspaper shortly after the veterans returned home. Coffin observed that the site of Pickett's repulse was a "spot where a monument ought to be reared" and stated, "Right into the faces of the foe flashed the muskets of the Massachusetts men." He ended with a sentence that would prove bittersweet for the men of the 15th, 19th and 20th regiments: "By the side of the new avenue, laid out by the Battlefield Association, along the ridge will stand the monuments of these Massachusetts regiments which did their full share in the mighty struggle." [38]

Everything about the battlefield grew exponentially in these first decades after the Gettysburg Battlefield Memorial Association was born. The amount of preserved land increased and veterans became more interested in memorializing their actions on the field. Each unit had its own ideas about where its monument should be placed and the story it should tell. Another indication of the veterans' growing interest in the battlefield was the increased attention paid to Gettysburg as a place to visit. One of the Association's goals, a local newspaper stated, was ". . . to secure accurate historical designations of the field so that the visitor can intelligently study it." It was difficult for the preservation organization to satisfy these demands, and its job became even harder over the years. [39]

Consequently, as the various states began to take steps to memorialize of their military units' activites on the battlefield, the Association felt the need to exert more control over who erected monuments, where these memorials were placed, and what information was imparted on them. The Association clearly took its role as guardian of historic truth very seriously. In March 1884, the preservation organization decided that it had become necessary for it to grant approval prior to erection of any permanent "tablet or monument" on land owned by the Association. Furthermore, to ensure historical accuracy, all inscriptions would have to be approved by the Association's Superintendent of Tablets and Legends. If any veterans' group disagreed with a decision, there was an appeals process available to the organization's Board of Directors. During this same month, members of the Association visited portions of the field, planning to purchase land where various monuments would be located. [40]

As a direct result of the Massachusetts veterans' October 1883 excursion, iron posts and tablets sprang up all over the battlefield, temporarily marking locations where Bay State regiments and batteries had fought. Erected in the fall of 1884 and standing above the ground at a height of six and one half feet, these markers had to suffice until more permanent monuments could be erected. [41]

In March 1884, the memorializing process of the battlefield received financial impetus when the legislature of the Commonwealth of Massachusetts appropriated $500.00 for each organization that had fought at Gettysburg. This sum enabled each unit to properly honor its record on the field by the erection of a monument. John Bachelder prophesied that the day would come when all units that had fought at Gettysburg would have a memorial. [42]

At the annual gathering of the 15th's Regimental Association held in October 1884, the unit's Gettysburg Committee was charged with receiving the funds from the Commonwealth and seeing that a suitable memorial was constructed and placed to recognize the accomplishments and sacrifices of its troops. In addition, Thomas Hastings felt it would be appropriate for a memorial to be erected at Gettysburg to the memory of the fallen Colonel Ward; his suggestion was met with enthusiasm. [43]

During this same timeframe, the annual gathering of the 19th Massachusetts Regiment Association took place at the Grand Army Hall in Haverhill, Massachusetts. This association also had a Gettysburg committee. Its members had made a thorough study of the unit's position on the battlefield, and subsequently stated where they believed the 19th's monument should be placed. They reported that the 19th had been ". . . one of the most prominent in the line of battle on that great day." A design for the memorial was proposed and approved. William R. Driver, George E. Teele, John G. B. Adams, John Chadwick, Arthur F. Devereux and William Hill, all veterans of the 19th, were chosen to make sure that the plans for the erection of the monument were successfully accomplished. Teele was one of the two men who had designed the monument; the other was John P. Reynolds, also a veteran of service with the 19th. [44]

At a meeting in July 1885, the directors of the 15th Regiment's Association determined to create a second committee, in addition to the Gettysburg Committee, for the purpose of raising funds to create a monument to mark the place where Colonel Ward had been mortally wounded. The Commonwealth's earlier $500.00 appropriation did not include funds for such a monument. The goal of the combined effort of 15th veterans, common citizens, and members of the Worcester City Guards, a militia unit, was to raise an additional $550.00 for that worthy cause. The new committee would also be responsible for contacting and cooperating with civic leaders in the Worcester environs. [45]

Events now moved quickly. At the 15th's 1885 annual meeting, held in Worcester on September 17, David Earle was again chosen to travel to the battlefield to insure that foundations were constructed at the locations selected by the representatives of the regiment. Part of his responsibility on the trip was to purchase land where the memorial to George Ward would be placed. Consequently, twenty square feet was bought from Simon Codori, the farmer who owned the land in question, and this was given to the Gettysburg Battlefield Memorial Association. [46]

Many veterans and their families from numerous Massachusetts organizations were scheduled to travel to Gettysburg on October 5, 1885. This excursion was planned as a grand celebration of the Commonwealth's participation in the battle, and was to culminate with the dedication of numerous regimental and battery monuments. However, since Charles Devens, first colonel of the 15th Massachusetts, could not attend, it was decided the regiment's trip should be postponed until the following year. Approximately 50 men expressed the intention of returning to the field at that time. [47]

The term "comrade" was used quite often during the post-war years as a salutation between veterans, or by one aging soldier about another old friend. These men had shared experiences and developed a closeness that civilians could never fully understand. At reunions and gatherings such as the September 17, 1885, annual meeting, men rose and stood in respectful silence and remembered those who were no longer present with them on earth. Letters were read from veterans unable to attend, or in some cases, from their widows. At the 1885 meeting, a photograph of a comrade who had recently died was passed around. The picture had been sent by A. C. Plaisted, who, as a 19-year-old private, had survived the bloodiest moments at the Copse of Trees. [48] This feeling of comradeship, born in camp, on the march and in battle, played an integral role in how the veterans felt about each other and treated one another in the post-war period.

The 1885 annual gathering also included a visit to the Boston Marble and Granite Company in Worcester. The group marched there and, after scrutinizing their monuments, the veterans praised the maker, Andrew O'Connor. They also took time to look over other regiments' memorials then being constructed. Upon their arrival, they met the wife of one and the mother of another of their fallen comrades. Mrs. Emily Ward, widow of the hero colonel, was acknowledged with raised hats. The entourage also recognized Mrs. Susan E. Alger. Her son Warren had joined the 15th at age 21, trading his job as a mechanic for that of a foot soldier. Corporal Alger did not survive the war; he died in the Confederate prison at Andersonville, Georgia, on August 14, 1864. One can only imagine the pain of the loss of a husband and of a son that still lingered within the two women, as they viewed the memorials. [49]

The monuments to the 15th regiment were transported without fanfare to the battlefield by the Boston Marble and Granite Company in early October 1885. Word of the 15th's decision to delay its visit had apparently not reached Gettysburg, as the September 29 issue of the *Star and Sentinel* announced that the regiment planned to dedicate its monument, "facing Pickett's charge," during the week of October 5, 1885. By the following week, that bit of misinformation had been corrected. The October 6 edition informed its readers that the dedication would not take place until the following summer. The newspaper stated that the "beautiful" monument containing "the Second Corps Badge and 15th Massachusetts" had been placed "near the copse of trees . . ." and that it was constructed of ". . . Quincy granite, the shaft being highly polished and having inlaid an Italian marble bass-relief of a private soldier with his gun at the ready." A monument to Colonel Ward, readers learned, had been erected where he fell ". . . on the railroad, not far from the Emmitsburg Road, and is made of Quincy granite, containing an Italian marble bust of Col. Ward, inlaid, which is said to be a correct representation of him." In case people missed the point, the article further stated, "Both monuments are fine specimens of artistic skill, and will be admired by all persons of good taste." [50]

While the 15th Association postponed its trip to the battlefield, more than a dozen other Massachusetts organizations did make the trek in September and October 1885, and dedicated monuments to commemorate their service to the Union cause. During mid-September, representatives from Smith Granite Company of Westerly, Rhode Island, erected the monument to the 19th Massachusetts, in preparation for its October dedication ceremony. The foundation for the monument to the 20th Massachusetts was also laid during this time. One of the local papers stated that due to its great weight, the memorial would not be placed until the winter. [51]

There was a great deal of activity on the battlefield that fall. According to the *Star and Sentinel*, "A person could hardly drive in any direction from the town without meeting men busily engaged in erecting additional monuments." This flurry of activity was caused by approximately 200 excursionists, from twenty-six organizations, who arrived from Boston at Gettysburg's Washington Street railroad station on the evening of October 6. Their special train arrived earlier than expected, catching the local welcoming citizens off guard. The Eagle Hotel was again the headquarters for the visit, and many of those who had made the locating trip in 1883 returned to see their vision fulfilled. [52] Interestingly, on the very day the Massachusetts veterans arrived, the *Star and Sentinel* reported that a skull of an unidentified soldier had been discovered on the battlefield. [53]

The next day was devoted to exploration, as the tourists spent pleasant sunlit hours wandering over the battlefield. About 50 members from the various units took an early morning train to Sharpsburg, Maryland, site of the bloody battle of Antietam. They returned that evening, many with relics gathered from that battlefield. Plans called for those organizations dedicating monuments to do so on October 8, with the following day being celebrated as "Massachusetts Day." According to the agenda, the organizations were to dedicate their monuments in a specific order, with each unit transferring the memorial to Edward J. Russell, Chief of Staff to Massachusetts Governor George Robinson. Edward Russell, as a 28-year-old carpenter, had enlisted on July 12, 1861, with the rank of sergeant in Company F of the 15th Massachusetts. Two years later, as captain of Company D, he had suffered from sunstroke on the march to Gettysburg. It is hard to believe that he ever imagined that over twenty-two years later, he would play an integral part in the process of ultimately transferring his state's monuments to the care of an organization such as the Gettysburg Battlefield Memorial Association. [54]

However, plans do not always go as desired, and rain began to fall during the night. October 8 dawned "raw, rainy and cheerless." While the weather caused the elaborate timetable to be discarded, the veterans were determined to honor their fallen comrades and did so by individual unit, despite the rain. Even though the 15th Massachusetts Association was not present as an organization, Edward Russell and Henry Dudley examined and accepted the memorials to the regiment and to Colonel Ward on behalf of the unit. A Gettysburg newspaper reported that the 15th planned on a reunion in 1886 and hoped to have its first commanding officer, Charles Devens, as the main speaker. [55]

Veterans, family and friends of the 19th Massachusetts also dedicated their unit's monument on that damp and dismal day. The monument was not located along the eastern side of the paved Hancock Avenue, where it stands today, a little more than 120 yards south by south-east of the Copse of Trees. Rather, it was placed on the grass immediately south of the trees. Visitors faced west toward the former Confederate lines to read its inscription, with the still unnamed road behind them to the east. Consequently, today's visitor not only finds the monument in a different location, but also must face in the exact opposite direction to read its message. On October 8, 1885, the monument to the 15th Massachusetts regiment stood closest to the road, and the foundation for the 20th Massachusetts memorial lay a few yards to the west, nearest to the stone wall. [56]

A Gettysburg newspaper reported that the 19th's monument was a substantial granite block, about five foot square and eight feet high. An 1886 guidebook described it more fully: "The monument has a base of four by four and three-fourth feet and nearly two feet thick having rough quarry faces. From this base rises a solid granite block of peculiar shape. Rising perpendicularly from the base of about eighteen inches it then rapidly slopes in on one face, until at the top, the width is not more than one-fifth of the base. Upon the surface of this slope is cut in bold relief a bugle from which is suspended by a chain a knapsack with rolled blanket. On the polished surface of the knapsack is the trefoil, and within the coil of the bugle is the regiment's number in sunken letters on a polished disk. Surmounting the monument is a granite plinth upon which rests a cartridge box carved from a block of granite." On the polished face of the upper stone that still rests on the base was cut the inscription: "THE 19th REG'T MASS VOL INFTY OF THE 3rd BRIGADE - 2nd DIVISION - 2nd ARMY CORPS STOOD HERE ON THE AFTERNOON OF JULY 3rd 1863." [57]

The Regimental Association of the 19th chose these words, acceptable to the Gettysburg Battlefield Memorial Association, which also agreed with the location of the monument. The words "STOOD HERE" visually jump out at the viewer, since they are on a line by themselves. The importance the regiment felt with regard to its actions on the third day of battle is unmistakable, as there is no mention of the unit's fighting on July 2, 1863. Today, the words are more than confusing—they are misleading, in light of the monument's present location. They now make it appear that the unit remained in its position in the second line of Hall's brigade as Pickett's men pierced the Union line around the Copse of Trees. Under these circumstances, it is almost impossible for the casual visitor to view the monument today and understand the 19th's actions on the fateful afternoon of July 3. The very words selected by the regiment to draw attention to its members' sacrifice and bring honor to the memory of those who fell now serve to obscure those deeds and that memory. [58]

The 19th Massachusetts' October 8, 1885, dedication ceremonies were presided over by Joseph Sawyer, a member of the monument committee, and by George Barry. Sawyer was a 19-year-old dentist from Boston when he enlisted as a musician in the 19th's Company D on July 26, 1861. At age 21, George Barry had mustered into the regiment's Company E on August 22, 1861, with the rank of second lieutenant, leaving his home in South Boston and his job as a bookkeeper. In his talk, Barry emphasized the historic importance of where the regiment had fought on July 3, and concluded by reading an original poem. There was also a speech by the apparently ever-present Charles Carleton Coffin; he recounted the regiment's actions during the conflict, which he considered to be one of the three major turning points of American history. Coffin also pointed out the great importance of the site where the memorial now stood. [59]

Archibald Higgins who, as a 21-year-old blacksmith, had enlisted from Andover as a private in the 19th's Company A on July 26, 1861, and Charles Tibbetts, a 21-year-old shoemaker from Georgetown when he enlisted in Company C of the 19th on August 17, 1861, were also present and took part in remembering the deeds of the regiment. Sawyer transferred the monument to the care of George Patch, formerly a private in the 19th; he accepted it on behalf of Regimental Association President George Teele, who was not present. Patch vowed to pass on its ownership to the Commonwealth of Massachusetts later in the day. An 1886 guidebook later stated: "[T]he monument marks approximately the spot which has been appropriately styled 'The High-water Mark of the rebellion.'" During the ceremony, Coffin took credit for coining that phrase, claiming it was first written in his dispatch to the *Boston Journal*, sent right after the battle had ended. [60]

At 2:00 p.m., the veterans, along with their ladies and other guests, gathered at the Skelly G.A.R. Post in Gettysburg, where the memorials were formally transferred to Edward J. Russell. Russell, acting on behalf of the governor, accepted them in the name of Massachusetts. (Henry Dudley represented the 15th and George Patch the 19th during this process.) At that time, the veterans registered their gratitude and appreciation for Governor Robinson's support in the memorial process and thanked the local veterans of the G.A.R. Post for their hospitality. [61]

The celebration continued that evening, with the G.A.R. band escorting the veterans and their entourage from the Eagle Hotel to the Courthouse. This event had been organized by John M. Krauth, and was filled with music, song and speeches. Edward Russell spoke on behalf of Massachusetts, expressing gratitude for such a pleasant sojourn in Gettysburg. George Patch was passionately praised for a speech filled with "rich humor and sound sentiment." George Barry read another original poem. Others gave battle histories of various units. D.A. Buehler, representing the Gettysburg Battlefield Memorial Association, described the goals and principles of his organization, in an attempt to clear up misconceptions held by some in attendance. Those misconceptions were not reported in the local newspaper; one can only imagine if Russell, Patch and Barry had any inkling how their regimental associations would conflict with the preservation organization in only a few short years. The evening of good fellowship ended with the singing of "Auld Lang Syne." [62]

Although it was no longer raining, "Massachusetts Day," October 9, 1885, arrived "still raw and ugly." As the formal proceedings would not commence until 1:00 p.m., the morning was spent visiting the battlefield. At the appointed hour, a procession of veterans, other visitors and local citizens, led again by the G.A.R. band, marched from the Eagle Hotel to the National Cemetery. Most of the visiting ladies rode in carriages filled with flowers provided by women of Gettysburg. From the cemetery gateway, a dirge filled the afternoon air as the group made its way to the graves of the 158 Massachusetts soldiers. As the silent and reflective crowd, some crying, placed flowers on the grave of each fallen son of Massachusetts, sunlight fell on the battlefield for the first time in days. The only other sound was that of the intonation of prayer. [63]

Closing ceremonies were held at the Courthouse, which was crammed to capacity. Speeches were delivered recounting the process that the Commonwealth of Massachusetts had followed in memorializing her veterans. John Bachelder then told in some detail of the part played by each Massachusetts unit during the battle. George Patch was the keynote speaker of the day. He expounded on Massachusetts' role in the war and told of the sacrifices her sons had made to gain ultimate victory. He gave the reasons behind the war and touched upon the on-going national healing process. Then he spoke of the monuments: "On this field the old Bay State's best blood was shed, and here today by the silent granite and sculptured marble does she honor their devotion." In his closing words, Patch declared that the monuments would be "perpetual memorials of her gratitude and affection" and prophesied that generations would come and draw ". . . inspiration from the memories of the past. . . ." [64]

George Patch's words were well received and interrupted by applause on numerous occasions. Edward Russell then formally transferred all the newly dedicated monuments to the Gettysburg Battlefield Memorial Association. The gathering broke up after the singing of "My Country, 'tis of thee." Early the next morning a train, added to the schedule just for the veterans and their families, carried the contingent toward home, each individual undoubtedly carrying many personal memories of the visit to Gettysburg. [65]

The following spring marked the onset of the long-awaited trip organized by the 15th Massachusetts Regimental Association to visit some of the glorious scenes of their youth. A group of 155 veterans, families and friends assembled in Worcester during the afternoon of Monday, May 31, 1886. Appropriately, it was Decoration Day. Announcements about the trip had been spread through circulars and newspapers. In addition to 50 former soldiers of the 15th Massachusetts, 21 men representing 17 other Civil War organizations also joined the excursion. Of the 82 civilians on the trip, 19 were women. [66]

The first leg of the journey took the tourists by train from Worcester to New London, Connecticut, where they boarded the steamer "City of Worcester." Silk identification badges were distributed, blue for the 15th's veterans and crimson for guests. Old comrades renewed acquaintances and enjoyed violin music played by Charles May, late of the regiment's Company A, while lounging on the steamship's after-deck. They reached their next stop, New York City, at 7 a.m. on Tuesday morning, before enjoying breakfast at the Jersey City, New Jersey, depot dining rooms. Afterward, a special four-car

Pennsylvania Railroad express train carried the pilgrims to Philadelphia. A twenty-minute pause for lunch followed their 11:30 a.m. arrival. Then they were off to Harrisburg, a 105-mile ride accomplished in three and a half hours by another special train. Gettysburg was now only some 50 miles distant. After a short delay, the train was transferred to the Cumberland Valley Railroad line for the final portion of the trip. The excursion passed through Carlisle, arriving at Gettysburg at 5:30 p.m. on June 1, 1886. It was later reported with obvious pride that the 440-mile trip between Worcester and the battlefield had been completed "without accident or delay." [67]

In Gettysburg, there was no establishment large enough to house the entire group. Therefore, while the Eagle Hotel was considered the expedition's "Headquarters," the McClellan House and several other places also accommodated the visitors. A meal was waiting for them upon arrival. After dining, some took advantage of the remaining daylight to stroll around the town or see the parts of the battlefield within walking distance. Throughout military history, during the immediacy of battle, soldiers are generally aware only of what impacts them as individuals and what occurs in their immediate vicinity. The so-called "big picture" eludes a soldier while death flies through the air. Consequently, that evening many from the tour took the opportunity to hear an illustrated lecture at the "Opera House" on the Battle of Gettysburg, given by local Civil War guide William D. Holtzworth, a veteran of service with the 87th Pennsylvania Volunteer Infantry Regiment. According to the *Star and Sentinel*, Holtzworth displayed "stereoptican views of monuments and prominent features of the field." It further declared: "What 'Billy' don't know about the battle isn't worth knowing." [68]

June 2, 1886, dawned cloudy with a threat of rain that, fortunately, never arrived. Undaunted by the possibility of inclement weather, the group left their accommodations early in the day and boarded 35 horse-drawn carriages for a tour of the battlefield, under the guidance of former Sergeant Holtzworth. The earthworks on East Cemetery Hill were the first stop. This was followed by a series of halts that included Culp's Hill, Spangler's Spring and the National Cemetery, where 17 of their comrades lay buried. [69]

The National Cemetery might have caused some confusion among the returning veterans, since some men's names may not have been readily recognizable on grave markers. Errors had occurred during the initial burials and a few soldiers originally identified as members of the 15th Massachusetts were not, until much later, determined to be from other units. In addition, some men's names were misspelled. [70]

It was a short journey from the National Cemetery to the itinerary's next point of interest—the umbrella-shaped clump of trees. For almost eight months, the 15th's monument had been standing along the southern edge of the Copse of Trees near the edge of the battlefield road. Unveiled the previous October, one of the very early memorials dedicated along Cemetery Ridge had been that of the 19th Massachusetts, which stood directly to the west of the 15th's monument.   Further to the west of the 19th was the base of the 20th Massachusetts, awaiting completion and dedication later in the month. Earlier visitors, as tourists are sometimes wont to do, had decided to indulge in souvenir hunting in order to make commemorative canes from the copse's tree limbs; as a consequence of this desecration, a sign nailed to one of the trees now warned of a $50.00 fine for disturbing the trees. [71]

As the veterans and their companions climbed down from their carriages, they gravitated toward the 15th's monument; their silk badges clearly identifying them as belonging to the 15th's excursion. The scene was recorded for posterity in a photograph taken by local Gettysburg photographer William Tipton. [72]

After an opening prayer, Charles Devens began the dedication ceremony. Devens recounted the 15th Massachusetts' history from its enlistment through the Battle of Gettysburg, down to its 1864 muster-out in Worcester. As he described the war years, the former general also mentioned the 19th and 20th Massachusetts and their roles in the conflict. He stressed that the regiment's monument on the field of Gettysburg was dedicated not only to those who fell on "this immortal field" or while engaged in any other of the unit's battles but, in a larger sense, to all those who had stood in harm's way during the war, whether or not they suffered wounds or death. In his speech, Devens emphasized that he felt that the Commonwealth of Massachusetts deserved great credit for its role in preserving the memory of her sons by funding memorials such as the one before them, and for her role in caring for these men, both during and after the war. He praised the cause of freedom for which the Union soldiers fought, and while professing no feeling of rancor toward the former enemy, damned their cause as being wicked. Devens also left a message for all those who would come in later times to view the monument: "It tells of bravery and valor, but it tells of more than these, for it tells of duty and patriotism, and it summons all who look upon it hereafter to answer their call." [73]

Other speeches followed. John Kimball, who had commanded the 15th at Antietam, stressed that the monument stood on "the very spot" where the

Confederate attack had been repulsed; Kimball called the location sacred, "hallowed by the blood of our brave comrades." George Joslin, Ward's successor as regimental commander at Gettysburg, spoke with pride of how the regiment, although reduced in numbers from its beginning days at Worcester, had become "thoroughly good soldiers" in the crucible of war. The unit's commander at the Battle of Fredericksburg, Chase Philbrick, had not been present at Gettysburg; consequently he felt it inappropriate to speak at length. He simply expressed his pleasure to "meet the men of the old Fifteenth on this consecrated ground." George F. Hoar, United States Senator from Massachusetts, had planned to be present, but was unable to attend due to his official duties. David Earle read a letter from Hoar, which expressed the senator's regret for his absence; it was filled with honor and praise for the men of the 15th. [74]

After the dedication service ended with the singing of "America," the assembled veterans and guests completed their tour of the 1863 Union line of battle. Following stops at Little Round Top, Devil's Den, the Peach Orchard and the Wheatfield, the party halted one final time. Just east of the Emmitsburg Road was the monument to Colonel George Ward; more speeches were given there to remember the regiment's fallen leader. [75]

The last oration of the day was the only one made by someone not intimately associated with the regiment. John Krauth, Esquire, was the secretary of the Gettysburg Battlefield Memorial Association; he accepted responsibility for the two monuments on behalf of that organization. Krauth recounted the Bay State's contribution to the Union cause and to the ultimate victory. He spoke not only of Massachusetts' representation on all parts of the field at Gettysburg, but also made special mention of the conspicuous role her sons had played in repelling the assault of July 3. Krauth closed his discourse with sweet words that would turn sour in just a few short years: "The Memorial Association cordially congratulates and thanks you for these beautiful additions to the many historic memorials erected on this field. We promise you that we will carefully watch and guard them, that they may be perpetual memorials to the heroism, courage, sacrifices and patriotism of the gallant Fifteenth Massachusetts volunteers and their knightly commander." The full day's activities ended with the singing of "In the Sweet Bye and Bye" and everyone returned to the hotel for dinner. [76]

During the rest of the party's stay at Gettysburg, the visitors saw portions of the field missed during the grand tour, including areas of the fighting that took place on July 1, 1863, as well as the locations of the headquarters of both commanding generals. They climbed Big Round Top and visited the site of the II Corps hospital where George Ward had breathed his last. Some enjoyed relic hunting, with minnie balls and shell fragments being picked up on the battlefield, not only where the regiment had fought, but also at other areas deemed of "special interest" by the individual veterans. [77]

On the morning of June 3, due to pressing business at home, Charles Devens had to return to Worcester. The entire group accompanied him to the railroad station, where he gave a farewell speech expressing his disappointment at not being able to complete the trip. [78]

That afternoon, the excursionists bade Gettysburg goodbye and left for Hagerstown, Maryland; they arrived there that evening, after stopping on the way at the Indian School at Carlisle Barracks. After visiting the scenes of the bloody fighting on the fields outside Sharpsburg, some of the contingent went directly to Washington; others visited Harpers Ferry and the Bull Run battlefields. While at the battlefield of Antietam, members of the party paused in the National Cemetery, where many of the 15th's dead lay, and decorated their graves. The veterans then gathered on the field at the location where the regiment had fought; an attempt by a local photographer to record the visit proved unsuccessful. Again, as at Gettysburg, minnie balls, shell fragments and remnants of equipment were picked up and kept as memorials of that terrible day almost 24 years past. [79]

Upon arriving in Washington, the reunited segments of the excursion broke up into small groups in order to tour the city's numerous places of interest. Many Massachusetts elected officials joined them at one time or another throughout the day, including Senator Hoar, who guided them through some of the Capitol's sites. While many of the party remained in Washington, slightly over half the group entrained for Leesburg, Virginia at 5:00 p.m. on June 5. Two hours later, they arrived at the town near which the regiment had suffered so dearly; in its initial war experience at the Battle of Ball's Bluff on October 21, 1861, the 15th Massachusetts had lost over half of its 625 officers and men. Fortunately, their Virginia hosts received this visit in a more kindly fashion—with flowers and song rather than shot and shell. The next day, the battlefield and its small cemetery, together with the locations where the regiment had trekked or camped prior to and after the battle, were visited. Mrs. Ward and her eldest son George were particularly moved to see where the late colonel had been wounded; they also visited the homes in which his left leg had been amputated and where he had recovered. [80]

One veteran on the 1886 excursion was George Rockwood, who had enlisted in the 15th at age 38 in 1861 and served as captain of Company A. Captured during the Battle of Ball's Bluff and transported to Richmond, he was held with other officers in the Liggon & Co. tobacco building. There, on November 12, 1861, Rockwood was chosen by lot as one of fourteen officers to be held as hostages. A Confederate privateer named Walter W. Smith was at that time incarcerated by Union authorities in Philadelphia under penalty of death. Confederate Acting Secretary of War Judah P. Benjamin retaliated to this sentence by decreeing that one Union officer would be similarly held for execution and that thirteen others were to be detained in cells "reserved for prisoners accused of infamous crimes." These thirteen were to suffer the same fate as Confederate privateers imprisoned in the North. Seven of the men, including Rockwood, were taken to the Henrico County Jail and placed in an eleven by seventeen-foot cell, where the captain's health deteriorated quickly. Captain Henry Bowman of the 15th's Company C and the 20th Massachusetts' Colonel W. Raymond Lee and Major Paul Revere were also held in this cell. [81]

Fellow officers, who had remained comparatively healthy, petitioned unsuccessfully to replace ill comrades such as Rockwood, who was suffering from typhoid fever. The captain's imprisoned comrades feared for his life. The intervention of a Confederate officer resulted in Captain Rockwood's transfer to a Richmond hospital, and quite possibly saved his life. After his eventual exchange, George Rockwood finally returned to the 15th in January 1862. [82]

George Rockwood was active in the post-war Grand Army of the Republic, but over the years his health continued to decline. In 1882, he reported that he could not work a quarter of the time. His pension file, like those of many other veterans, illustrates a continuing struggle for funds. An 1889 notation in this file revealed ". . . that he cannot furnish the testimony of a Commissioned Officer, First Sgt., or any enlisted man of his Co, as their whereabouts are unknown and those that were with him in prison in Richmond, Virginia of his Co. are dead or unknown to him." In 1890, Rockwood was receiving a Federal pension of $10.00 per month; by 1895, it had risen to $15.00. A fellow veteran wrote of him in 1891: "Each Memorial Day he comes to Sterling and the remarks of the comrades has been, 'The Captain has failed since last year.' He has been unable to march with us for the last four years." George Rockwood died on April 18, 1896. [83]

The 1886 pilgrimage was, in effect, Rockwood's last hurrah. Although he had not been present on the field of Gettysburg in 1863, the monument to the 15th Massachusetts dedicated on that battlefield was as much for him as for anyone else from the unit. Many of those participating in the excursion had not been present during those bloody July days. Each man's war story was unique. However, the monument at Gettysburg served to bring them together as one, regardless of their individual experiences.

Early on June 7, the group reunited at the Leesburg railroad station, accompanied by a large contingent of local citizens, and took the train for Washington. They were met there by the balance of the party; at that point, the official tour ended. Some began the return journey to Massachusetts almost immediately, while others lingered in Virginia, going on side trips to Fredericksburg, Mount Vernon and Bull Run. Those remaining did not depart for their northern homes until June 12, 1886. [84]

S hortly after the 15th's travelers returned home, former members of the 20th Massachusetts traveled to Gettysburg to dedicate their monument. Its base had been constructed the previous October but the monument itself had not been installed until the morning of June 21, 1886. The focal point of the memorial, an eight-foot tall, 30-ton, puddingstone boulder, makes this monument distinct and unique on the Gettysburg battlefield. The boulder, donated by the city of Boston, had been shipped by rail from West Roxbury Park to be erected by the Smith Granite Company. With the combined effort of horses and man-power using a pulley system, the stone had been unloaded during the preceding week from a railroad car onto a well-built wagon, near where the track crossed the avenue close to the George Weikert home. By the evening of June 19, it was ready to make the short trip northward to the Copse of Trees, where its journey finally ended. The boulder stood a few yards to the west of the 19th Massachusetts' memorial, adjacent to the low stone wall. Together with the monument to the 15th Massachusetts, it was on a roughly east-west line just south of the Copse of Trees. The gigantic rock came to rest on a base seven and a half feet square, composed of three massive hunks of Westerly granite. The complete monument rises almost twelve feet over the battlefield. On the monument's face is the carved trefoil of the II Corps, with the designation "20th Mass Infantry." [85] No documentation has been located by the authors giving any details of the dedication ceremony itself, if one indeed did take place.

(In 1897, Gettysburg historian John Vanderslice wrote that the puddingstone used in the 20th's monument came from a playground in

Roxbury, Massachusetts, where the men of the regiment once frolicked as children. Over time, the sentimental story has become a part of Gettysburg's historiography. However, research done by the authors in preparing this work has failed to substantiate any part of this account, other than the fact that the stone itself came from West Roxbury Park. The unit's post-war chronicler stated, "With the exception of the men enlisted in Nantucket . . . , no particular locality was represented in the regiment." In addition, none of the men on the 20th's monument committee had grown up in Roxbury. Puddingstone itself is indigenous to the Boston basin, but the exact reason it was used in the regimental monument is unknown.) [86]

On July 3, 1886, another event that was to have an impact on the ultimate locations of the three Massachusetts monuments—in particular that of the 15th regiment—occurred. During a reunion of Captain Andrew Cowan's 1st New York Independent Battery on the field of Gettysburg, the veterans selected as the site for their unit's proposed monument a position only a few yards to the east of the 15th's memorial. Once erected and dedicated one year to the day later, the three-inch Ordnance rifles of the battery pointed directly at the 15th's monument. [87]

Almost immediately after the dedication of the 20th's memorial, the first change in the way the Massachusetts regiments would be remembered on the historic landscape occurred. On this occasion, however, the change was one precipitated by the men of the 19th. J. E. Roach, representing the Smith Granite Company which had erected the monument in 1885, made a "slight adjustment" in the location of the memorial. This move was based on comments by visiting regimental survivors, who felt the initial position south of the Copse of Trees between the 15th and 20th Massachusetts monuments did not accurately reflect the route taken by the unit to repel Pickett's men. Consequently, the monument was moved to a new foundation directly east of the Copse of Trees, along the western edge of the battlefield avenue. The monument was placed so that any one reading the inscription would be facing the trees themselves. [88]

Visits to the field of Gettysburg, made not only by the veterans who fought there, but also by former Civil War combatants who did not even participate in the battle, were common in the following decades. In an 1889 speech, a veteran from another state explained the draw and importance of the Gettysburg monuments, words that clearly applied to the feelings of the men of the three Bay State regiments: ". . . [T]hese monuments are not to commemorate the dead alone. Death was but the divine acceptance of life freely offered by every one. Service was the central fact. That fact, and that truth, these monuments commemorate." He eloquently summed up the commonality of their war-time service for all veterans: "Those who fell here – those who have fallen before or since – those who linger, yet a little longer, soon to follow; are all mustered in one great company on the shining heights of life. . . ." [89]

In the closing months of 1886, the veterans of the 15th, 19th and 20th Massachusetts regiments most likely felt a grand sense of accomplishment. They had visited the fields of their youth where they made history and acted to ensure that the sacrifices of their fallen comrades were honored and, more importantly, would be remembered by the generations that followed them. They probably felt that their place in history was secure. Sadly, they were wrong. Within a year, the Gettysburg Battlefield Memorial Association initiated a process that would change how the actions of these three regiments would be perceived by generations down to the present day. The Association believed its actions were in the best interests of preserving the integrity of the Gettysburg battlefield. They believed the actions taken would organize the memorial process and help the visitor to better understand the battle. The men from Massachusetts did not see it that way.

Copse of Trees, ca. 1882.

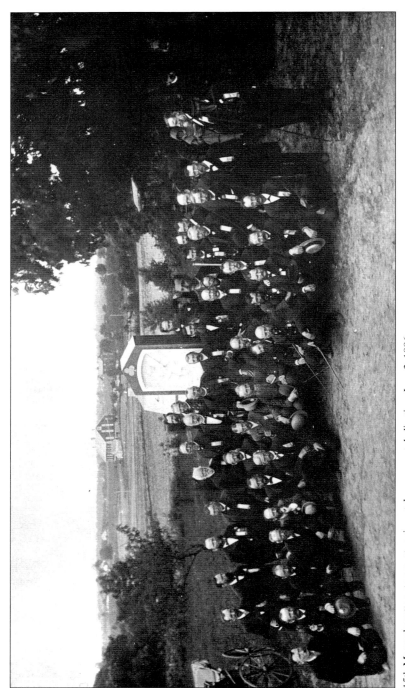

15th Massachusetts veterans at regimental monument dedication, June 2, 1886.
(Note: The monument to the 19th regiment and the base of the 20th's monument in the background.)

15th Massachusetts veterans, families and friends at dedication of monument to Colonel George Ward, June 2, 1886.

15th Massachusetts veterans at Washington Street train station, Gettysburg, Pennsylvania, June 3, 1886.

(l-r) "High Water Mark" showing monuments of 20th, 19th and 15th Massachusetts, ca. 1886. *(Note: The 19th Massachusetts monument is in its original position.)*

(l-r) "High Water Mark" showing monuments of 20th, 15th and 19th Massachusetts, ca. July, 1887. *(Note: The monument to the 19th is in its second and "correct" position.)*

15th Massachusetts monument in first position by Copse of Trees by Charles Tipton, ca. June, 1886. *(Note: White marble bas-relief of soldier.)*

15th Massachusetts monument in present position. *(Note: Bronze bas-relief of soldier.)*

Colonel George Ward monument by Charles Tipton, ca. June 1886. *(Note: White marble bas-relief of Ward.)*

Colonel George Ward monument. *(Note: The bronze bas-relief of Ward.)*

19th Massachusetts monument in original position. *(Note: The Cordori Farm is in the background.)*

19th Massachusetts in third and present position.

20th Massachusetts in present position.

"High Water Mark" ca. 1892.

15th Massachusetts veterans at Copse of Trees during the 1898 reunion.

(l-r) Plaques to 20th, 15th and 19th Massachusetts at Copse of Trees.
(Note: Although the order of the plaques is correct, they do not accurately mark where the regimental monuments of the 15th and 19th regiments originally stood.)

6

Fallen Through the Cracks of History

1887 into the Twenty-first Century

s more and more veterans' groups requested placement of monuments, it became increasingly difficult for the Gettysburg Battlefield Memorial Association to maintain what it considered to be a coherent and orderly presentation of these memorials on the field. The directors feared that erecting monuments throughout the now-historic ground without any kind of logical arrangement would result in a chaotic setting, causing confusion rather than clarifying the troop movements for visitors. In order to fulfill their vision, John Bachelder moved to make the Association's regulations more stringent.

At a May 1887 Association executive meeting, Bachelder asked for the formation of a committee to study the possibility of moving any existing monument that did not adhere to a "line of battle" philosophy. At the December 16, 1887, meeting, it became a requirement that any unit wishing to place a monument on Association property would have to erect it along the line held by the regiment in its line of battle. It would be permissible, however, to place markers denoting secondary or advanced positions, as approved by the Association. [1]

Three members of the Executive Board in attendance at the meeting were personally familiar with the three Massachusetts regiments and their monuments. John Krauth and Charles Buehler had both been involved when the Bay State veterans visited the battlefield in 1883 to select the locations where their memorials would be erected. Krauth had even accepted the 15th's monument on behalf of the Memorial Association when it was dedicated in 1886. The guide during that excursion was none other than William D. Holtzworth, another member of the Association's Executive Board. [2]

Throughout 1887, the entire area around the Copse of Trees became more important as a focal point of the battlefield. In the spring, discussions between Confederate veterans and the Gettysburg Battlefield Memorial Association were held regarding the possible placement of a monument to Confederate Brigadier General Lewis Armistead. This commemorative marker was to be placed at the location where the general had fallen mortally wounded within the Union lines, just to the north of the Copse of Trees. In July 1887, the Association authorized the installment of a "suitable and substantial iron fence" encircling the Copse of Trees. The previous February, John Bachelder had been asked to begin work in planning a descriptive tablet, which would identify the troops and action that had taken place in and around the trees. Now at the July meeting, he was directed to submit his plans to the Executive Committee for approval. Most important from the perspective of the 15th, 19th and 20th veterans was the decision and authorization to, wherever possible, move any monument on the land owned by the Association to "their proper position in line." [3]

One can almost picture these guardians of the battlefield standing at the Copse of Trees, looking at the newly-dedicated monument to Captain Cowan's battery and the memorial to the 15th Massachusetts, only a few yards in its front. The phrase "Double Canister at 10 Yards" on the New Yorkers' monument must have made it look like the men from the Bay State had been the target of Cowan's guns. To the Association's members, the necessity for clarifying this confusing situation was obvious. [4]

As 1887 came to a close, the infrastructure of the battlefield continued to develop and take shape. The name "Hancock Avenue" was finally proposed for the thoroughfare that ran, and still runs, along Cemetery Ridge. Also, the die was cast in determining how history would view the role that the three Massachusetts regiments played in the action on July 3, 1863. The Gettysburg Battlefield Memorial Association instructed its Committee on Locations and Inscriptions to implement the decision made at the July executive meeting and to notify the representatives of the regiments whose monuments were projected for a change in location. A number of specific rules and regulations indicated that the Association knew its decisions would cause repercussions within the veteran community. [5]

Of these recommendations, the following are the most germane to the story:
• "All persons are forbidden under penalty of law, to place, change or remove any stake or marker on the grounds under control of the Memorial Association, without the knowledge and consent of the Superintendent of Grounds.
• Any one who shall construct any foundation for, or erect any monument or memorial upon the grounds of the Association, before the Superintendent of Grounds shall have designated the place and given a permit, will be regarded as a trespasser and be amenable to the severe penalties, provided for in the Charter of the Association.

• The Superintendent shall not permit the erection of any monument or memorial until its location and the inscription to be placed thereon, shall have been approved by the proper committee of the Association.
• They must be on the line of battle held by the brigade unless the regiment was detached, and if possible the right and left flanks of the regiment or battery must be marked with stones not less than two feet in height." [6]

In March 1888, the Commonwealth of Massachusetts decided to fund flank markers for the 21 Massachusetts units which fought at Gettysburg. This action was in step with the Memorial Association's desire to present a regiment or battery's total position within a battle line, and thus give the visitor a better understanding of the amount of ground the unit actually held. [7]

At a meeting held in Philadelphia in early May 1888, representatives of the 72nd Pennsylvania Regimental Association went before the Pennsylvania Soldiers' Monument Commission and made it known that they wished to erect a monument near the stone wall in the "Bloody Angle." The Keystone veterans had noted the locations of the three Massachusetts regimental monuments by the Copse of Trees. However, members of the governing committee objected to the proposed position and the matter was tabled without reaching any decision. [8]

Undaunted, on July 3, 1888, representatives from the 72nd Pennsylvania Regimental Association approached the Gettysburg Battlefield Memorial Association and requested that a monument be placed on what they felt was the front line of their position, located just to the north of the Copse of Trees by the low stone wall. The Association rejected this petition and selected a different site on the crest of Cemetery Ridge, on the east side of Hancock Avenue, located some 94 yards from the desired position. They also advised, as per Association policy, that an advanced marker could be authorized for placement at the 72nd's preferred site. Although some local newspapers initially reported that the dispute had been resolved, the Pennsylvanians determined to fight the preservation organization's verdict. This decision had a much larger impact than for just the Pennsylvania veterans alone. The philosophy of how the battlefield would be preserved and presented to posterity was now being challenged. [9]

The action of the 72nd Pennsylvania Association was the impetus that the directors of the Gettysburg Battlefield Memorial Association needed to finally move monuments that the organization felt did not adhere to its "brigade line" policy. On September 25, 1888, the minutes of the Memorial Association included the following resolution: ". . . [T]he Superintendent of Grounds be instructed to have the Monuments of the Massachusetts regiments, erected at the copse of trees, at once removed to their proper positions in line of battle." [10]

As a direct result of the 72nd's request and the Pennsylvanians' reaction to the Association's denial, on July 26, 1888, John Bachelder wrote to the president of the 20th Massachusetts Association. Bachelder advised him that the Association was "contemplating" moving the 20th's monument, as well as those of the 15th and 19th regiments. [11] The resolution of the Memorial Association became public knowledge, at least in Gettysburg, when the *Compiler* reported on October 2, that the monuments to the three Massachusetts regiments would be moved ". . . to their brigade line to the south of the Clump of trees." [12]

On the same day, the *Star and Sentinel* noted that the United States Congress had passed a resolution which permitted the iron fencing surrounding Washington's Lafayette Square to be relocated to Gettysburg, pending approval of the necessary expenditure. [13] Part of that fence was later used to protect the trees in the famous copse from the depredations of souvenir hunters.

Less than a month later, at the annual meeting of the 15th Massachusetts Association, held on October 20, its members learned of the Association's intended action. They received a copy of the July 26 letter sent by Bachelder to Robinson. Apparently, no letter was sent directly to the 15th Massachusetts, or if sent, was never received.   The 15th acted on October 22, 1888, after a meeting of its directors and officers, held at Thomas Hasting's office. On that date, General Charles Devens wrote a letter in reply to the Gettysburg Battlefield Memorial Association. [14]

Although he was not a veteran of Gettysburg, Devens wrote with a passion befitting his past role as the regiment's first commanding officer. This letter writer was not just some disgruntled old private soldier, but a past attorney general of the Commonwealth of Massachusetts and a former brigadier general of the Union army. The letter was simply addressed, "To the President & Directors of the Gettysburg Battlefield Memorial Association." Its tone was nothing if not angry. [15]

Devens informed the preservation association that his regimental organization had learned with "great astonishment and regret" that the relocation of their Gettysburg monument was under consideration. He made it crystal clear that this information had not even come from the Gettysburg Battlefield Memorial Association, but through another affected unit, the 20th Massachusetts. Devens reported that the regimental association of the 15th was incredulous that such action could even be under deliberation without any contact between the organizations. He explained that both as an association and as individuals, the members of the 15th were unanimous in expressing disapproval of any site change for their monument. To show that this statement was not just empty rhetoric, Devens emphasized that the 15th would utilize "all honorable means" to keep the monument at its present location. [16]

Devens then launched into a post-war history lesson, relating how the 15th had been entrusted by the Commonwealth of Massachusetts with putting up its monument and how it had met that obligation. He reminded the Memorial Association that the site selected for the 15th's memorial had been approved by it and that some of the same members of the regiment who were now writing to object about any relocation had been present, along with members of the preservation society, when the spot was accepted. Devens left no room for any rebuttal argument about a misunderstanding concerning the site. [17]

He continued building his case for keeping the monument where it was by stating that the present location accurately confirmed the historic events of July 3, 1863, as ". . . it is on the exact place occupied by the Regt at the decisive struggle which closed the great battle of Gettysburg with victory. . . ." He related that over half the soldiers of the regiment, including the colonel, George Ward, had fallen during the battle and pleaded: "In their name as well as our own we urge that the monument stand where they fell mingling their life blood with the soil of Pennsylvania." The veterans of not only the 15th Massachusetts, but all the other units of the II Corps who rushed to repel Pickett's men at the battle's critical stage, Devens declared, would be robbed ". . . of their just claim to honor and renown." [18]

Although the 15th had no authority to express the feelings of other affected units, Devens indicated that he felt assured that their opinions would mirror those of his regiment. In order to cover all possible rebuttals to his argument, Devens attacked the rationale he believed was behind the Gettysburg Battlefield Memorial Association's motivation for moving the monuments. He referred to John Bachelder's letter to the 20th Massachusetts, in which Bachelder cited the maneuvering of carriages between closely placed monuments as a difficult undertaking for visitors, and the fact Bachelder felt that the numerous memorials around the Copse of Trees presented a congested and confusing image. Devens wrote sarcastically: "As to the first it is not possible that this slight inconvenience will not be readily submitted to, and it is to be hoped that all who visit them will not only be willing but anxious to descend from their carriages and stand for a moment on a spot made sacred in the cause of liberty by the blood of so many brave men: As to the second, it is enough to say that the final struggle was confused as well as terrific, and that it is much better that the monuments should so far as possible represent the historic truth with accuracy than that they should be regularly aligned." [19]

Charles Devens ended by "Earnestly protesting against any change in the location of the monument to the 15th Regt {Mass} on behalf of the Association we represent and on our own behalf. . . ." It was signed by Devens, as president of the regimental association, as well as Samuel Fletcher, Edward A. Rice, Luther D. Goddard, Thomas J. Hastings, Henry E. Smith, William H. Andrews, Amos Bartlett and David M. Earle. [20]

On November 5, 1888, Charles Buehler, vice president of the Memorial Association, responded to Devens' letter. He wrote that he believed his organization had done everything possible to meet the wishes of the units that had fought at Gettysburg. He admitted that the sites for the monuments, not only to the 15th, but also the 19th and 20th regiments, were selected with the agreement of all the involved organizations. However, he added, ". . . [I]t was afterward discovered that a serious mistake had been made, that the marking of the field to suit the wishes of individual organizations to indicate special movements would lead to inextricable confusion and then make the historical features of the struggle unintelligible." [21]

Other veteran organizations, Buehler explained, had requested permission to place monuments, after a similar fashion, as that permitted to the Massachusetts units. These requests had been denied, thus giving the impression, according to Buehler, that the Massachusetts regiments had received preferential treatment over units from other states. He further related, "Indeed one Regt, the 72nd Penna, having made claim to a position which would not be historically correct, upon being notified that their claim could not be allowed, have gone even to the length of instituting suit against the Association, to compel us to accede to their demand and one reason governing them they say is that we have allowed Massachusetts Regts privileges desired to them." [22]

Mr. Buehler continued his defense of the Association's actions by telling the 15th that it had been determined "several years ago" that it was essential to "adopt some well defined rule to which we could unflinchingly adhere." That rule ". . . was to require all monuments to occupy positions in line of battle & to let legends on the monuments describe special and varying movements. When monuments are completed this can be done, <u>and is being done</u> by special markers [emphasis in original]." [23]

In a further attempt to get the 15th's representatives to see the controversy from his perspective, Buehler made reference to a large tablet then being planned for placement at the Copse of Trees "near to the spot occupied by the 15th Regt." John Bachelder was responsible for this tablet. It was to include a special legend that "will give all that you can desire, and in a way that will be much more intelligible." [24]

Charles Buehler continued to try and strengthen his argument by stating that the location of the 15th's monument "hitherto" had been sited a short distance in front of the memorial to Captain Cowan's 1st New York Independent Battery. Since that monument, by consensus, was sited properly, it seemed obvious that the Massachusetts regiment could not have been present at that spot at the same time during the fight as the New York artillerymen. To disarm one possible 15th argument, Buehler wrote that there was apparently a mistaken belief that Bachelder felt that it was impossible to have so many monuments located by a "single driveway." He assured the 15th that nothing so frivolous would have motivated the Association. Their goal was ". . . historical accuracy . . . [and] . . . honor and glory to the heroes who fought and won this field." In a postscript, Buehler wrote that he had forgotten to mention that the "present site" of the 15th's monument "is not in the rear but in front of the old position," and "to the left" along the stone wall, nearly in line with the memorial to Colonel Ward. [25]

This letter was read at a subsequent meeting of the officers and directors of the 15th Association. Although Charles Buehler never directly said the 15th's monument had already been moved, his postscript certainly made it appear that such was the case. Consequently, another letter was sent shortly thereafter to the Memorial Association by the 15th, requesting clarification. [26]

While this drama was playing out, the Gettysburg Battlefield Memorial Association faced action on another front. Without notifying the Association, workmen dug a foundation for the new 72nd Pennsylvania monument, not on the crest of Cemetery Ridge on the east side of Hancock Avenue, as required by the preservation organization, but next to the stone wall, some 283 feet to the west. Upon learning of the excavation, representatives of the Association contacted the local police and several members of the 72nd Regimental Association were arrested for trespassing. [27]

In a letter dated December 7, 1888, sent to Secretary Edward A. Rice of the 15th's Regimental Association, Buehler responded to the unit's inquiry about where their monument was now located. The veterans' worst fears were realized. Buehler claimed not to have possession of his original letter, so he could not confirm if the monument had been moved by the time of his November 5 correspondence or not. However, Buehler stated, "[T]hey are now in the new positions." He then listed the positions of Union regiments along the low stone wall. From north to south were the monuments of the 71st Pennsylvania, 69th Pennsylvania, 59th New York, 7th Michigan, 20th Massachusetts, 19th Maine, 15th Massachusetts, 1st Minnesota and 82nd New York. "It is the universal opinion of all," Buehler wrote, "that the present positions cannot but be satisfactory to all: the 15th was moved to the front and left along the stone wall with the flank markers in position also." In one last attempt to convince the veterans that the monument reconfiguration was a benefit, he stated, "[A] large bronze tablet is ordered to be erected at the Copse of trees, showing the varying measurements of the different organizations." [28]

Charles Buehler and the Gettysburg Battlefield Memorial Association found themselves in the middle of a real dilemma, and while not lying outright, he certainly did not relate all he knew about the plans to relocate the memorials. In fact, the monuments of the 15th and 19th Massachusetts were moved in the period between Buehler's two letters, as noted in the November 27, 1888, edition of the *Compiler*. The 20th's monument had not as yet been relocated, probably because of the logistics of moving the large stone. [29] An additional two weeks passed before the same newspaper reported that the preservationists had contracted ". . . for the removal of the 20th Mass 'pudding stone' monument to its proper position, the time for the work not yet decided." [30]

When all was said and done, the monument of the 15th Massachusetts rested along the front line of General Harrow's brigade line, some 235 yards south of the Copse of Trees. The 20th's memorial was positioned in Colonel Hall's front line, approximately 125 yards south of the trees. The 19th's stone was placed along the east edge of Hancock Avenue, in the second line of Hall's brigade, some 119 yards from the trees. [31]

Shortly after receipt of Buehler's latest correspondence, the 15th Association learned of a coming reunion of the 20th regiment. David Earle and Thomas Hastings were appointed to contact both the 19th and 20th Massachusetts Associations, to determine if they knew that their monuments had been relocated, and if so, how they planned to react to the relocation. [32]

Charles Buehler apparently believed that a greater amount of communication from the preservation organization had reached the Massachusetts veterans than had actually occurred. In a letter to John Bachelder, he expressed amazement that Arthur Devereux of the 19th was not aware of the proposed "tablet" to be erected at the Copse of Trees, mentioned in his correspondence to the "protestants." [33] Devereux, in a letter written two years later to Bachelder, stated that he had "permitted" the movement of his regiment's monument. However, it is unclear if this permission was granted prior to the monument actually being moved, or as an after-the-fact acquiescence. No documentation has been uncovered concerning the 15th or 20th Massachusetts associations' indicating any earlier permission or approval for the relocation of their monuments. [34]

Subsequently, David Earle attended the 20th's reunion and discovered they were unaware their monument had been moved. He reported back to the 15th that their fellow veterans were "thunderstruck" at his message as "they supposed as we did, that they would be notified before a change of location was made." It seems safe to say that Buehler was incorrect when he had stated, "It is the universal opinion of all that the present position cannot but be satisfactory to all." [35]

The men of the 72nd Pennsylvania had obviously seen where the monuments of the 15th, 19th and 20th Massachusetts had been placed initially. These Keystone State veterans were determined to have their view of history reflected in the location of their new memorial. While the men from distant Massachusetts wrote letters attempting to right what they considered a wrong, the Pennsylvanians took the fight one step further. In early 1889, representatives of the 72nd filed a lawsuit against the Gettysburg Battlefield Memorial Association, in an attempt to gain the legal right to place their monument near the stone wall. [36]

The official fight of the 15th Massachusetts, through government channels, peaked in early March 1889. At a meeting of the 15th's regimental association, it was reported that John Bachelder had requested that the Commonwealth of Massachusetts set aside funds in order to erect ". . . a Tablet at the Copse of Trees bearing the names of the Regts who were near it in the fight. . . ." This tablet would become known as the "High Water Mark" monument. The 15th naturally desired to find out, if possible, what inscription referencing the regiment was to be on this marker. David Earle and Thomas Hastings were appointed to yet another committee, this one to work toward ". . . preserving the memory of the part taken by the Regt on the day of the final charge of Pickett's Division at the Battle of Gettysburg." With the appropriation of this money, the regimental records state, ". . . that ended all the Association could do in the matter." [37]

In the ongoing legal battle with the Pennsylvanians, the Gettysburg Battlefield Memorial Association filed its own motions. At the end of March 1889, the 72nd received the bad news that their suit had been dismissed by the Adams County Court of Common Pleas. The Pennsylvanians counterattacked and appealed the decision to Pennsylvania's Supreme Court, which ended up reversing the lower court's ruling. The case consequently was remanded to the trial court, with instructions from the appellate court to take testimony based on the original lawsuit and resolve the matter. On September 23, 1889, a Master in Equity was appointed by the local court and witnesses began to be called. [38]

As the plaintiff had, and still has, the burden of proof, the representatives of the 72nd Pennsylvania called their witnesses first. Their goal was to present testimony substantiating the fact that the 72nd did indeed fight near the stone wall and deserved to be permitted to place its monument there. Almost all the men called had served with the 72nd during the Battle of Gettysburg. Their testimony again and again supported the claim that they fought at or near the stone wall. In addition, none of the witnesses remembered seeing any supporting troops from Massachusetts or New York coming to their aid. This portion of the proceedings occurred over a several-day period in October 1889. [39]

The case resumed two months later. Two of the witnesses called to testify on behalf of the Gettysburg Battlefield Memorial Association were Arthur Devereux and William Hill, both formerly of the 19th Massachusetts. Each man traveled to Philadelphia to have his testimony taken; this was done on December 10, 1889. At the time Devereux, then 53 years old, was living in Marion, Indiana, and was involved in constructing a National Home for Soldiers. Hill resided in Salem, Massachusetts, and worked for the Edison Illuminating Company of Boston. Under normal circumstances, one might ask why these two ex-soldiers would care where the veterans of the 72nd Pennsylvania placed their monument on the Gettysburg battlefield? Why, one might wonder, would they travel such distances in the midst of winter? It is highly likely that both men were angry that the memorial to their regiment had been unceremoniously moved in 1888. Now one year later, the

72nd Pennsylvania was attempting to place its monument in an advanced position, something that had been denied to the 19th Massachusetts. The irony was that the New England veterans were testifying on behalf of the very organization that had caused their anger in the first place. [40]

Both men stressed that they saw the 72nd Pennsylvania only along the crest of Cemetery Ridge, and not down at the stone wall, as the 19th Massachusetts, together with the 42nd New York, had rushed from their positions south of the Copse of Trees to help blunt the Confederate breakthrough. In cross-examination, plaintiffs' counsel attempted to discredit their accounts of the admittedly confused event. Neither man retreated from his conclusion that the only units seen by them in the "Bloody Angle" by the stone wall, in addition to their own regiment and the 42nd New York, were the 69th and 71st Pennsylvania. [41]

Devereux was asked if his regiment had erected a monument. Receiving an affirmative answer, plaintiffs' counsel inquired if he knew its location. The witness replied, "I do not know." The former commander was evasive when asked why the 19th had not erected a monument by the stone wall, if in fact they had fought in the area. It is not known if Devereux visited Gettysburg after the 19th's monument was moved in 1888, but he certainly knew more than he was willing to share with the plaintiffs' attorney about his regiment's monument history and its current location. [42]

It is telling to note that two other defense witnesses were Alexander Webb, commander of the brigade to which the 72nd belonged, and Charles Banes, an original member of the 72nd, who served as brigade assistant adjutant general during the Battle of Gettysburg. Webb testified in the December 1889 session. Banes was called when the testimony concluded in April 1890. Both of these men participated in the dedication of the first 72nd Pennsylvania (Philadelphia Brigade) memorial in 1883, which is located on the military crest of Cemetery Ridge, some 120 feet east of where the 72nd wanted to place its new monument. It was Charles Banes, in response to General Webb's orders, who had led the 72nd forward from its reserve position behind the crest of the ridge. Banes stated under oath that the new position was slightly in advance of where the 1883 memorial was, and still is, located. Webb testified that, in his professional opinion, the monument to the 72nd Pennsylvania belonged on the crest of the ridge. Banes, although sympathetic to the men of the 72nd, felt that only a portion of the 69th Pennsylvania was at the stone wall, and not men of the 72nd regiment. This testimony placed the 72nd between where the Pennsylvanians wanted their monument and the position desired by the Gettysburg Battlefield Memorial Association, who desired to erect it an additional 163 feet to the east. [43]

Several former soldiers from the 69th and 71st Pennsylvania were also called by defense counsel to give their accounts of the battle. In their testimony, all refuted the claim of their fellow Pennsylvanians. [44]

John Bachelder was also one of the witnesses called by the defense during the April 1890 session. He related his background as a historian of the battle from the time he arrived in Gettysburg, shortly after the fighting ended, up through his current role as a director of the Gettysburg Battlefield Memorial Association. Bachelder explained how the Association determined that no monuments should be permitted in the trees themselves, as they were the focal point of Pickett's Charge. However, monuments had been permitted in the vicinity of the trees. Specifically listing the 15th, 19th and 20th Massachusetts, he explained that after permitting their monuments' placement, the Association's Board of Directors realized that ". . . a very large number of others had left their position in the line of Battle and had also gone up to that point." The preservationists now recognized that as 13 Union regiments had fought in the area, if monuments were permitted for all of them, the resultant congestion would make it difficult for anyone to understand what had occurred during this critical part of the battle. [45]

Bachelder explained how after numerous discussions with officials in Washington, D.C. and army officers, it was decided to place monuments only on lines of battle rather than at points of actual combat. He further stated that inscriptions on monuments and separate markers were permitted, describing a unit's movement and its subsequent fighting. He testified that the "embarrassing question" of the problem of the three Massachusetts monuments already being placed was resolved when, after explaining the regulations and their reasons to the Massachusetts organizations, they, "as good law-abiding citizens," permitted their monuments to be moved. [46]

Fortunately for John Bachelder, Arthur Devereux and William Hill were not present to hear this perspective of events. It is interesting to note that no one from either the 15th or 20th regiments testified during this case, as it is likely that they would have considered this statement of Bachelder's to be a bald-faced fabrication.

Under cross-examination, Bachelder admitted that he was the architect of the brigade line plan of monumentation. He further explained why he felt that all regimental monuments along Hancock Avenue should be placed on one side or the other of the road, depending on their place in the brigade formation. This was his rationale for the location of the placement of the 72nd monument. [47]

Plaintiffs' counsel further attacked Bachelder's credibility on the basis that he was not present at the Battle of Gettysburg, was not even a veteran and that all his knowledge was second-hand. Finally, he was forced to admit that the Commonwealth of Pennsylvania had the authority to place a monument "wherever it pleases." [48]

The court weighed the evidence throughout the balance of 1890. A final decision was issued in December of that year. The court found that men from the 72nd had indeed fought and died at the stone wall. It not only permitted the 72nd Pennsylvania to place its monument there, but also specifically forbade the Gettysburg Battlefield Memorial Association from ever moving it. There the distinctive monument of a Pennsylvania Zouave wielding a clubbed musket remains to this day. [49]

From far-away Marion, Indiana, exactly one year to the day after his court testimony, an anguished Arthur Devereux wrote John Bachelder, advising him that he had seen the decision of the court in his local newspaper. He asked for information about the case and the rationale behind the decision, since his paper provided no in-depth analysis. In an understated, possibly sarcastic vein, he wrote: "[I am] naturally a little curious to know." Devereux rhetorically asked about the worth of documented evidence and wanted to learn ". . . the value of a Monument . . . when it attempts to enforce a lie?" In another question to which he surely knew the answer, he asked if the 19th's monument could be moved back " . . . where it belongs or must it stay back where it gives no idea of the service performed by it?" Devereux lamented ever giving approval for his monument to be relocated under Gettysburg Battlefield Memorial Association policy, if that action were to end in ". . . a travesty of truth." Although not placing blame on the Association, Devereux did ask for a response and ended with this threat: "There will be lots of troubles grow out of this if not mended." [50]

I n the midst of all this controversy, on May 18, 1891, John Bachelder presented his plans for the establishment of a "High Water Mark" tablet to the directors of the Gettysburg Battlefield Preservation Association, who immediately approved them. His vision of developing the Copse of Trees as the focal point of the battlefield was now close to fruition. [51]

In a last attempt to reverse the decision in the 72nd Pennsylvania case, the preservation organization appealed to Pennsylvania's Supreme Court. The high court upheld the lower court's ruling on June 5, 1891, thus ending the legal battle. On July 4, 1891, amid much celebration by the Pennsylvania veterans, their monument was dedicated twenty feet from the stone wall. [52] The brigade line policy of the Gettysburg Battlefield Memorial Association had been broken and its officials were embittered at this defeat.

However, the real losers in the case were the men of the 15th, 19th and 20th Massachusetts. For more than a century, a very important fact seems to have been overlooked by historians who have studied this matter. The Gettysburg Battlefield Memorial Association required the 72nd Pennsylvania to erect its monument at a position some 283 feet to the east of where the regiment wished it placed. This site, just below the crest of Cemetery Ridge, on the east side of present-day Hancock Avenue, was where the unit had been held in reserve during the cannonade preceding Pickett's Charge. That location would have been every bit as misleading to the Pennsylvanians' subsequent actions as the present location of the 19th Massachusetts monument is to understanding the Bay Staters' movements on July 3, 1863.

The trial testimony clearly showed that the Pennsylvania regiment had moved forward and stood firm on a battle line near the site of the 1883 brigade monument; there it took most of its casualties. Although speculation, one can only wonder if there would ever have been a controversy if John Bachelder and his associates had picked that site for the Pennsylvanians' memorial, and agreed to place an advance marker at the stone wall. Would the 72nd have gone to all the trouble to file suit in that event? Consequently, would the Massachusetts monuments still be on the grass immediately south of the Copse of Trees? The answers are of course moot, but interesting nonetheless. [53]

In order to mollify the anger of the men of the three Bay State regiments, John Bachelder and the directors of the Association moved to erect bronze markers, denoting the forward positions taken by the units after their rush to the trees. These were installed on October 15, 1891. The *Boston Daily Globe* announced the event under the heading, "Bay State Valiant Heroes." Columns in both the *Daily Globe* and Gettysburg's *Star and Sentinel* defended John Bachelder against what was considered severe and unfair criticism by the veterans. Some old soldiers had felt that Bachelder had not tried to prevent the Gettysburg Battlefield Memorial Association's relocation of their memorials. The article in the Gettysburg newspaper put the best possible face on the matter, stating that the markers were placed "near" where the memorials had been originally located. In addition, the three regiments had "... the unique distinction of having not only their brigade but also their advanced position marked." The Boston newspaper mistakenly reported that the tablets were "... located on the exact spots upon which the regular regimental monuments stood. ...." Both papers explained that the monuments had been moved back to the brigade line to meet the requirements of the Gettysburg Battlefield Memorial Association. [54]

The Massachusetts newspaper reflected the bitter feeling over the 72nd's success in placing its monument by the stone wall. The article specifically pointed out that it was the 19th Massachusetts and 42nd New York regiments which had rushed forward to repel General Pickett's men when the Pennsylvanians "refused to advance." During the dedication of the 72nd's monument, one of the speakers had implied that the four Confederate flags captured by members of the 19th Massachusetts had been taken from the dead hands of Pennsylvanians. That statement, the article continued "... was a lie, pure and simple. ...." John Bachelder's tablets would set the record straight for all time: "The Massachusetts tablet will be seen and read by the visitor, while the 72nd memorial will not be noticed on account of its distance from the road." [55]

Unfortunately, the placement of these markers did not, in fact, represent exactly where the monuments had been erected by the veterans. As stated earlier, in 1885 and 1886, all three monuments were installed in a line just south of the Copse of Trees. Facing north, the 20th Massachusetts was on the left, with the 15th Massachusetts closest to the road and the 19th Massachusetts in the middle. In July 1887, after objections by members of the 19th as to the accuracy of that location, their monument was moved to a position directly to the east of the Copse of Trees. That position now conflicted with John Bachelder's new "High Water Mark Tablet," which had recently been erected and was scheduled to be dedicated the following month, on the anniversary of Lincoln's famous Gettysburg Address. Consequently, the 19th's plaque was placed, not where its monument had been, as that location would have been directly in front of Bachelder's monument, but was positioned where the 15th's monument had originally stood. This caused the 15th's marker to be placed in the original location of the 19th's monument. Only the marker of the 20th Massachusetts truly represents the site originally selected by the unit's veterans.

With the 19th's memorial moved out of the way, Bachelder's High Water Mark monument dedication ceremony was highly anticipated, with possible attendance by President Harrison and various Northern governors. However, the ceremony was postponed later that month, and was not in fact held until the following June. [56]

The markers, fabricated in statuary bronze by the Henry Bonnard Bronze Company of New York, were 16 by 38 inches in size, with the Massachusetts State coat of arms at the top, and mounted on posts over eight feet tall. Funding was provided by the Massachusetts State Legislature. The markers' inscriptions correctly described the advance of the three regiments in maneuvering from their brigades' lines to the Copse of Trees. The 19th's marker also gave credit to and included the movement of the 42nd New York. [57]

In an attempt to continue to soothe the veterans' frayed feelings, John Bachelder immediately sent copies of the newspaper article describing the erection of the tablets at the Copse of Trees to some of the Bay State veterans. Edmund Rice, one of the Medal of Honor recipients from the 19th Massachusetts, wrote from Chicago on October 21, 1891, thanking Bachelder for the article describing the action near the trees ". . . where so many of us were gathered in a crowd as if we were after a football." Rice also complimented Bachelder for his work in writing a history of the battle and sent him some personal information which he felt might be of some use to the historian. [58]

One month after the markers were erected, Arthur Devereux, writing from Cincinnati, Ohio, also sent a letter to Bachelder, in which he expressed his favorable reaction to the installation of the markers. In Devereux's words, the placement of the bronze tablets ". . . is most satisfactory to myself and has settled any discontent among my men some of whom failed to be convinced of the reason for carrying back the monument." He praised the preservationist and his fellow directors for fighting against the placement of the 72nd Pennsylvania monument and placed no blame on them for losing that struggle. Devereux admitted that he was "getting reconciled" to the Pennsylvanians' victory, but could not resist one last parting shot: "It blazons their shame and the story will be told to all comers and they might have seen the waters of oblivion roll over it but for their own action." [59]

The monuments and advance markers of the 15th, 19th and 20th Massachusetts now apparently rested at their final sites. The regimental associations still watched over their monuments and took responsibility for their care. However, events that affected these memorials continued to unfold. Some of these changes had a bearing on how the regiments' actions during the battle would be viewed by visitors and historians in the ensuing years.

On June 2, 1892, John Bachelder's "High Water Mark" Tablet was finally dedicated with great fanfare. The 1272-pound bronze book listed the commands of both armies on its open pages; individual participating units were enumerated on the north and south panels. Flanking the massive book were two bronze cannon, complete with stacks of cannon balls. An iron fence protected the trees from souvenir hunting tourists. The platform, built to hold the numerous dignitaries, including Massachusetts Governor William Russell, was built south of the Copse of Trees. Covered chairs were provided for about 2,000 members of the audience; it was also estimated that nearly that many stood during the ceremony. In all, some 8,000 visitors flocked to Gettysburg for the historic event. [60]

At the dedication ceremony, Bachelder, who, in 1868, had first coined the term "High-Water Mark," recounted the events of the great assault and repulse of July 3, 1863. The list of speakers also included many who had fought on the field that day, but none spoke from the three Massachusetts regiments, who had struggled and bled where the visitors sat in covered chairs and enjoyed the strains of martial music played by John Philip Sousa and his Marine Band. [61]

In May 1893, a three-member Gettysburg National Military Park Commission was appointed to serve under the auspices of the United States War Department and care for the Gettysburg battlefield. John Bachelder was selected as one of the first three commissioners. This organization co-existed with the Gettysburg Battlefield Memorial Association until those first preservationists ceded their holdings to the Federal government in May 1895. The record of the Association then became part of the historiography of the Battle of Gettysburg. [62]

Consequently, it was to the park commissioners that Gustave Magnitzky, representing the 20th Massachusetts veterans, sent an inquiry dated January 20, 1895. The Bay Staters had decided to approach the Commission with a request to move their monument ". . . to the most advanced position occupied by the regiment during the battle." Magnitzky, showing some latitude in the proposal, added a fall-back caveat by asking that the New Englanders be permitted to at least erect something conspicuous on that site, by putting ". . . a more prominent marker on that position, something in the shape of a reduced Bunker Hill Monument, about five or six feet high, with a suitable inscription." As subsequent actions proved, Emmor B. Cope, the Commission's engineer, misunderstood this request, in that he thought Magnitzky meant the 20th's skirmish line's position of July 2, 1863, and not the plaque near the Copse of Trees. [63]

Also in 1895, someone from the 15th Massachusetts Association discovered that the George Ward monument had been damaged and contacted the Gettysburg National Military Park Commission about repairing it. Initially, some confusion ensued as to which of the 15th's monuments was involved. Once again, Emmor Cope, the Commission's engineer, wrote to Chairman John Nicholson, and reported that nothing was wrong with the memorial on Hancock Avenue. He further stated that although it appeared to be in good repair from the road, he had not examined the one on the Emmitsburg Road. [64]

In actuality, the marble bust of Colonel Ward had been damaged by the elements and the monument itself needed some painting and base stabilization. Nine additional letters written over the next two plus years have survived, detailing the process of repairing the memorial. At one point, it was felt that the entire shaft would have to be returned to Massachusetts. However, in the end, a replacement bronze bust of the colonel was produced in Massachusetts and freighted to Gettysburg, for installation by a local workman recommended by the Commission. The Gettysburg National Military Park Commission was certainly a no-frills organization, as Commissioners John Nicholson and William Robbins, together with Engineer Cope, personally removed the marble medallion on November 25, 1896. It was subsequently shipped to New England, where it was placed on display in G.A.R. Post Number 10 in Worcester, Massachusetts. The tenor of all of the communication between the organizations was friendly and respectful; it was detailed to the extent that David Earle actually sent bolts for the bust installation from Massachusetts to Gettysburg. Although the Commission worked closely with the 15th Association in regard to seeing that the repairs were carried out, it was the veterans themselves who bore the financial responsibility. Today's visitor will find the bronze replacement bust of the fallen Colonel George Ward gazing out toward the Emmitsburg Road, looking toward the position of the advancing Confederates. [65]

A s the battlefield developed and visitation increased, foot and carriage paths cut by tourists evolved into dirt roads. In 1895, the Gettysburg National Military Park Commission worked to construct new roads and im-

prove existing ones. Hancock Avenue was in the process of being converted
from a dirt road into a 25-foot wide thoroughfare of various size stones, com-
pacted by 14-ton steam rollers. Two additional 20-foot wide roads were laid
out, one to the north of the Copse of Trees and one to the south. The northern
one, known as Webb Avenue, was in fact a loop. It left Hancock Avenue
where a portion of the 71st Pennsylvania had fought, traveled next to the
stone wall to the west, and then south to where the 1891 72nd Pennsylvania's
monument stands. Finally, it returned to Hancock Avenue near the location
of the 1883 72nd Pennsylvania monument. [66]

The second road, named in honor of Brigadier General William Harrow, left Hancock Avenue by the monument to Captain Cowan's New York
battery, and continued past the three markers to the 15th, 19th and 20th Massachusetts. Where it reached the stone wall, it turned south; at this point, it
roughly paralleled Hancock Avenue. Harrow Avenue passed the monuments
of the 59th New York, 7th Michigan and 20th Massachusetts of Colonel Hall's
brigade, and then the monuments to all the regiments of Harrow's brigade. It
finally rejoined Hancock Avenue where the major road curved east, near where
Major General Winfield Scott Hancock was wounded on July 3, 1863. This
work was completed in 1896. [67] The monuments of the 42nd New York and
19th Massachusetts of Hall's second line are located along Hancock Avenue.

Finally, on February 11, 1896, over a year after Gustave Magnitzky's
letter inquiring about the placement of a more conspicuous marker for the
20th Massachusetts, E. B. Cope wrote an internal memorandum to the commissioners explaining Magnitzky's request. Since he had apparently not understood what Magnitzky meant by "advanced position," Cope addressed both
the 20th's skirmish line's position of July 2, and the unit's movement to the
Copse of Trees on July 3. One immediate problem was that the Federal government did not even own the land near the Codori barn to which the 20th's skirmishers had advanced on the second day of the battle. Cope also advised the
Commission that after reading Captain Henry Abbott's post-battle report, he
learned that the 20th had gone to the Copse of Trees to help repel General Pickett's
Virginians. The engineer either forgot, or was oblivious to, the 20th's monument
history, as he recommended against any marker (that in fact had already been
there for over four years) at the Copse of Trees. Cope felt that the trees could not
be considered an advanced position and that ". . . a marker here would compli-
cate the present arrangement of the monuments and markers in the vicinity of the
"High Water Marker." Cope concluded that the unit should either attach a
bronze tablet to the regiment's monument, explaining the skirmishers' ac-

tions on July 2, or that land should be purchased at the site near the Codori barn and a descriptive marker erected at the advanced position. [68]

The matter came to an end with a May 11, 1896, memorandum between Commissioner Charles Richardson and Chairman John Nicholson. On the Park Commission, Richardson had replaced John Bachelder, who had passed away on December 22, 1894. He wrote that, based on official reports, the 20th's monument was located at the correct position, which represented where the regiment had been in line of battle. More importantly, based on the normal expectation of the duties of a skirmisher line, the men, although they had performed well, had not achieved at a level that would warrant a separate marker. Richardson concluded, as had Cope, that too many markers "beyond what is necessary to indicate important positions" only resulted in bewilderment for the visitor. He felt that if the unit wanted to record the actions of the skirmish line on July 2, it should add a plaque to the present monument, instead of erecting a new memorial. [69] No further correspondence has been located concerning this matter during this period. However, nothing was added to the 20th's regimental monument, and no memorial or marker representing the actions of the skirmish line was erected.

The 15th Massachusetts Regimental Association was a very active organization, holding their annual reunions in Worcester on the anniversary of the Battle of Ball's Bluff. Also, in addition to the 1886 battlefield tour during which the Gettysburg monuments were dedicated, the group again visited Gettysburg in 1898 and 1900. David Earle was the driving force behind the 1898 trip. A photograph of the veterans taken at that time shows the men in front of the Copse of Trees, facing toward the former Confederate lines. It is interesting to note that the photograph was taken at that location. No picture has been found of the group at the regimental monument, now located some 235 yards due south of the trees. The veterans obviously still felt the almost mystical lure of the Copse of Trees and the sacrifice there of their comrades-in-arms. [70]

The primary purpose of the 15th Massachusetts Regimental Association's 1900 excursion was to dedicate their monument on the Antietam battlefield. The successful Gettysburg trip in 1898 had left a balance of $300.00 in the association's coffers; this was the genesis of the movement to memorialize the unit's sacrifice on that bloody September day in 1862. Edward Russell served as the trip's leader. George W. Ward, one of Colonel Ward's sons, wrote a history of the event, which was published in 1901. If anything, the bond among the men of the 15th Massachusetts seemed to have grown stronger over the years following the Civil War. [71]

Twelve of the men who participated in the 1886 expedition once again mustered for another jaunt into their collective past. As is the norm with organizations of this nature, formed to represent and remember a specific period in time, some had "gone to the great bivouac beyond." However, 44 men, representing every company and the field and staff of the regiment, made the trip, which left Worcester's Union Station on September 14, 1900. They were accompanied by another 26 veterans who had served in other Civil War units, as well as by many additional family and friends. [72]

Upon arriving in Gettysburg, the excursionists met other tourists; including United States Senator George F. Hoar, the group now numbered over 200. As on previous trips, a tour was undertaken; during the next two days, all parts of the famous battlefield were visited, including the National Cemetery, where fallen comrades were remembered with floral offerings. Colonel Ward was honored with a speech by his son George, and with flowers placed by his son Robert at the memorial where their father had received his mortal wound. At the behest of his friends and comrades, David Earle spoke at the Copse of Trees. His speech lasted for over an hour. In it, he described the 15th's desperate actions in the fighting on July 2 and 3, 1863. The excursion history clearly stated: "One of the important points touched upon was the displacement of the 15th Regiment Monument from its honored position at the Copse of Trees to a point south never occupied by this command." Later that evening, Senator Hoar spoke passionately to the assembled gathering at the Adams County Courthouse about the 15th and the cause for which it fought. [73]

Early the following day, everyone gathered for the trip to Sharpsburg, Maryland. It happened to be September 17, the 38th anniversary of the Battle of Antietam. After dedicating the regiment's beautiful monument on the field, which lists all 118 men who were killed in action or died of wounds, the sight-seers toured the battlefield. [74] Their mission to remember their fallen comrades complete, the veterans and friends returned to Massachusetts, after stops at Harpers Ferry, Washington D.C. and the Ball's Bluff battlefield. [75]

One result of the 15th's excursion was to bring to the surface the festering wound of the placement of its regimental monument at Gettysburg. The veterans were still angry and had apparently not given up all hope of securing justice for their unit's memory. Shortly after returning to Worcester, David Earle wrote to the Secretary of State for the Commonwealth of Pennsylvania. He requested a copy of the charter of the Gettysburg Battlefield Memorial

Association, as well as the names of the organization's directors and officers in 1884. The letter was forwarded to a local school teacher and former director of the Memorial Association, Calvin Hamilton, with instructions to respond to Earle. Hamilton immediately went to see William Robbins, a commissioner of the Gettysburg National Park Commission, who in turn wrote to the chairman of the Commission, John Nicholson. Robbins informed Nicholson that Hamilton would send Earle the names of the 1884 directors, making a notation next to the names of those who had passed away. Hamilton planned to direct Earle to John Vanderslice's published work, *Gettysburg Then And Now,* for information about the preservation organization's charter. Robbins warned Nicholson: "So you see those fellows seem bound and determined to get up a movement concerning the position of their monument." Apparently Senator George Hoar had also entered the fray on behalf of his friends, as Robbins also mentioned that the politician had not responded to a letter he had written and suggested that Nicholson contact him. However, on second thought, Robbins ended his letter with the observation that ". . . perhaps we should wait until they show their hand." [76]

George Hoar was more to the 15th Massachusetts' veterans than merely a politician currying favor with his constituents. Although not a veteran, he was one of them in almost every sense of the word. His association with Charles Devens dated back to before the Civil War and his brother-in-law had fought and died as a member of the 15th at the Battle of Antietam. On December 14, 1900, the senator wrote a nine-page, double-spaced typewritten letter to John Nicholson, in response to one written to him on September 24. He apologized for not writing sooner, not only because of the exigencies of running a re-election campaign, but also because he had wanted to meet with members of the 15th Massachusetts before responding. [77]

Hoar began by straightening out Nicholson's misconception that anyone ever complained that the monument to Colonel George Ward had been moved by any of the organizations responsible for the development or governance of the Gettysburg battlefield. He stated unequivocally that the memorial was still situated where it had been erected, and had never been relocated. [78]

The senator then launched into a step-by-step recitation in which he described how the regimental association, with the full understanding and approval of the Gettysburg Battlefield Memorial Association, located and erected their monument. Hoar even stated that the veterans, and not the preservation organization, had had initial reservations about the spot chosen, because of possible crowding with other memorials. He went so far as to quote the preservationists' own rules and regulations governing the placement of monuments. Furthermore—and important when considering the later rationale used for moving the monument—Senator Hoar declared that the position by the Copse of Trees ". . . was on the line of battle held by the brigade to which the 15th Regiment was attached, and it was so erected in full compliance with the rules then existing. . . ." [79]

After presenting his argument that the Memorial Association had been wrong in moving the monument, Hoar proceeded to assault the current location of the 15th's memorial. He stated that it, and all the monuments of Harrow's brigade, were placed incorrectly. According to Hoar, during the battle all the units had held positions further east, on the other side of Harrow Avenue. He chided Nicholson, writing that if he wanted to be accurate about the position prior to rushing to the Copse of Trees, all the brigade's monuments should be moved. [80]

The senator used the very words of the Memorial Association to damn its actions. Hoar quoted liberally from the speech accepting the 15th's memorial by Association Secretary John Krauth, citing the promise to "watch and guard" the monument. Sarcasm dripped from Hoar's pen: "Now the way in which that memorial was watched and guarded was to remove it, without notice to the Regiment that had erected it under the direction of the Memorial association. . . ." To emphasize that the removal of the 15th's monument had in no way occurred to correct any historical inaccuracies, Hoar called Nicholson's attention to the bronze tablet erected near where the monument had originally been sited. He reminded the commissioner that the marker validated the actions of the 15th on July 3, 1863. [81]

In order to respond to a statement made by Robbins in a September 28, 1900, letter, Hoar made it clear that David Earle had never blamed the National Park Commission for moving the 15th's monument. The Memorial Association, and only that organization, was responsible for that deed. Hoar did take exception to Robbins' opinion that the 15th had moved to the Copse of Trees only ". . . as the Confederate column was overwhelmed and went to pieces. . ." and that they and other Union regiments ". . . really had no part in this final struggle. . . ." Hoar questioned whether that statement was fair, considering the 60% casualties suffered by the 15th Massachusetts at Gettysburg. (Interestingly, on September 28, 1900, Williams Robbins also recorded his personal views about Hoar's arguments in his journal. In his opinion, Robbins felt that the Gettysburg Battlefield Memorial Association had ". . . found a ridiculous number of Monuments beginning to cluster at 'High Water Mark' where the Reg'ts did not fight." Naturally, this private thought was never communicated to Senator Hoar.) [82]

The senator ended his lengthy epistle by restating that the regiment had moved to the trees during the heat of battle and how the Memorial Association, including historian John Bachelder, had promised to protect and preserve their subsequently-placed monument. He assured Nicholson that he believed that Robbins was ". . . an honorable and gallant gentleman . . ." who would not ". . . do any man, least of all any soldier, an injustice." He asked that his letter to Nicholson be shared with Robbins. The overwhelming evidence, however, sustained the original monument location and ". . . in violation of that pledge, the monument was moved. It was moved to a place the regiment never occupied. It was moved without hearing or notice." [83]

On December 29, 1900, John Nicholson sent Senator Hoar a measured response. He showed considerable political acumen of his own by never really addressing the salient points of Hoar's letter. Nicholson wrote that someone (he was unsure if it was a member of the 15th regiment or a visitor) had, indeed, accused the National Park Commission of moving the Ward monument. However, he was pleased and grateful that they both agreed that the memorial was never relocated. He assured the senator that he was aware of the content of John Krauth's speech of 1886 and was also fully cognizant of the deeds of Massachusetts soldiers during the Battle of Gettysburg. With regard to the senator's claims of injustice, Nicholson simply stated that he was sure that Major Robbins would write ". . . and at that point I think I may safely leave the matter." [84]

The final changes to any of the regimental monuments honoring the 15th, 19th and 20th Massachusetts were initiated almost forty years after the battle. On February 20, 1903, Charles Peirson, representing the 20th regiment, responded to a letter from John Nicholson, as part of an ongoing dialogue concerning a tablet that Peirson wished attached to that monument. This dialogue apparently had its genesis in the attempt made by Gustave Magnitzky eight years earlier to augment the regiment's battlefield actions through additional memorialization. It is clear in retrospect that Magnitzky had, indeed, referred to the 20th's position at the Copse of Trees and not to the skirmishers' position of July 2. Peirson's response contained the exact wording he desired placed on the tablet, and was detailed to the point of not only including the size of the tablet, but also of the letters themselves. These words clarified the actions of the regiment and its cost in casualties in the fighting on July 2 and 3, 1863, especially the movement ". . . TO ASSIST IN REPELLING THE CHARGE OF PICKETT'S DIVISION [emphasis added]." Paul Revere, Henry Ropes and Sumner Paine, the three officers who perished during the battle, were all specifically listed by name. [85]

Nicholson answered on March 2, 1903, with a few changes, including altering "Pickett's Division" to "Longstreet's Corps." Peirson immediately incorporated the changes and sent the commissioner a final draft on March 3, 1903. Nicholson placed his endorsement on the document on March 4, and sent it on to the War Department for final approval; this was granted two days later and received back in Gettysburg on March 12, 1903. [86]

Consequently, due to the efforts of Charles Peirson, of the three Massachusetts' monuments, only the words on the 20th's memorial actually inform visitors of what occurred on July 3, 1863. Indeed, the 15th's monument has nothing on it describing the regiment's role in the fight. In its present position, the inscription on the 19th's monument is incorrect and, as a result, misinforms the visitor. Only the tablets at the Copse of Trees serve the purpose of enlightening those who visit the battlefield.

During the summer of 1903, the observance of the battle's 40th anniversary brought many visitors to the field and heightened interest about Gettysburg throughout the nation. However, the role of the three Massachusetts regiments was lost within the larger scope of the great battle. For instance, an article in the *Star and Sentinel* about Pickett's Charge made no mention of the 15th, 19th or 20th Massachusetts. [87]

The Massachusetts veterans continued to be responsible for maintaining their regimental monuments during the ensuing years. Just as the marble bust on the memorial to the 15th's Colonel Ward had been damaged by the elements in the previous decade, the 15th's regimental monument likewise deteriorated in 1906. It was E. B. Cope of the Gettysburg National Military Park Commission, who, on January 17, 1906, discovered the damage, which he determined had been caused by expansion of the marble bas-relief of the soldier. Cope felt that merely repairing the monument and reusing the marble would only result in additional damage. Consequently, he suggested replacing it with one of bronze. On May 9, 1906, John Nicholson sent Cope's report, along with a blueprint of the monument, to the Adjutant General of

Massachusetts. Nicholson asked that the report be forwarded to the 15th Massachusetts Regimental Association ". . . for such action as they may think proper." The Regimental Association, in coordination with the Commission, did as suggested and brought the monument back to Worcester, where the broken marble soldier on the monument's face was replaced with a bronze replica, a process that was completed in 1907. [88]

As the 20th century progressed, age took its inevitable toll on the veterans of the Blue and Gray. However, the bonds formed in warfare remained strong until the very end. The importance of this relationship among the veterans was understood by their sons and daughters. For example, on December 29, 1917, Eliza Converse, the daughter of the 15th's Josiah Converse, wrote a quick note to the son of Colonel George Ward. She related that "Papa" had died that morning and asked that Mr. Ward ". . . notify other interested friends and comrades . . ." of the funeral arrangements. In describing the feelings of the survivors as their compatriots died, one veteran wrote, "Year after year the comrades of the dead follow, with public honor, procession and commemorative flags and funeral march—honor and grief from us who stand almost alone, and have seen the best and noblest of our generation pass away." [89] Finally, only the monuments remained.

In August 1933, the War Department transferred all of its holdings to the National Park Service, where responsibility for the nation's military parks resides to this day. At some point during the early 1950s, someone (exactly who is not known), at Gettysburg National Military Park apparently decided that the plaques representing the movements of the 15th, 19th and 20th Massachusetts on July 3, 1863, were extraneous, and had them taken down and placed in storage. Possibly this action occurred because all three units had monuments nearby, but here again the exact rationale for the plaques' removal is unknown. Consequently, this tangible evidence describing the roles played by the three Massachusetts units in repelling Pickett's Charge disappeared from the face of the battlefield. [90]

As described earlier, a "well trodden footpath" had been paved during the years 1895-1896 to facilitate visitation to the monuments of Hall's and Harrow's brigades. After World War II, however, most travelers came to Gettysburg by automobile, rather than by train, and toured the battlefield following the designated stops along a car tour route. In the early 1970s, officials at Gettysburg National Military Park removed Harrow Avenue completely, to "encourage people to explore the landscape on foot." This paved surface was now replaced with sod. [91] However, if one stands at the south side of the Copse of Trees and looks southward along the line of the monuments of Hall's and Harrow's brigades, the outline of the old roadbed can still easily be discerned.

In fact, most visitors drove past the monuments to the 15th, 19th and 20th Massachusetts as they gravitated to the official automobile stop at the "High Water Mark" and the "Bloody Angle." The story of the 72nd Pennsylvania's actions on July 3, 1863, became well known, in large part due to the lure of the statute of the Zouave soldier with the clubbed musket located near the stone wall. The memorials to Lieutenant Alonzo Cushing's Battery "A", 4th U. S. Artillery and Confederate General Lewis Armistead's mortal wounding, also north of the Copse of Trees, are visited by almost all who come to the battlefield. The monuments to the three Massachusetts regiments, and indeed all those to the units of Hall's and Harrow's brigades situated south of the Copse, faded into the background. Those tourists who did walk along the battle line gained little in the way of understanding the role of any of these regiments during Pickett's Charge.

I n early 1993, the Civil War Round Table of Eastern Pennsylvania, Inc., was looking for a worthy historic preservation project. This group of Civil War history enthusiasts, based in the Lehigh Valley area of Pennsylvania, had built a reputation as a strong proponent of battlefield preservation since its founding in 1978. Throughout the years, the Round Table had previously worked with various private land acquisition organizations, as well as the National Park Service, toward that end. [92]

That quest led to Kathy Georg Harrison, Senior Historian at Gettysburg National Military Park. Ms. Harrison had long felt that the Park's action in removing the Massachusetts plaques had been "obviously misguided" and wished to ". . . return these three markers (and their regiments) to the measure of prominence that they deserve." Unfortunately, in the decades following the posts and plaques being put into storage, the iron supports for the 15th and 19th Massachusetts had disappeared. Replacing the plaques had been approved by the Regional Director of the National Park Service in October 1985, but a lack of funding had precluded the Park's replacing them. Because of this, Ms. Harrison suggested that the Round Table might wish to adopt the plaque restoration as a project. [93]

The Lehigh Valley group readily agreed and in April 1993 donated $600.00, followed by an additional $600.00 in June 1993, to fabricate the new posts needed to support the plaques of the 15th and 19th Massachusetts regiments. As a result, all three tablets were reinstalled that fall. In fact, in the re-installation process, one of the posts even struck an original monument foundation. [94]

Finally, after an absence of approximately forty years, visitors to the Gettysburg battlefield were once again able to learn from these silent sentinels of the roles played by the 15th, 19th and 20th Massachusetts in repelling the assault of Pickett's Virginians well over a century ago. The gallantry displayed by the men of these three Massachusetts units, as related in this study, is meant to complement, rather than diminish, the actions of the other Union and Confederate soldiers who fought in the gigantic struggle known as the Battle of Gettysburg. In the post-war period, the men who served on the Gettysburg Battlefield Memorial Association and the Gettysburg National Military Park Commission served honorably, under difficult conditions, trying to balance the sometimes emotional opinions of the veterans with their own vision for the battlefield as a memorial. However, the Gettysburg Battlefield Memorial Association, in attempting to defeat the maneuvers of the veterans of the 72nd Pennsylvania in placing its monument, did the Massachusetts veterans a great disservice. When the veterans questioned their plans, the preservation organization stalled and misled them until their monuments were moved to the "brigade line." Worse, they made it seem like the New Englanders readily approved and agreed with the relocation of their monuments. [95] The goal of the Memorial Association in placing monuments on a "brigade line" was a valid one, and the battlefield today is clearly more easily understood because of that organization's work. However, the Association's actions in 1888 helped to create a void in the historiography of this battle concerning the Bay Staters' participation, especially on July 3, 1863. The authors have attempted to honor the men of the 15th, 19th and 20th Massachusetts who were involved in that struggle and to fill that void. They deserve nothing less.

7

Personal Epilogue

hroughout this book, the post-battle and/or post-war fates of most of the Bay State men who have been discussed have been described in detail, whether in previous chapters or in the footnotes. However, some of key figures in the fighting done by the 15th, 19th and 20th Massachusetts have not had their complete stories told. This chapter will attempt to do that.

George Joslin was discharged from the 15th Massachusetts on July 11, 1864, when his three-year term of service expired. His rank when he mustered out was still that of lieutenant colonel. After the Battle of Gettysburg, Joslin was promoted to the rank of colonel, with an effective date of July 4, 1863, but he was never officially mustered in at that rank. [1]

His personal life after the war was marred by tragedy. Joslin's first wife, with whom he had three children, died of disease in 1868. His second wife, whom he married in 1872, was placed in an insane asylum in 1878, where she remained for the rest of her life, leaving Joslin to raise his children alone. [2]

After spending three years in Chicago, in 1869, George Joslin moved back to Massachusetts. He found employment with the Customs Service at the port of Boston. In 1871, Joslin was promoted to assistant appraiser of merchandise at the port. He remained in this position until his retirement in 1895. [3]

In September 1866, Joslin began collecting a Federal disability pension of $15.00 per month. He suffered from the effects of being shot in his right wrist at the Battle of Antietam. A government examining physician noted that Joslin's right hand was permanently drawn inward and that he had very little movement in it. By the time of his death at his home in Dorchester, Massachusetts, on November 21, 1916, George Joslin's pension had been increased to the sum of $30.00 per month. [4]

On January 29, 1917, heart disease brought death to the 15th Massachusetts' David Earle after a six-month illness, at the age of 78. For the previous 13 years, the well known and popular Earle had been a messenger and doorkeeper on the Republican side of the United States Senate. The "Boys in Blue" were now old men; four other members of Worcester's George H. Ward Grand Army of the Republic Post Number 10 had already died since the beginning of that year. [5]

The measure of Earle, the man, can be taken from two life experiences. When he was wounded at the Battle of Antietam, Earle refused an order to leave the field and seek medical treatment, staying on the firing line until he was hit again. The second ball struck him in the chest near his heart, but was fortunately deflected by a rib and ended up by his shoulder blade. The ball was cut out with a penknife by his brother and was later placed in a Masonic charm that Earle kept and carried on his person for the rest of his life. [6]

After the war, during the years 1867 to 1871, Earle served as deputy collector of internal revenue for the district of Worcester. He remained in that job until he took on the duties of deputy sheriff of Worcester, which he held for 18 years. In the midst of that tenure, Earle was appointed by the governor as warden of the Massachusetts state prison at Concord, and spent over a year in that position. [7]

Earle's character is further demonstrated by an experience he had in his job as warden. Upon assuming his duties, Earle had to deal with mutinous prisoners, who had started to rebel under the previous administrator. Facing down men who had just been yelling and rioting and had threatened to rip out his heart, David Earle, showing the same kind of courage exhibited in his Civil War service, stood next to a pathway taken by 600 unfettered criminals. These men walked within easy reach of him in the prison yard, yet he remained undaunted and untouched. [8]

During his long life, David Earle, in addition to his faithful service to the 15th Massachusetts Regimental Association, was a member of many other veteran and civic organizations. He was remembered for his "unflinching courage" and revered for "his faithfulness to duty and readiness to assist in any way possible to help make the paths of others easier." David Earle was survived by his wife, Lola, four sons and a daughter. He is buried in the Walnut Grove Cemetery, located in North Brookfield, Massachusetts. [9]

On February 27, 1864, Arthur Devereux had resigned his commission as colonel of the 19th Massachusetts to take care of "private affairs" and returned to civilian life. In recognition of his gallantry and dedicated service, on March 13, 1865, Devereux was brevetted brigadier general of volunteers. Following the war, Arthur Devereux started a contracting business. His firm built dry docks in Brooklyn, Boston and Portland, Maine; they were among the largest in the country in the 19th century. He also invented a type of coal-moving machine, which made it easier and quicker to load coal onto ocean liners and warships. [10]

In the late 1880s, Arthur Devereux moved to Cincinnati, Ohio, where he was elected to the state legislature and subsequently made acting governor of the state. He was also selected to build the National Soldiers' Home at Marion, Indiana, a task which he accomplished "with great care and perfect system." [11]

His health began to deteriorate after the war, since he suffered from asthma, scurvy and rheumatism, which he attributed to the effects of the "swamp fever" contracted in the 1862 Peninsula Campaign. Devereux filed for a Federal disability pension in the early 1890s. In the accompanying documentation, he stated that he was then living in "circumstances of poverty." His pension application was granted, and beginning in December 1890, Devereux began receiving a monthly pension of $15.00. [12]

Arthur Devereux died at his home in Cincinnati on February 13, 1916, from heart disease. He left behind his widow, Clara, whom he had married in 1859, and two surviving children. According to a contemporary obituary, Devereux had the reputation of being "a thorough military man, a strict disciplinarian, but at the same time had one of the most lovable natures." [13]

It is clear from reading through hundreds of pension files at the National Archives that Post-Traumatic Stress Disorder is not an affliction limited to veterans of modern wars. The pension records show that one of the many Civil War soldiers who suffered from this disease was Ansel Wass, lieutenant colonel of the 19th Massachusetts at the Battle of Gettysburg. Wass had sustained a concussion and severe bruising of his neck and back caused by the explosion of a shell over his head during the cannonade that preceded Pickett's Charge. He was able to return to duty with the regiment on August 28, 1863, and was wounded in the right foot at the Battle of Bristoe Station on October 14, 1863. Wass was promoted to the rank of full colonel, effective February 2, 1864, and took command of the 19th that month, when Arthur

Devereux resigned. [14]

However, Ansel Wass never regained his full health after his Gettysburg wound, and even had to spend most of the 1864 Overland Campaign in an ambulance, following behind his regiment. He received little sympathy from one of the brigade surgeons, who commented critically on Wass' absence from the unit on a number of occasions. On June 8, 1864, after Wass had been away from the 19th for a few days, the doctor wrote, "It is a very unfortunate thing for an officer's reputation to be sick at such a time. He had better keep with his command as long as he can stand – do anything but go to the rear." On July 28, 1864, Wass, who, by that time, had gone home sick, was discharged, as his three-year term of service having expired. [15]

Two days later, Wass joined the 60th Massachusetts Volunteer Infantry Regiment with the rank of colonel; he served until being mustered out on December 29, 1864. Ansel Wass was promoted to the rank of brevet brigadier general on March 13, 1865, for "gallant and meritorious services" during the war. After his discharge, he immediately filed for and began receiving a Federal disability pension of $15.00 per month. According to the testimony of those who knew him, before the war Ansel Wass was a "bright active young businessman." After his return to Boston, Wass suffered from chills, nausea, constant severe headaches and depression. A physician who examined him termed the former officer a "physical and mental wreck." [16]

Wass' post-war occupation was as an employee in the Boston Customs House, where he spent hours staring silently at the walls of his office. He was also subject to delusions and fits of terrible temper tantrums, and was determined by another doctor to be in a "low state of mind." In 1878, Ansel Wass was removed to the Boston Lunatic Hospital, where he lived on a periodic basis for the rest of his life. Wass died in Boston on January 24, 1889, at the age of 55. He lies in Portland, Maine's Evergreen Cemetery, next to his wife, Emily, who survived him by 38 years. Written on the top of his tombstone are the words, "BREV BRIG. GEN." and on the bottom, simply, "Member of 19th Mass Regt.". [17]

On June 30, 1865, when his term of service expired, Lieutenant Colonel Edmund Rice, the last commander of the 19th Massachusetts, was mustered out of service. On July 1, 1866, Rice joined the Regular Army with the rank of first lieutenant, despite still suffering from the effects of his Gettysburg leg wound. He immediately received three brevet promotions, to the ranks of captain, major and lieutenant colonel, for "gallant and meritorious services" at the Battles of Antietam, Gettysburg and the Wilderness, respectively. He was also granted a Bachelor of Science degree in 1874 from his alma mater, Norwich University, backdated to 1859. [18]

Throughout the rest of his army career, Rice served at various posts in the West, in the Spanish-American War, in which he commanded the 6th Massachusetts Regiment, and in the Philippine Insurrection, where he led the 26th United States Volunteer Regiment. He was credited with the invention of the Rice Trowel Bayonet, the Rice Knife Intrenching Bayonet, the Rice Stacking Swivel, and the Rice Clothing Roll, all of which were used by the United States Army and Navy. By the time of his retirement on August 14, 1903, at the age of 61, Rice had attained the rank of brigadier general. [19]

After leaving the service, Edmund Rice lived in Boston and Wakefield, Massachusetts. He died of heart disease in Wakefield on July 20, 1906. A grand funeral procession took place in Boston; many dignitaries, including the governor of Massachusetts, participated. His casket lay in state in the Massachusetts State House's Hall of Flags, where, among thousands of other mourners, it was viewed by 25 veterans of the 19th Massachusetts. The coffin was then borne by train to the National Cemetery at Arlington, Virginia, where Rice was laid to rest. Edmund Rice was eulogized as being "noted for his winning personality, his fidelity to duty, his solicitude for the comfort and well-being of the men under his command and his ability and bravery," a fitting tribute for one of the heroes of the Battle of Gettysburg. [20]

Like Rice, another of the 19th's Medal of Honor recipients at Gettysburg, Sergeant Benjamin Jellison was also mustered out on June 30, 1865. After the war, he worked as a messenger in the Massachusetts Senate. Jellison's health began to worsen in the late 1880s, as he suffered from heart disease, rheumatism, chronic diarrhea, and had constant pain in his liver, disabilities which he attributed to the vicissitudes of his four-year service in the Civil War. He began receiving a United States government pension of $10.00 per month in 1890. In addition, a Federal statute of April 1916 authorized a monthly stipend of $10.00 to all living recipients of the Medal of Honor, which Jellison used to supplement his pension; at that time, his pension benefits were $35.00 per month. Benjamin Jellison died in April 1924 at his home in Reading, Massachusetts, at the age of 78 of "pernicious anemia." He is buried in the Elmwood Cemetery in Haverhill, Massachusetts. [21]

The surviving government records are not as detailed on the post-war lives of the 19th's other two surviving Medal of Honor recipients. Joseph DeCastro was also mustered out on June 30, 1865, and returned to his wife in Boston. However, on July 19, 1870, he left home and enlisted in Troop L of the 6th United States Cavalry Regiment. His wife filed for and was granted a divorce on the grounds of "abandonment." On April 8, 1874, DeCastro was discharged from the cavalry with the rank of sergeant. He died in New York City on May 8, 1892, of a cerebral hemorrhage. [22]

Private John Robinson of the 19th's Company I was wounded and captured on June 22, 1864, during the initial stages of the Petersburg Campaign. After his release, he was mustered out of service on February 1, 1865, and returned to his home in Roxbury. Robinson went back to his pre-war occupation of rope-making, but claimed that he had to abandon his business due to a lack of strength in his right hand, caused by the gunshot wound suffered in the fighting before Petersburg. Unfortunately, the Federal pension board did not believe him, and disallowed his claim. On November 30, 1883, John Robinson died of pneumonia in Boston, leaving a wife and two children. [23]

One of the most tragic post-war fates of any man in the 15th, 19th and 20th Massachusetts was that suffered by George Macy of the 20th, the unit's lieutenant colonel at the Battle of Gettysburg. Macy had lost his left hand as a result of being shot in the fighting on July 3, 1863, and had also been wounded in both legs at the Battle of the Wilderness in May 1864. Due to the injuries to his legs, Macy was on convalescent leave until August 1864. Unfortunately, shortly after he returned to active duty, on August 14, 1864, at the Battle of Deep Bottom, Macy was severely injured when his horse was shot and fell on him. In this incident, he suffered severe bruising and contusions to his chest and abdomen. [24]

Macy was able to return to duty again in October 1864. For the rest of the war, he served as a brigade commander and then as the Provost Marshal of the Army of the Potomac. A fellow officer left this description of Macy in the Grand Review of the Army of the Potomac held in Washington D. C. on May 23, 1865: "Now rides the Provost Marshal General, gallant George Macy of the 20th Massachusetts, his [left] arm symbolized by an empty sleeve pinned across his breast." [25]

After the war, George Macy received two promotions by brevet. The first, to that of brevet brigadier general, with a post-dated effective date of August 14, 1864, was for "distinguished conduct at the Battle of the Wilderness and at Deep Bottom, Virginia." The second promotion, to the rank of brevet major general, as of April 9, 1865, was for "gallant and meritorious services during the recent operations resulting in the fall of Richmond, Virginia, and the surrender of the insurgent army under General Robert E. Lee." [26]

Following his discharge from the army, Macy lived in Boston and found work as a secretary with the Suffolk Bank. As a disabled veteran, he also received a Federal pension of $30.00 per month. Unfortunately, on February 13, 1875, while climbing a set of stairs in his home, Macy was afflicted with an attack of vertigo, and lost his balance. Macy had been in the habit of carrying a pistol in his vest pocket for protection, as he said that "having but one arm he felt defenseless without it." When the general fell, the weapon discharged and the ball passed through his abdomen into his intestines. Macy briefly regained consciousness and, as reported by a Boston newspaper, "For four years during the war . . . [that] he should have had his life spared, though he had lost an arm, and now he was to pass away by the chance discharge of his own weapon, weighed heavily on him." [27]

George Macy died that afternoon at the age of 37. He was buried in Forest Hills Cemetery in Boston on February 16, 1875. Macy was survived by his wife and three children. [28]

As much as possible, the story of these three Massachusetts regiments at the Battle of Gettysburg has been told through the words of the men themselves. The focus has deliberately been placed on the so-called "common" soldier, the man at the sharp end who had to do the fighting. In that spirit, this work will end with the post-war fate of Private Chester Leonard of Company K, 20th Massachusetts, who was wounded by the same "friendly fire" from Battery "B", 1st New York Light Artillery, that killed Lieutenant Henry Ropes, his company commander, on the morning of July 3, 1863.

When Henry's brother, John Codman Ropes, visited Gettysburg in October 1863, he met Leonard, who was still there in a hospital recovering from his badly fractured arm. Leonard described for him how he had been wounded and how Henry died. Ropes found him ". . . [a] very nice young fellow, very kind and pleasant, and evidently truthful." [29]

After his discharge for disability in July 1864, Leonard began receiving a Federal pension of $6.00 per month. He initially found work on a Connecticut railroad. But soon, more misfortune struck him. In 1869, while working in a moving railroad car, he lost his balance. As his left arm was useless from the surgery performed in July 1863, he could not grab onto anything quickly enough to prevent his fall. He landed directly on his right arm, fracturing it at the elbow. The damage to the limb was so severe that the right arm had to be amputated at the shoulder. [30]

Now completely helpless, for the rest of his life, Leonard had to rely on family members to aid him in dressing and undressing, feed him and help him perform his bodily functions. Chester Leonard died on January 20, 1914, in Hartford, Connecticut, at the age of 71. [31]

Surely, he was one of the last casualties of the Battle of Gettysburg.

APPENDIX I
James H.Tenney Narrative

In sifting through literally hundreds of pension documents at the National Archives, many fine nuggets of information that have been used in this book were unearthed. However, one soldier's account stood out as a model of clarity and detail. This excellent narrative merits separate publication, rather than being broken up and cited in small sections within the main work. It is included to give the reader the full perspective of one man's story of his wounding at the Battle of Gettysburg, his ordeal in the battle's immediate aftermath and the physical struggle to recover from his injuries so that he could return to duty with his unit. It is presented unedited, as recorded by a Notary Public in Stark County, Ohio, in October 1899.

The soldier in question is James H. Tenney of Company B of the 15th Massachusetts. Tenney was born in Dudley, Massachusetts, in June 1838. He was working as a mechanic in Fitchburg, Massachusetts, when he joined the 15th on August 11, 1862. In the fighting at the Copse of Trees on July 3, 1863, Private Tenney sustained a gunshot wound approximately four inches above his right knee. The ball entered the back of his leg and was removed later that afternoon on the field. Fortunately, no bones were broken; after a prolonged hospitalization, Tenney was able to return to the 15th in February 1864. He was not able to do full duty, as his leg had not regained its complete mobility. Consequently, Tenney was transferred to guard duty at division headquarters, where he served until July 28, 1864, when he was discharged for disability. James Tenney then returned to Massachusetts and began collecting a Federal pension of $4.00 per month.

After his discharge, Tenney found work as a toolmaker in several sewing machine factories and watch companies. He moved to Ohio from Massachusetts in 1888, and worked for a cash register company and as a watch tool maker. His occupation allowed him to sit at a work bench and remain off his damaged limb as much as possible. James Tenney died in Canton, Ohio, on June 10, 1913. By that time, his pension had been raised to the sum of $27.00 per month. This is his story.

"James H. Tenney, Company B, 15th Regt. Mass. Inf. Vols.,
On this __ day of October A. D. 1899, personally appeared before me, a Notary Public, in and for aforesaid county, duly authorized to administer

oaths, James H. Tenney, aged sixty-one years, a resident of Canton in the County of Stark, and State of Ohio, well known to me to be reputable and entitled to credit, and who being duly sworn, declares in relation to aforesaid case as follows:

That he is the claimant for Re-Issue and Increase of his pension under the General Law, and in reply to your circular call of Sept. 26th, 1899 (the same herewith returned) he makes the following statement:

I was wounded in right thigh at Battle Gettysburg, Pa., July 3rd, 1863. On the morning of that day my regiment, the 15th Mass. Infantry, was held in reserve, occupying a position in the rear of our second line of battle on Cemetery Ridge. The reason of our being held in reserve at this time was on account of the heavy loss the regiment had sustained on the previous day, while supporting skirmishers.

This was at the time of Longstreet's advance. Our position being on the Emmittsburg Road. More than half of our regiment were killed, wounded or taken prisoners at that time. Among those killed was our Colonel, George H. Ward, of Worcester, Mass. The fact of our having lost so many men the day before (including more than half of our commissioned officers) led us to believe that we would not be called into action that day, but little did we know what was in store for us. At about one o'clock P. M., the Rebs opened up with all the artillery they could bring to bear on us, and kept it up for one hour. Under cover of this demonstration Pickett's men advanced. My regiment was not engaged until the Rebs had succeeded in breaking our line, having captured two pieces of artillery just to the right of where we lay, perhaps ten rods distant. By that time we were on our feet and by the "Right flank, Double quick," went for them. I heard no orders at that time and do not think there were any given. It seemed as though every man had taken it upon himself to drive them from those guns. We rushed upon them and then it was every man for himself. They only got their hands upon the guns but could not hold them. Our men coming in from the right and left outnumbered them, and they were forced to give way contesting every inch of the ground until they reached the stone wall where they made a stand. We followed them up loading and firing all the time and calling on them to surrender.

It was at this time and when within about three rods of the stone wall that I was wounded in the right thigh. I fell to the ground but was soon on my foot again, not realizing then that I was wounded, but more as though some one had hit me with a sharp stick. I think I had not loaded and fired my gun but once after I was wounded before my leg began to pain me so that I could not bear my weight on it. My shoe was full of blood and my pant's leg was saturated with blood. I put the butt of my gun under my arm for a crutch and tried to get back to the rear. It was slow business and several times I fell. Then I would try to crawl or drag myself along. I had gone about twenty or thirty rods in that way when I suppose I fainted, as I found myself there on the ground when I came to my senses. The battle was all over and the only thing to disturb the quiet was the moving of artillery and galloping of horsemen over the field. All around and about me were the dead and dying. In trying to get back to the rear of our position I had worked myself towards the left of our line and could recognize none of those about me, in fact there were more dead and wounded of the enemy than there were of our own. There were four Rebel officers within forty feet of where I lay and it was from one of them that I learned that we had gained the day.

My wound had stopped bleeding and had stiffened so that I could not move my leg in the least without causing me a great deal of pain. I was looking for some one to do something for me or to help me to a hospital, and soon saw the surgeon of my own Regt., F. Le Baron Monroe,[1] crossing the field at a little distance. I called to him twice before he heard me, and he came to me, saying, "You belong to my regiment, what are you doing here," at the same time taking a knife from his pocket and ripping my pant's leg the whole length of the seam. Then he examined my leg and found where something had gone in, but no place where it had come out. He then told me that whatever had hit me was still in my leg, and as soon as I reached the hospital to call the attention of the surgeons to it, and have it removed. I then told him I wanted it removed at once. He then said he had nothing with him, but was going after his instruments when I called him as stated above. I then made him promise to come back to me, and he did so. And after spreading out his instruments he probed my wound but could not locate anything. He then commenced pressing my leg with his thumbs, and after a time said he found something that did not belong there, keeping his thumb on the spot, and with his other hand he again tried to reach it with his probe, but was unable to do so. He told me then that it would have to be cut out, and that I must wait until I reached the hospital. I insisted on his cutting it out then and there as I did not know when I would get to a hospital. His objection to the operation at that time was that I was liable to bleed to death as I was already weak from loss of blood.

The Doctor tried hard to reason with me, but I would not have it that way, telling him it was hot weather, and the sooner it was out the better. After using his lance, with another instrument he brought out a piece of my pants and the next time he brought out an ounce ball in such a shape one would hardly know what it was. (I still have the ball.) Calling for my handkerchief the Doctor tied it in a hard knot around the leg above the wound, and inserted my bayonet, giving it one twist and after telling me to hold on to the bayonet and keep my wound wet took his departure. This occurred late in the afternoon, but before darkness. I had no trouble in carrying out the Doctor's instructions, as I was suffering too much pain to sleep. Was fortunate in having my canteen full of water and could keep my wound wet, but had to ease up on the bayonet during the night. Could hear the ambulance wagons moving about all that night picking up the wounded, but it was morning before they reached me, and carried me to the general hospital, so called, more than three and a half miles distant. This hospital was in a piece of woods and was without tents or shelter of any kind, excepting the shelter of the trees over our heads. I was taken from the ambulance and carried some thirty or forty feet from the road and placed on the ground with my rubber blanket around me, and my haversack under my head for a pillow. I soon fell asleep and when I awoke it was daylight again, and they were still bringing in the wounded. While asleep some one had relieved me of my haversack, with what few rations I had left, with knife, fork, spoon, tin plate and cup, leaving me with only my rubber blanket and canteen. Some time during the fore part of the day I was found there by George A. Harwood, Drum Major of my regiment, who was also a member of my Company "B." Harwood procured the assistance of Daniel Pierce,[2] 'Fifer', who was also a member of my company, and another musician, and they carried me back from the road to higher ground, where I found J. B. Mathews, Henry M. Carpenter and George L. Boss,[3] all of Company B, of my regiment. We were laid side by side and all were wounded in the thigh or hip. Boss was wounded in the hip by a piece of shell and died some time during the following night. He was lying next to me, and had had nothing done for his wound up to the time he died. Note: Harwood and Mathews both lived to get home, but have since died. Have not heard from Pierce or Carpenter since the war.

A drizzling rain followed the Battle and we were cold and chilly. Water was dripping on us from the branches of the trees over head and the ground became wet under us. About dusk on that evening Boss worked himself down to a fire that had been built just below us, wrapped his blanket around him and died there (as above stated). Harwood and Pierce buried him. The next two days was bad weather. Still raining enough to keep us wet and the stench from our wounds and bloody clothing was something awful. I then discovered that my wound was alive with white maggots. They were crawling up and down my leg. This was the sixth day of July. After my being wounded, to add to our discomfort there was an amputating table located just below, and not over forty feet from us, and we knew not how soon we might receive an invitation from those in charge to come down and have a leg sawed off. That table was run day and night while we were there, with different reliefs of surgeons, and we had to lay there and see it all.

No rations were dealt out to us as our supply trains had not put in an appearance. Cattle were driven into camp and slaughtered. Kettles were procured from farm houses in the neighborhood and they made what they called soup. It was without salt or seasoning of any kind, but served to keep us alive.

Friday, July 7th, opened nice and pleasant, the sun came out and it was not long before we were steaming hot and it was nothing uncommon to see men sick and vomiting on account of the stench. Early on that day the surgeon in charge came among the men and advising all who could get conveyances or who had legs and could use them to go to Littlestown by all means, telling them that it was only seven miles distant, was on the B & O Railroad, and the government had control of the road and if we could get there we would be put on trains and taken to Baltimore, Washington or Philadelphia, where we could have good care, telling us that our supply trains had not come up, that the surgeons had nothing to do with, and that if we remained there thousands of us would die in those woods. Those words had their effect, and every one who could travel was soon on the road.

Soon after this an old German farmer came among us, and in conversation with him we found that he owned the ground we were on, as that was part of his farm. He owned a team but we could not get him to take us to Littlestown until we had promised to pay him $5.00 a man and guaranteed to make him up a load, which we did, and in half an hour he came on with his team, consisting of an old mare and a colt that was not broken, hitched up together. The wagon was one of the old Pennsylvania kind, long bed, setting square on the axles. There was some straw in the wagon, and eleven of us took chances in getting to Littlestown. Mathews, Carpenter and myself with eight others. It was a corduroy road most of the way and I thought Mathews would not live to get there. In lying on the wet ground he had contracted rheumatism in both his legs and he suffered greatly. Every jump the colt made would make him scream. It was a paying trip for the old Dutchman as he received about fifty dollars for his trip. Those who had money paying for those who had none. In the condition we were at that time money was no object.

It was about noon when we reached Littlestown. The old man drove around through the different streets trying to find some place to take us under cover, but the town was full of wounded men, and every available place seemed to be taken, so we ordered him to drive back to the depot, where we were taken from the wagon and placed on a brick side walk in the hot sun by the side of the depot. The people of the town gave us something to eat and drink, but we had nothing for our wounds, and we suffered a great deal lying there on those hot bricks in a boiling hot July sun.

Mathews was so bad that he arranged with a citizen to take him home and care for him until his wife could come out to him. He was wounded in both thighs and was suffering from rheumatism too. He bid us good bye, and they carried him away. He lived to get home, but was a cripple for life, being obliged to use crutches, as we afterwards learned. As before stated it was about the middle of the day of the 7th of July that we reached Littlestown, and Carpenter and I laid on that brick side walk until noon of the 8th without having anything done for us. Then we were put into box cars with some straw thrown on the floor. It was my fortune to be one of the first to be put into one of these cars and was taken to the forward end and given space to lie down.

I do not remember much about the journey, though I have a faint recollection of our train stopping twice on the way. Did not know when we arrived at Baltimore, but have since learned that we arrived there about ten o'clock in the evening of the same day. I had been overlooked and was taken from the car an hour after all others had been carried to different hospitals. I was aroused by some one singing out "All out of this car," on opening my eyes I saw the light of a lantern thrust into the car door. I knew enough to make a noise when two men, one of them a policeman, jumped into the car and pulled me out upon the platform in a hurry. They just had me safely landed when the train started back to Littlestown. Then they told me that it had been more than an hour since the last man had been taken to the Hospitals, and they supposed every one was off the train. After consulting together what they would do with me I was put upon a stretcher and taken to West Building Hospital, arriving there at midnight. Was placed upon an elevator and assigned to ward "I" on the second floor, where a member of my own company, Kilburn Howard, was ward master. [4] I was first taken to the bath room and all my clothing removed, and was given a thorough scrubbing from head to foot. Then they put a nice white shirt on me and carried me into another room and laid me on a table where the surgeon came in and dressed my wound. This was the first surgical treatment for my wound since the surgeon cut out the ball on the battlefield, on July 3rd, this being on the early

morning of July 9th. And to the exposure, starvation and lack of medical attendance, and care, etc., as above narrated he attributes his disease of the nervous
system and heart with general debility, and for which he has applied for re-issue
and increase of his pension.

After my wound was dressed as above stated, I was then placed in bed,
"between two sheets," and then they brought me a light lunch. If there is anything on earth like unto heaven that bed was heaven to me. It was well along the
next day before I woke up. My wound was dressed as soon as I had my breakfast, and again in the afternoon. Was in this hospital about one week, being sent
from there with others and a couple of days later found me at McDougall General
Hospital at Fort Schulyer, N. Y., Ward 5, Sec. B.

I did not get as good treatment here as I had been getting at Baltimore, Md.
Instead of my wound being examined and dressed two and three times a day as it
had been there, it was only looked after once a day, and some days not at all.
Myself and others procured sponges and washed and dressed our own wounds, a
good share of the time. One reason for our doing so was that the nurses in our
ward (three in number) had more patients than they could take proper care of.
Another reason was that there were quite a number of cases of gangrene in our
ward, and we did not care to have the same sponges used on us which had been
used on them. One very bad case, that of Daniel Kearn [5] of the 111th New York
Vols., the calf of his leg being nearly all eaten away by the gangrene. My wound
was a long time healing permanently as pieces of my pants had been driven into
my leg with the ball. The threads of which kept working out, and even after it
healed over, it would break anew, and commence discharging again, and continued that way for many weeks.

After the Battle of Gettysburg the hospitals were overtaxed for some time,
and the Doctor in charge of my ward No. 5, Section B, had 160 patients under his
charge. About October 29th, a squad of one hundred or more were sent to their
regiments. My name was on the list but the doctor pronounced me unfit for
service, and I was left there. I then commenced to assist some about the ward in
the hospital, and about December 17th, 1863, was detailed as nurse in the ward
although I was still quite lame from my wound and had to use a cane in walking.

On Jan. 6th, 1864, received a furlough for fifteen days, and started for my
home in Fitchburg, Worcester County, Mass., arriving there the next morning.
On Jan. 22nd, started on my return to the hospital. On reaching New York City
went to the New England Rooms where I met a Sergeant from McDougall Hospital who informed me that the hospital was broken up and that the patients had
been transferred to Davis Island, N. Y., and the next day (Jany. 23rd) I reported at

Davis Island, and two or three weeks later a call was made to send all available men to their regiments.

A board of examiners was therefore selected from the surgeons of the hospitals and examinations were in order. The surgeon of my ward was on the board and when I responded to my name was told to go back to my quarters. I insisted on going to my regiment, when he took me to one side and gave me quite a lecturing, saying I was unfit for field service and ought to know it, that I would be sent back if I went to the front, would never be fit for service in the field, and that if I would give up going he would make me ward master, and that I did not need to see any more fighting. I remember of telling him I would not stay in a hospital if he would make me a Major General. He did not like this and told me to go where I pleased.

Thursday afternoon, Feby. 11th, 1864, about three hundred of us were sent by steamer Thomas P. Day to Bedloe Island, this being a sort of depot for convalescents returning to the field. On Feby. 15th myself and other convalescents to the number of about 150 were taken on board the Admiral Dupont, and then steamed to Governor's Island where we took on board 305 deserters and bounty jumpers. On Tuesday, Feby. 16th, about sunset we left New York Harbor for Alexandria, Va. As we left the harbor, four deserters jumped overboard. One was killed by the paddle wheel, two were drowned and one escaped.

We had a rough night on the water. The gang way was stoved in, and a foot of water in the hold driving the men from the lower berths. All were seasick, deserters stealing and robbing the men of their money and valuables. We arrived off Fortress Monroe on the afternoon of the 17th and on the afternoon of the 18th we run to the mouth of the Potomac River, when we anchored for the night. On the 19th we run up the river, which was full of floating ice, arriving at the dock at three o'clock P. M. Here the deserters were turned over to a guard from the Fort. Several of them trying to escape, but were captured and brought back. The rest of our party marched to Camp Distribution, about four miles distant, arriving there at sun down. Was there sent with others for the 2nd Army Corps and soon rejoined my regiment near Stevensburg, Va., Feby. 24th, 1864. Having been away from my regiment for seven month and twenty days. When I left the hospital I had a cane but had thrown it away before reaching the Regiment, and although I was quite lame I had made up my mind to make no complaint, but to do whatever duty fell to me saying nothing . . ." [6]

APPENDIX II

*Chronology of Events Impacting the Monumentation Process
of the 15th, 19th and 20th Massachusetts Volunteer Infantry Regiments,
as Reported Through Newspapers, Gettysburg Battlefield Memorial
Association Records or Letters, with approximate dates.*

1880, March 11

Legislation passes in the United States Congress authorizing metallic tablets on the Gettysburg battlefield. The Gettysburg Battlefield Memorial Association (GBMA) must give its approval before the act can become law and markers will only be placed on land owned by the GBMA.

1881, July 13

The GBMA contemplates constructing a "broad and handsome" avenue to Little Round Top, beginning on the Baltimore Pike and running along the northwest line of the National Cemetery, then taking in Ziegler Woods, and following the Union battle line.

1882, June 14

Gettysburg newspaper reports that the GBMA will mark positions of Pennsylvania units prior to the upcoming Grand Army of the Republic encampment

1882, July 12

The new Battlefield Avenue opens to travel from the Taneytown Road to Little Round Top.

1882, July 12

Pennsylvania G.A.R. encampment is the largest in the history of the organization.

1882, September 20

A Commonwealth of Pennsylvania charter for a railroad from Gettysburg to Round Top, 3 miles in length, is granted at Harrisburg. The capital expenditure is $25,000.00. A corps of engineers starts a survey of Little Round Top.

1883, May 2

Representatives of the 72nd Pennsylvania Volunteer Infantry Regiment locate the position for a monument on the battlefield, along the new avenue, near the center of General Hancock's line, which they occupied at the time of Pickett's Charge. It is to cost $500.00 and will be dedicated at the time of coming G.A.R. encampment.

1883, July 11

The Commonwealth of Massachusetts appropriates $5,000.00 to be used to place unit monuments on the Gettysburg battlefield, but the money has not been yet distributed to any of the organizations.

1883, August 15

The surviving members of the Massachusetts regiments which took part in battle of Gettysburg are requested by Governor Benjamin Butler to meet to determine what purchases, etc., should be made with the $5,000.00 recently appropriated to the GBMA.

1883, August 15

The encampment of the G.A.R., Department of Pennsylvania, will commence on August 25. All indications are that it will be the largest encampment ever held in the state, and that there will be sizable delegations from the various posts throughout Pennsylvania.

1883, August 22

The 72nd Pennsylvania has erected a handsome granite memorial stone on the avenue near the point of Pickett's assault on the Union lines. Appropriate ceremonies will be held during the week of the encampment.

1883, August 27

The 72nd Pennsylvania Regimental Association unveils a beautiful granite monument on the ground of the last assault of July 3, 1863. Former General Alexander Webb gives the keynote address.

1883, September 19

Track-laying for the Gettysburg and Harrisburg Railroad progresses rapidly, with about 50 men laying 1/2 mile of track daily. It is hoped that the road will be completed and cars running to Gettysburg by the latter part of November.

1883, September 26

Arrangements are being made in Gettysburg for the terminus of the new railroad. The depot building will be located on the corner of Washington and Railroad Streets. The railroad will be extended to Little Round Top for excursion purposes. In the neighborhood of Round Top, a good deal of money will be spent to put up commodious pavilions and other buildings to accommodate sightseers and to make the grounds attractive and inviting.

1883, October 24

The Massachusetts Legislature makes an appropriation of $5,000.00 to the GBMA; a portion of it is to be expended to erect a tablet or tablets to mark the positions held by Massachusetts soldiers. The committee charged with indicating these positions has arranged a trip to the battlefield. The veterans arrive in Gettysburg on October 24, 1883.

1883, October 27

Several board members of the GBMA visit the positions of Massachusetts regiments to obtain title to such land as does not belong to the association. Some of the positions to be located are: The 15th regiment in field of Simon J. Codori along the avenue where Gen. W.S. Hancock was wounded, and the 19th and 20th regiments on the avenue to the left of the 72nd Pennsylvania monument.

1883, October 31

A local newspaper reports that the visit by the Massachusetts veterans was a huge success.

1883, November 7

The plans for the new railroad depot are ready. It is believed that the laying of ties and rails will begin shortly at the end of the rail line.

1883, November 14

Well-known war correspondent and author C. Carleton Coffin, who had accompanied the Massachusetts veterans in October, reports his observations in the *Boston Daily Globe*. He highlights the battlefield movements of all Massachusetts units. When describing the action around the Copse of Trees, he writes, ". . . We come to the spot where a monument ought to be reared, with this inscription: 'Here was a turning-point in the world's history, where it was decreed that this government of the people should not perish from the earth.'" He ends by stating that, "By the side of the new ave., laid out by the Battlefield Assoc. along the ridge will stand the monuments of these Massachusetts regiments which did their full share in the mighty struggle."

1884, February 5

Gettysburg newspaper reports that interest in the Gettysburg battlefield continues to increase and that Pennsylvania and Massachusetts have appropriated funds to erect monuments. "No battlefield of the war—in fact, no battlefield in the world has been as carefully studied or as much written about as that of Gettysburg." It relates that the GBMA's aim is to preserve the lines and designate positions "held by both armies," in order to secure accurate historical designations of the field so that the visitor can intelligently study it and that "[I]t is hoped that in due time the positions held by both Union & Rebel troops will be properly designated."

1884, February 26

The new railroad line completed to Gettysburg amid much fanfare.

1884, March 24

Commonwealth of Massachusetts grants funds to certain organizations for the erection of monuments on the battlefield of Gettysburg, including the 15th, 19th and 20th regiments.

1884, March 25

A report is submitted by the committee appointed to secure the positions occupied by Massachusetts troops. GBMA resolves: "[T]hat hereafter no tablet or monument shall be permanently erected on grounds held by this Association without permission from the Board of Directors; nor until its legend has been approved by the Superintendent of Tablets and Legends, subject to an appeal to the Board of Directors."

1884, April 1

Article reports that the GBMA Board visited locations around the battlefield with the aim of buying land where memorials are to be placed. Newspaper again reports that interest in the battlefield has been increasing and that the visit by the Massachusetts veterans last Fall has "awakened" interest in that state.

1884, April 1

Local newspaper predicts that the newly-completed railroad line will enable many people to visit Gettysburg.

1884, April 8

Newspaper article entitled "Massachusetts to the Front" reports that Massachusetts has made another appropriation of $12,500.00 (in addition to the $5,000.00 in 1883) for the erection of monuments. It also states: "The Old Bay State cherishes the memory of her fallen heroes & means that the world shall know it."

1884, April 21

The new railroad's regular passenger train begins to run on the Gettysburg and Harrisburg Railroad.

1884, August

(Exact date unknown) Annual reunion of 19th Regimental Association held in Grand Army Hall, Haverhill, Massachusetts. Design of monument presented and approved. Location fixed, committee formed to follow through to erection.

1884, September 23

Newspaper reports that 30 iron posts and tablets, to indicate the positions of Massachusetts regiments during the battle, have been received and will be put in position.

1884, October 7

The Massachusetts iron markers put up, with posts standing 6 1/2 feet out of the ground.

1885, September 17

The excursion of many Massachusetts veterans to Gettysburg to dedicate their monuments scheduled to start October 5, 1885. The 15th Massachusetts Regimental Association decides to undertake an excursion in the spring or summer of 1886. Since the sites for its two monuments had previously been determined, a representative was sent to Gettysburg to see that the foundations were set at the designated spots. The Regimental Association visits foundry where monuments are being made.

1885, September 22

Mr. Roach of Smith Granite Company of Westerly, Rhode Island, placed the monument of the 19th Massachusetts in position the previous week.

1885, September 29

Newspaper incorrectly reports that the 15th Massachusetts plans to dedicate its monuments the week of October 5, 1885.

1885, October 6

Gettysburg newspaper describes the two monuments of the 15th Massachusetts and reports that the foundation for the 20th monument had been laid. The monument of the 20th will not be placed until winter. Article describes the arrival of the Massachusetts contingent for the dedication of numerous monuments, including that of the 19th regiment.

1885, October 8

19th Massachusetts monument dedicated at the Copse of Trees.

1885, October 20

Newspaper reprints George Patch's Massachusetts Day Speech. (Patch served with the 19th Massachusetts.)

1886, May 18

Newspaper article anticipating the arrival of the 15th Massachusetts veterans mistakenly reports that the unit will dedicate its monuments on June 1, 1886.

1886, May 31 - June 12

The 15th Massachusetts veterans undertake their excursion to the battlefields of Gettysburg, Antietam, Ball's Bluff and to Washington, D.C.

1886, June 1

Both Gettysburg newspapers report the arrival of the 15th's veterans. "The 15th Massachusetts monument will be dedicated the next morning. Ex-Attorney General Devens will deliver the address. It is located on the Avenue, facing Pickett's Charge." One article misidentifies the regiment as the 15th Connecticut.

1886, June 2
15th Massachusetts monument dedicated at Copse of Trees. Monument to Colonel George H. Ward dedicated near the Emmitsburg Road.
1886, June 8
Lengthy account of 15th's dedication printed in Gettysburg newspaper.
1886, June 22
Mr. Roach has completed the erection of the 20th Massachusetts monument. *Compiler* newspaper states that boulder was placed on June 21; with the aid of pullies, teams and well-directed labor, it was transferred from car to wagon. (No contemporary account has been found detailing an actual dedication ceremony for the 20th's monument.)
1886, July 4
Cowan's New York Independent Battery holds a reunion and selects a site for its monument. (This decision will have an impact on the future of the 15th, 19th and 20th monuments' locations.)
1886, July 13
Last week Mr. Roach, for the Smith Granite Company, moved the 19th Massachusetts monument from where it stood between the 20th's and 15th's, on the south side of the Copse of Trees, to a new foundation just to the east of the trees. Complaints from the 19th's veterans precipitated the move.
1887, February 27
Executive Committee of GBMA instructed to have a fence placed around the Copse of Trees. Also, John Bachelder requested to prepare an appropriate and suitable tablet descriptive of the action and the commands engaged at the Copse of Trees.
1887, May 5
Bachelder moves to appoint a committee to consider the advisability of removing any monuments which have been erected out of line to their correct position on the line of battle. Further, that hereafter, any regiment erecting a monument on GBMA ground would be required to place it on position held by the regiment in line of battle. They would not be prohibited from erecting secondary or advanced markers, as approved by GBMA.
1887, July 3
Cowan's New York Battery monument dedicated at the Copse of Trees.
1887, July 12
The GBMA resolves that a "suitable and substantial" iron fence be placed around the Copse of Trees on the main avenue. The Superintendent of Tablets is requested to prepare, at his earliest convenience, a tablet descriptive of the engage-

ment at that point and submit it to the executive committee. It is also determined to move all monuments on the grounds of the Association to their proper positions in line, wherever said removal is practicable.

1887, November 4

The GBMA formally names the avenue running from the Taneytown Road to the base of Little Round Top "Hancock Avenue."

1887, December 16

GBMA resolves to notify the proper regimental officers of the proposed changes in the location of certain monuments erected upon the field. The following rules and regulations are also adopted: "1. All persons are forbidden under the penalty of law, to place, change or remove any stake or marker on the grounds under the control of the Memorial Assoc without the knowledge & consent of the Superintendent of Grounds. 2. Any one who shall construct any foundation for, or erect any monument or memorial upon the grounds of the Assoc, before the Superintendent of grounds shall have designated the place & given a permit, will be regarded as a trespasser and be amenable to the severe penalties, provided for in the Charter of the Assoc. 3. Superintendent shall not permit the erection of any monument or memorial until its location & the inscription to be placed thereon, shall have been approved by the proper Committee of the Association."

1888, April 19

Commonwealth of Massachusetts resolves to spend $1,200.00 to procure and mark the flanks of 21 Massachusetts regiments and batteries.

1888, May 8

At a meeting of the Pennsylvania Soldiers' Monument Commission in Philadelphia, the 72nd Regimental Committee presents a claim to be permitted to place their monument at the stone wall in the corner of the "Bloody Angle," on the right of the position occupied by the 69th Pennsylvania during the battle. The committee of the 69th Pennsylvania enters a protest against allowing the claim and the matter will be further considered before it is decided upon.

1888, July 3

72nd representatives go before GBMA and ask that their monument be placed on the front line. GBMA selects site on crest of Cemetery Ridge for the 72nd Pennsylvania and advises that an advance marker could be authorized. The 72nd Pennsylvania decides to fight decision.

1888, July 10

Newspaper account erroneously reports that the 72nd Pennsylvania's dissatisfaction with the position assigned for their monument was settled by allowing them to place a marker at the advanced position at the stone wall, and claimed that during the battle the regiment reached the stone wall. The monument, a fine bronze statute, will stand at the east side of the avenue above the position of the brigade monument, on the brigade line. The article states that out of the disputed question has grown a rumor of want of harmony between the GBMA and the State Commission, which is wholly without foundation.

1888, August 14

Another newspaper account indicates that the 72nd Pennsylvania had secured the approval of the Philadelphia Brigade to locate their monument in the rear of the battle lines of the 69th and 71st Pennsylvania.

1888, September 25

The GBMA acts in response to the action of the 72nd Pennsylvania and resolves that its Superintendent of Grounds be instructed to have the monuments of the Massachusetts regiments already erected at the Copse of Trees removed at once to their "proper positions" in line of battle.

1888, October 2

United States House and Senate pass resolution approving that fence from Lafayette Square be sent to Gettysburg as soon as appropriation is approved.

1888, October 2

Newspaper reports that the GBMA at its last meeting directed Superintendent N.G. Wilson remove the 15th, 19th and 20th Massachusetts monuments from where they now stand, to their brigades' lines south of the Copse of Trees.

1888, October 22

The 15th Massachusetts Association learns from a copy of a letter sent by John Bachelder the previous July to Charles Robinson, President of the 20th's Regimental Association, that the GBMA contemplates moving monuments. Consequently, a representative of the 15th writes letter to GBMA questioning whether or not this is true and protesting any such move.

1888, November 5

Charles Buehler responds to the 15th and explains why GBMA felt monument should be moved and relates problems with other regiments, including the 72nd Pennsylvania. He mentions that a marker can be placed explaining the movements of the regiment, but the letter is not clear as to whether or not monuments have already been moved. Consequently, the 15th Massachusetts Association decides to write again to ascertain exactly what has occurred.

1888, November 27

According to the *Compiler*, the 15th and 19th Massachusetts monuments are moved from their position at the Copse of Trees to their brigades' lines, a few hundred yards south, in the vicinity of the Vermont brigade monument. The 20th Massachusetts "pudding stone" will also be moved in the same direction.

1888, November 30

Charles Buehler writes to John Bachelder and states that he was surprised that Arthur Devereux of the 19th Massachusetts was not aware of the proposed tablet at the Copse of Trees.

1888, December 7

Charles Buehler confirms to the 15th that their monument and flank markers were moved and mentions again that a special plaque can be installed explaining the regiment's movements. The 15th Association sends representatives to 19th and 20th regimental meetings and discovers they did not know their monuments had been moved.

1888, December 11

72nd Pennsylvania has purchased land west of the Bloody Angle from Mr. S. J. Codori. The regiment's representative directs that their monument be placed where the GBMA has forbidden it.

1888, December 11

For the purpose of finishing some New York monument work for the Smith Granite Company, Mr. J. E. Roach arrives in Gettysburg. While there, he contracts with the GBMA for the removal of the 20th Massachusetts "pudding stone" monument to its "proper position," the time for the work not yet decided. (The exact date of the monument's relocation is not known.)

1888, December 18

Newspaper reports that the previous week workmen had placed the foundation of 72nd monument at its present position near the stone wall. There had been no indication that GBMA had rejected this position, but the Association called police and had the parties arrested for trespassing.

1889, March 7

The 15th Massachusetts Regimental Association discusses Colonel Bachelder's proposal to get the state legislature to fund $500.00 for the markers. 15th Association appoints committee to meet with legislature. Shortly thereafter, the funds are appropriated, ending the association's ability to do anything further about the location of its monument.

1889, March 23

Suit filed by representatives of the 72nd Pennsylvania dismissed by Adams County judge.

1889, June 3

Upon appeal, the Pennsylvania Supreme Court reverses the decision and sends case back to lower court for a formal answer to the suit and a conclusive determination. Arthur Devereux and William Hill (both members of the 19th Massachusetts) testify during the ensuing trial.

1890, May 10

John Krauth of the GBMA dies. He had promised to protect the monument of the 15th when he accepted it on behalf of the Association on June 2, 1886.

1890, December 10

Arthur Devereux writes John Bachelder asking for details of newspaper account of 72nd Pennsylvania's winning court case. Wants to know on what grounds they won. Can he move the 19th's monument where it belongs? He permitted it moved back but is upset by the travesty. Ends with "There will be lots of troubles grow out of this if not mended."

1890, December 15

GBMA loses appeal, which consequently allows 72nd to place their monument at the advanced position.

1891, May 18

John Bachelder submits a plan for the "High Water Mark" Tablet at the Copse of Trees. Plan approved.

1891, June 5

GBMA appeals 72nd Pennsylvania case to Pennsylvania Supreme Court, which affirms lower court decision.

1891, July 4

72nd Pennsylvania monument dedicated at advanced position.

1891, July 7

Article in *Star and Sentinel* critical of the 72nd for the placement of its monument. Another article reports that some of the 72nd men present for the dedication admit that the monument belonged near the 1883 memorial.

1891, July 14

Philadelphia Inquirer criticizes the *Star and Sentinel* article.

1891, August 25

Special report by GBMA printed in its records, explaining the entire controversy with the 72nd Pennsylvania.

1891, September 29

The granite and bronze work for the "High Water Mark" monument at the Copse of Trees arrives and the structure is in course of erection.

1891, October 6
Star and Sentinel states that High Water Monument was put in place the previous week. Dedication planned to take place on November 19, 1891.

1891, October 13
Compiler announces the dedication of the "High Water Mark Tablet," designed by John Bachelder, to take place on November 19.

1891, October 16
The Boston Daily Globe, under title "Bay State Valiant Heroes" in a byline Gettysburg, October 15, states that the tablets of the 15th, 19th and 20th Massachusetts are finished and are being set today. Article describes the tablets. It incorrectly states that they are on the exact spots where the regimental monuments had been located previously. Severely criticizes the 72nd Pennsylvania.

1891, October 20
John Bachelder was in Gettysburg last week superintending the placement of the three Massachusetts markers. Newspaper reports that the monuments were originally located near where the markers are now located.

1891, October 21
Edmund Rice of the 19th writes to John Bachelder and thanks him for the description of new tablets sent to him from a *Boston Daily Globe* article.

1891, October 27
John Bachelder announces the postponement of the dedication of the "High Water Mark" monument from November to next year.

1891, November 15
Arthur Devereux of the 19th writes John Bachelder, stating that the erection of the tablets is most satisfactory to him and has settled discontent among the veterans. Devereux relates he is reconciled to the 72nd's monument, which will be their monument to "shame."

1892, June 2
High Water Mark monument dedicated. Thousands of people present. Platform erected south of the Copse of Trees for guest speakers.

1893, May 25
The Gettysburg National Park Commission is created under the direction of the United States War Department. This organization co-exists with the GBMA.

1895, January 20
Gustave Magnitzky of the 20th Massachusetts requests information from the Gettysburg National Park Commission about steps necessary either to move the

regimental monument forward to its most advanced position or place an additional monument at that advanced position.

1895, May 22

The Directors of the GBMA vote to convey all of its property and holdings to the United States War Department, and the organization passes into history.

1895, September 17

An internal document of the Gettysburg National Park Commission remarks that an engineer on its staff tried to find the monument of the 15th Massachusetts, which is reported to be damaged. The regimental monument on Hancock Avenue was examined and found to be not in bad condition. The monument to Colonel Ward on the Emmittsburg Road was not examined, although it appeared to be satisfactory when viewed from the road.

1895-96

Permanent base for Harrow Avenue added because of all the visitor traffic. Webb Avenue created.

1896, February 11

Based on Gustave Magnitzky's earlier inquiry, the Gettysburg National Park Commission contemplates if the 20th Massachusetts should be allowed to place a more conspicuous marker at the Copse of Trees or place a small memorial on the site of the regiment's skirmish line position of July 2.

1896, May 1

Another internal Commission document determines that the present position of the 20th's monument is correct and as these skirmishers did their duty on July 2, 1863, no special treatment should be necessary, unless extraordinary action was involved. A tablet on the present monument will be acceptable, but not a separate marker.

1896, November 21

Because of water damage behind the marble medallion of Colonel Ward, David Earle of the 15th requests the Commission to return the monument to Worcester for repair.

1896, November 25

Commissioners Robbins and Nicholson, together with engineer Cope, drive to the monument of Colonel Ward, and at the request of the Regimental Association of the 15th Massachusetts, remove the medallion for shipment to Worcester to be cast in bronze.

1896, December 4

David Earle of the 15th writes to acknowledge the Commission's interest in the monument and states that the entire shaft does not have to be returned to

Massachusetts. Medallion will be returned to Massachusetts, repaired and then sent back to Gettysburg for placement on shaft.

1896, December 5

Internal Commission document indicates that a letter has been received from David Earle of the 15th and has just been answered, including the engineer's report, diagrams and measurements, in order to help the unit decide how to proceed.

1897, August 7

David Earle writes Commissioner Robbins that he had received a letter from a 15th Massachusetts member, who, while in Gettysburg, noticed that the Ward medallion was not in place on the shaft. Earle wants to know if anything is required from the Regimental Association to expedite the work. Earle expects to visit Gettysburg in the fall and would be pleased to meet with Robbins.

1897, August 9

Memo states that Earle letter of August 7 was received on this date. Robbins writes back recommending W.P. Dolly to do work for $3.00 and if the 15th Massachusetts would employ him, the Commission would deliver the tablet to him. (The Rule of the Commission is to gladly give information but not to perform or be responsible for work.)

1897, August 10

Commissioner Robbins informs Commissioner Nicholson of Earle's August 7, 1897, letter and his answer of August 9, since he felt it was the proper response.

1897, August 23

Earle sends new bolts for the Ward medallion, as suggested by the Commission, and trusts that they are of suitable dimension. He thanks the Commission for its kindness and mentions that he will be visiting the battlefield the next month with two brothers, "one of whom was in the battle with me and whom I have not seen for 24 years."

1897, October 30. 15th Regimental Association requests that the Commission allow it to make additional repairs to the Ward monument. Cost to be borne by the regiment and the workman to be approved by the Commission as someone known to them. Repairs made around the base, together with letter painting.

1897, November 3

Nicholson sends above request to the United States Secretary of War.

1900, September 14 – 20

15th's excursion to the battlefields of Gettysburg, Antietam, Ball's Bluff and to Washington, D.C. takes place.

1900, October 9

Representatives of the 15th ask the Commission for a copy of the Charter of the GBMA and for the names of the directors and officers who served in 1884. Commission members are concerned. One writes, "So you see these fellows seem bound to get up a movement concerning the position of their monument. Senator Hoar has not answered my letter. Maybe you'd better drop him a line - but perhaps we should wait until they show their hand."

1900, December 14

United States Senator George Hoar writes the Commission on behalf of the 15th Massachusetts. He recounts the history of the monuments at the Copse of Trees, the approval of the GBMA and their erection as well as their unannounced removal.

1900, December 29

Commissioner Nicholson responds to the December 14 letter of Hoar. Denies that the Ward monument had ever been moved. (Nicholson is confused between the regimental marker and the marker to Colonel Ward.)

1901

History of the 15th Massachusetts' 1900 excursion to Gettysburg published. In the section concerning the action of July 3, 1863, one of the important points touched upon was the displacement of the 15th regimental monument from its honored position at the Copse of Trees to a point south, never occupied by the command.

1903, February 20

Representative of the 20th Massachusetts requests the Commission to add a tablet to the monument describing the position of the regiment on July 2 and 3, 1863, the movement to the Copse of Trees and the unit's losses.

1903, March 3

Commissioners confirm improved inscription for proposed tablet of the 20th.

1903, March 4

Commissioners send letter with inscription to the United States Secretary of War for final approval.

1903, March 12

Receive approval of the inscription to be placed upon the tablet of the 20th Massachusetts. (The exact date that the tablet was added to the monument is not known.)

1903, July 8

40th Anniversary of battle observed. Newspaper article about Pickett's Charge does not mention the 15th, 19th or 20th Massachusetts.

1906, January 17
Gettysburg National Park Commission discovers that there was a crack in the marble bas-relief in the monument of the 15th Massachusetts.

1906, May 4
Internal Commission document indicates that the damage to the 15th's monument was caused by expansion of the marble bas-relief.

1906, May 9
Commissioners send a report to the 15th Massachusetts describing the damage to the marble bas-relief, which they feel cannot be repaired. They suggest replacing it with one made of bronze and ask for direction from the Regimental Association.

1906, October
After discussion, the 15th Massachusetts veterans bring the monument back to Worcester and plan to repair it at a cost of $500.00.

1906, November 2
President of the 15th informs the Commission that they have voted to repair its monument by furnishing a new die, which will replace the broken marble one with a replica in bronze. The directors assume that the work will be accepted by the Commissioners when the work is completed, which will be in December. 15th asks for an answer so that the regiment can close the contract with the granite company at the earliest possible date.

1933, August
The United States War Department transfers responsibility for the Gettysburg National Military Park to the National Park Service, where that responsibility resides to this day.

1950s
Markers to the 15th, 19th and 20th Massachusetts removed by the National Park Service as being "superfluous" at the Copse of Trees.

1970s
Harrow Avenue removed to encourage tourist foot traffic.

1993, Summer
Markers to the 15th, 19th and 20th Massachusetts reinstalled at the Copse of Trees through funding by the Civil War Round Table of Eastern Pennsylvania, Inc. to correct the previous injustice.

1996
Webb Avenue removed.

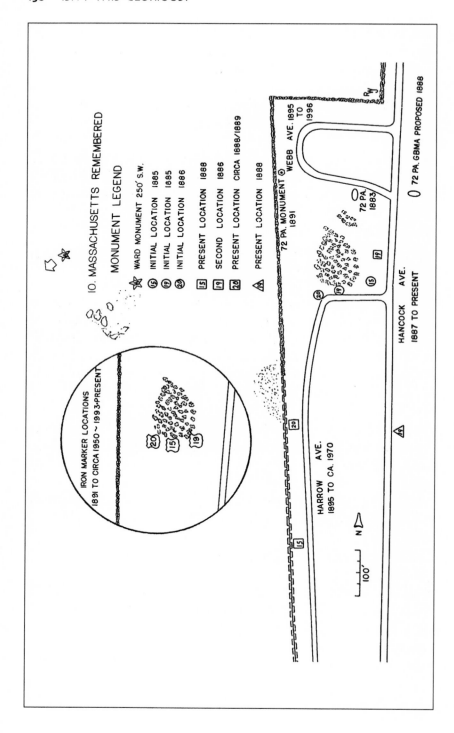

10. MASSACHUSETTS REMEMBERED

MONUMENT LEGEND

✮ WARD MONUMENT 250' S.W.

⑯ INITIAL LOCATION 1885
⑰ INITIAL LOCATION 1885
⑳ INITIAL LOCATION 1886

[15] PRESENT LOCATION 1888
[19] SECOND LOCATION 1886
[20] PRESENT LOCATION CIRCA 1888/1889

◬ PRESENT LOCATION 1888

IRON MARKER LOCATIONS
1891 TO CIRCA 1950 ~ 1993-PRESENT

72 PA. MONUMENT
1891

WEBB AVE. 1895
TO
1996

72 PA.
1883

72 PA. GBMA PROPOSED 1888

HANCOCK AVE.
1887 TO PRESENT

HARROW AVE.
1895 TO CA. 1970

N

100'

NOTES

Preface

(1) During the course of the Civil War, the 15th Massachusetts lost 241 officers and men killed or mortally wounded, the 19th lost 161 and the 20th 260. In addition to this total of 662, a further 403 officers and men in the three regiments died of disease. The 20th Massachusetts ranked first among Massachusetts regiments and fifth overall among Union regiments in battle deaths. William L. Fox, *Regimental Losses In The American Civil War 1861 – 1865* (Dayton, Ohio: Press of Morningside Bookshop, 1985), pp. 3, 122, 161, 163-164.

(2) Carol Reardon, *Pickett's Charge In History & Memory* (Chapel Hill, North Carolina: The University of North Carolina Press, 1997), p. 3.

(3) John M. Vanderslice, *Gettysburg Then And Now* (Dayton, Ohio: Press of Morningside Bookshop, 1983), p. 256; Glenn Tucker, *High Tide At Gettysburg* (Dayton, Ohio: Press of Morningside Bookshop, 1973), pp. 366-367; Edwin B. Coddington, *The Gettysburg Campaign: A Study in Command* (New York, New York: Charles Scribner's Sons, 1984), pp. 518-519; Noah Andre Trudeau, *Gettysburg: A Testing Of Courage* (New York, New York: Harper Collins Publishers Inc., 2002), p. 509.

(4) See Reardon, *Pickett's Charge In History & Memory*, pp. 108-130.

(5) Letter of John B. Bachelder to Winfield Scott Hancock, November 13, 1885, Sessler Collection, Folder D.15.8., Civil War and Underground Railroad Museum, Philadelphia, Pennsylvania.

(6) For examples of criticism directed toward John Bachelder, see Richard A. Sauers, "John B. Bachelder: Government Historian of the Battle of Gettysburg," *The Gettysburg Magazine*, no. 3, July 1990, pp. 122-126, and David M. McGlaughlin, "Monumental Litigation," *The Gettysburg Magazine*, no. 20, January 1999, pp. 125-126.

(7) Letter of Winfield Scott Hancock to Francis A. Walker, December 12, 1885, Sessler Collection, Folder D.15.17., Civil War and Underground Railroad Museum, Philadelphia, Pennsylvania.

Chapter 1

(1) Edmund J. Raus, Jr., *A Generation on the March - The Union Army at Gettysburg* (Lynchburg, Virginia: H.E. Howard, Inc., 1987), p. 35; Andrew E. Ford, *The Story of the Fifteenth Regiment Massachusetts Volunteer Infantry in the Civil War 1861-1864* (Clinton, Massachusetts: Press of W. J. Coulter, 1898), pp. 10-13, 36-37.

(2) Fox, *Regimental Losses,* p. 161.

(3) Harry W. Pfanz, *Gettysburg - The Second Day* (Chapel Hill, North Carolina: The University of North Carolina Press, 1987), p. 53.

William Harrow, a 40-year-old lawyer born in Kentucky and raised in Illinois, was living in Indiana at the outbreak of the Civil War. In April 1861, he was appointed captain commanding a company in the 14th Indiana Volunteer Infantry Regiment. Rising through the ranks, by July 1863 Harrow had become a brigadier general in command of a brigade.

John Gibbon, 36 years old in July 1863, although born in Philadelphia, Pennsylvania, was raised in North Carolina. He was a professional soldier who had graduated from West Point in 1847 and was serving as a captain in the artillery when Fort Sumter was fired upon. On duty with the Army of the Potomac from the time of its formation, Gibbon was promoted to the rank of brigadier general on May 2, 1862, and took command of this division in March 1863.

Winfield Scott Hancock, a 39-year-old native of Montgomery Square, Pennsylvania, was also a professional soldier, having graduated from West Point in 1844. Appointed a brigadier general on September 23, 1861, Hancock had fought with great gallantry in most of the Army of the Potomac's previous battles. He won the sobriquet "The Superb" at the Battle of Williamsburg in May 1862, and was promoted to the rank of major general on November 29 of that year. Hancock was given command of the II Corps after the Battle of Chancellorsville in May 1863, and led this storied unit onto the field of Gettysburg.

Ezra J. Warner, *Generals in Blue* (Baton Rouge, Louisiana: Louisiana State University Press, 1964), pp. 171, 202-203, 210-211.

(4) Pfanz, *Gettysburg - The Second Day*, pp. 53, 61; letter of Henry Abbott to John Ropes, August 1, 1863, MOLLUS (Military Order of the Loyal Legion of the United States) - Massachusetts Commandery Collection, <u>MS Am 1084</u>. By permission of the Houghton Library, Harvard University.

(5) Pfanz, *Gettysburg - The Second Day*, pp. 63-64; notation found on map

contained in the John Ropes Files. From the Massachusetts Military Histori-cal Society Collection, Howard Gotlieb Archival Research Center, Boston University, Boston, Massachusetts; Earl J. Hess, *Pickett's Charge - The Last Attack at Gettysburg* (Chapel Hill, North Carolina: The University of North Carolina Press, 2001), pp. 90, 92, 118.

(6) Pfanz, *Gettysburg - The Second Day*, pp. 380, 417; Lieutenant Colonel George C. Joslin, "Report of the Fifteenth Massachusetts Infantry at Gettysburg," United States War Department, *The War of the Rebellion: A Compilation of the Official Records of the Union and Confederate Armies,* 70 vols. in 128 parts (Washington, D.C.: Government Printing Office, 1880-1901), series 1, vol. 27, pt. 1, p. 423. (Hereafter cited as *OR*. All subsequent citations are from series 1.)

(7) Gregory A. Coco, *From Ball's Bluff to Gettysburg . . . And Beyond* (Gettysburg, Pennsylvania: Thomas Publications, 1994), pp. 32, 201; Ford, *Fifteenth Regiment Massachusetts Volunteers*, pp. 7, 155, 260, 374.

(8) Brigadier General John Gibbon, "Report of the Second Division of the II Corps at Gettysburg," *OR*, vol. 27, pt. 1, pp. 416; *OR*, vol. 27, pt. 1, p. 423.

(9) Pfanz, *Gettysburg - The Second Day*, pp. 124-148, contains a more de-tailed description of General Sickles' ill-advised advance.

(10) *OR*, vol. 27, pt. 1, p. 416.

(11) Pfanz, *Gettysburg - The Second Day*, p. 374; Thomas Cushion pension file, National Archives-Record Group 15. (Records cited hereafter as RG, NARA); Coco, *From Ball's Bluff to Gettysburg*, p. 199.

(12) *OR*, vol. 27, pt. 1, p. 423; Raus, *A Generation on the March*, pp.147-148; Pfanz, *Gettysburg - The Second Day*, pp. 374-375, 384.

Time was always very subjective in the Civil War, and the time of General Wright's brigade's assault was no exception. A modern author found con-temporary accounts indicating that the attack began anywhere from 5:00 p.m. to 7:00 p.m., and reached the conclusion that it "probably" stepped off from 6:15 p.m. to 6:30 p.m. Bradley M. Gottfried, "Wright's Charge on July 2, 1863: Piercing the Union Line or Inflated Glory?", *The Gettysburg Maga-zine*, no. 17, p. 71.

(13) The canister fractured the bone in Prince's left thumb, which was oper-ated on in the fall of 1863 while he was on medical leave in Boston. After the war, Albert Prince collected a Federal pension of $2.00 per month until his death in March 1881. (As a point of reference, in 1863, privates in the Union army were paid the sum of $13.00 per month, which in 2005, is the equiva-lent of approximately $190.00.) James Mahoney never filed for a govern-

ment pension. Ford, *Fifteenth Regiment Massachusetts Volunteers*, pp. 269-270, 358, 372; Albert Prince pension file, RG 15, NARA; http://www.eh.net/hmit/ppowerusd, Economic History Resources – How Much is That?; Bell Irvin Wiley, *The Life of Billy Yank* (Baton Rouge, Louisiana: Louisiana State University Press, 1971), p. 49.

(14) Ford, *Fifteenth Regiment Massachusetts Volunteers*, pp. 256, 280.

(15) Coco, *From Ball's Bluff to Gettysburg*, pp. 1, 7, 201.

(16) Pfanz, *Gettysburg - The Second Day,* pp. 374, 387.

(17) Pfanz, *Gettysburg - The Second Day,* p. 387; pension file of Gilman Whitcomb, RG 15, NARA; Ford, *Fifteenth Regiment Massachusetts Volunteers*, p. 270; Coco, *From Ball's Bluff to Gettysburg*, p. 202.

(18) James Huston was survived by his wife and three minor children, who collected a Federal pension of $36.00 per month. James Huston pension file, RG 15, NARA; John W. Busey, *These Honored Dead* (Hightstown, New Jersey: Longstreet House, 1988), p. 131; Captain John Darrow, "Report of the Eighty-second New York Infantry at Gettysburg," *OR*, vol. 27, pt. 1, p. 426.

(19) Ford, *Fifteenth Regiment Massachusetts Volunteers*, pp. 280-281; Abijah P. Marvin, *History of Worcester in the War of the Rebellion* (privately printed: Worcester, Massachusetts, 1870), p. 484; George H. Ward pension file, RG 15, NARA.

(20) *OR,* vol. 27, pt. 1, p. 423; Coco, *From Ball's Bluff to Gettysburg*, pp. 205, 236.

(21) Thomas H. Wentworth, ed., *Harvard Memorial Biographies* (Cambridge, Massachusetts: Sever and Francis, 1866), vol. 2, pp. 447, 452-454. In January 1885, Edward Chapin's mother Margaret applied for her son's back pay, but there is no indication that she ever received it, or filed for a Federal death pension. Edward Chapin pension file, RG 15, NARA.

(22) *OR*, vol. 27, pt. 1, p. 426: Raus, *A Generation on the March*, p. 72; John Rhodes, *The History of Battery B, First Rhode Island Artillery in the War to Preserve the Union, 1861 - 1865* (Providence, Rhode Island: Snow and Farnham, 1894), p. 203.

(23) Pfanz, *Gettysburg - The Second Day*, p. 387.

(24) *Boston Globe*, November 22, 1916; Ford, *Fifteenth Regiment Massachusetts Volunteers,* p. 38; George C. Joslin pension file, RG 15, NARA; Office of the Adjutant General of Massachusetts, *Massachusetts Soldiers, Sailors and Marines in the Civil War* (Brookline, Massachusetts: Riverdale Press, 1935), vol. 2, p. 193.

(25) The figure of 160 officers and men remaining in the ranks of the 15th

Massachusetts is an estimate, and has been reached through a review of the various compiled service and pension records at the National Archives.

(26) Ernest L. Waitt, comp., *History of the Nineteenth Regiment Massachusetts Volunteer Infantry 1861-1865* (Salem, Massachusetts: The Salem Press Company, 1906), pp. 1, 9-10; Fox, *Regimental Losses*, p. 163.

(27) Waitt, *History of the Nineteenth Massachusetts,* pp. 1, 247, 381.

Norman J. Hall, aged 26 at the time of the battle, was a professional soldier from Michigan who had graduated from West Point in 1859. After the Peninsula Campaign ended in July 1862, Hall was promoted to the rank of colonel and named commander of the 7th Michigan Volunteer Infantry Regiment, which he led until he took command of this brigade during the Battle of Antietam on September 17, 1862. Pfanz, *Gettysburg - The Second Day*, p. 70.

(28) Roger D. Hunt, *Brevet Brigadier Generals in Blue* (Gaithersburg, Maryland: Olde Soldier Books, Inc., 1990), p. 159; *Boston Globe*, February 14, 1906; Arthur F. Devereux pension file, RG 15, NARA; Waitt, *History of the Nineteenth Massachusetts*, p. 222.

(29) Colonel Norman J. Hall, "Report of the Third Brigade, Second Division, II Corps, at Gettysburg," *OR*, vol. 27, pt. 1, p. 436; Colonel Arthur F. Devereux, "Unpublished Report of the Nineteenth Infantry at Gettysburg dated May 1, 1878," p. 2, copy courtesy Gettysburg National Military Park (hereafter referred to as GNMP); Colonel Arthur F. Devereux, "Report of the Nineteenth Massachusetts Infantry at Gettysburg," *OR*, vol. 27, pt. 1, pp. 442-443.

As to Colonel Devereux having command of both his regiment and the 42nd New York on July 2 and 3, 1863, in a post-war account, he wrote, "It is right for me to say here that there was a disputed, and as yet unsettled, right of seniority between myself and Colonel Mallon [of the 42nd New York], but which never interfered with our personal relations, and it is due to the memory of so good an officer . . . to state that he frankly and cheerfully waived all claim on his part, and obeyed my orders without reserve the balance of that day and during the next." Colonel Arthur F. Devereux, "Unpublished Report of the Nineteenth Infantry at Gettysburg dated May 1, 1878," p. 2, copy courtesy GNMP.

General Humphreys' division was attacked by three Confederate brigades from Mississippi, Alabama and Florida, with the New Yorkers and Bay Staters being confronted by the Alabama and Florida brigades. Humphreys himself later wrote that he had requested the support of "a brigade, if possible" from II Corps commander General Hancock, and that the aide in question, Lieutenant H. C. Christiancy, had "judiciously posted" the 19th Massachusetts and 42nd New York. Pfanz, *Gettysburg – The Second Day,* pp. 376, 379-380; Brigadier General Andrew A. Humphreys, "Report of the Second Division, II Corps at Gettysburg," *OR*, vol. 27, pt. 1, p. 533.

(30) Colonel Arthur F. Devereux, "Unpublished Report," p. 2, copy courtesy GNMP; *OR*, vol. 27, pt. 1, p. 442. For more information on the gallant stand of the 1st Minnesota on July 2, 1863, see Pfanz, *Gettysburg - The Second Day*, pp. 410-414.

(31) *OR*, vol. 27, pt. 1, pp. 442-443; Colonel Arthur F. Devereux, "Unpublished Report," p. 2, copy courtesy GNMP.

(32) Charles Preston pension file, RG 15, NARA.

(33) Cornelius Linehan pension file, RG 15, NARA; letter of Cornelius Linehan to "Father," July 17, 1863, copy courtesy GNMP.

(34) Waitt, *History of the Nineteenth Massachusetts,* pp. 232, 392; *Massachusetts Soldiers, Sailors and Marines in the Civil War*, vol. 2, pp. 432, 485; W.F. Beyer and O.F. Keydel, *Deeds of Valor* (Stamford, Connecticut: Longmeadow Press, 1992), p. 236; Benjamin H. Jellison pension file, RG 15, NARA; Charles Rowe pension file, RG 15, NARA.

Charles Rowe had enlisted as a private in the 19th's Company K on August 15, 1862. After the Battle of Fredericksburg, Rowe had been promoted to color sergeant for his heroism in taking up the colors, which had fallen to the ground when the previous color bearer was hit. Because of his wounds sustained on July 2, Charles Rowe was never able to return to duty with the regiment. He was discharged on August 27, 1864, and began collecting a $4.00 per month pension from the Federal government. He died in Boston in 1915 at the age of 78. Waitt, *History of the Nineteenth Massachusetts,* p. 409; *Boston Herald*, December 24, 1862; Charles Rowe pension file, RG 15, NARA.

(35) Waitt, *History of the Nineteenth Massachusetts,* pp. 231, 407; *Massachusetts Soldiers, Sailors and Marines in the Civil War*, vol. 2, p. 454; John G. B. Adams, *Reminiscences of the Nineteenth Massachusetts Regiment* (Boston, Massachusetts: Wright & Potter Printing Company, 1899), p. 35; Edmund Rice pension file, RG 15, NARA; brief biography of Edmund Rice prepared by Norwich University, 1953. Norwich University Archives and Special Collections, Kreitzberg Library, Northfield, VT.

(36) Edmund Rice to Abner Doubleday, April 19, 1887, BV Doubleday, Abner, Reports of the Battles of Gettysburg, July 1st, 2d and 3d, 1863, New-York Historical Society, New York; Waitt, *History of the Nineteenth Massachusetts,* pp. 231-232; *OR*, vol. 27, pt. 1, p. 443.

(37) Waitt, *History of the Nineteenth Massachusetts,* p. 232; Edmund Roche pension file, RG 15, NARA; inscription on tombstone of John L. Hoyt, Hilldale Cemetery, Haverhill, Massachusetts; letter of Cornelius Linehan to "Father," July 17, 1863, copy courtesy GNMP; John Doherty pension file, RG 15, NARA; Charles Brown pension file, RG 15, NARA; Colonel James E. Mallon, "Report of the Forty-Second New York Infantry at Gettysburg," *OR*, vol. 27, pt. 1, p. 451.

(38) Colonel Arthur F. Devereux, "Unpublished Report," p. 3, copy courtesy GNMP.

(39) Richard F. Miller, "Brahmins Under Fire: Peer Courage and the Harvard Regiment," *Historical Journal of Massachusetts,* XXX (Winter 2002), p. 76; George A. Bruce, *The Twentieth Regiment of Massachusetts Volunteer Infantry 1861-1865* (Baltimore, Maryland: Butternut and Blue, 1988), p. vii; Fox, *Regimental Losses,* pp. 11, 164.

(40) Bruce, *Twentieth Regiment Massachusetts Volunteers*, pp. 1-3, 9-13, 136-137; Fox, *Regimental Losses,* p. 164.

(41) Bruce, *Twentieth Regiment Massachusetts Volunteers*, p. 446; Paul J. Revere pension file, RG 15, NARA; Wentworth, *Harvard Memorial Biographies*, vol. 1, pp. 219, 221-227, 234-235; Robert Garth Scott, *Fallen Leaves: The Civil War Letters of Major Henry Livermore Abbott* (Kent, Ohio: The Kent State University Press, 1991), p. 179.

(42) Scott, *Fallen Leaves*, p. 184.

Colonel Revere was suffering from lumbago and rheumatism. Nina Zannien, "The Civil War Reveres: A Family Story," unpublished article, p. 4, copy courtesy The Paul Revere Memorial Association, Boston, Massachusetts.

(43) Scott, *Fallen Leaves*, p. 186; Captain Henry L. Abbott, "Report of the Twentieth Massachusetts Infantry at Gettysburg," *OR*, vol. 27, pt. 1, p. 445; letter of E. B. Cope to Gettysburg National Park Commission, February 11, 1896, Records of the Gettysburg Nat'l Park Comm, Monuments and Markers, US Commission, vol. 1, GNMP Archives; letter of Henry Abbott to John Ropes, August 1, 1863, MOLLUS-Massachusetts Commandery Collection, MS Am 1084. By permission of the Houghton Library, Harvard University.

Despite sustaining two wounds in the fighting at Gettysburg, one in his left thigh and another which resulted in the amputation of the middle finger of his right hand, Henry L. Patten later returned to duty with the regiment and was promoted to the rank of major. On August 17, 1864, at the Battle of Deep Bottom, Virginia, Major Patten was shot in his left leg while establishing a

picket line. The gunshot caused such damage that the limb had to be amputated, but blood poisoning set in and caused his death on September 10, 1864,
at a hospital in Philadelphia. As Major Patten was unmarried, his parents
collected a pension of $20.00 per month from the Federal government. After
his death, Patten was recognized for his gallantry by a posthumous promotion to the rank of brevet brigadier general. Wentworth, *Harvard
Memorial Biographies*, vol. 1, p. 458; Hunt, *Brevet Brigadier Generals In
Blue*, p. 468; Henry L. Patten pension file, RG 15, NARA.

(44) *OR*, vol. 27, pt. 1, p. 436. The "interval" that Colonel Hall referred to in
his report, which he described as being ". . . nearly a quarter of a mile . . .
from the left of my position," may have actually been as much as a mile in
length. It stretched from the area north of Little Round Top to the position
held by Hall's left flank, just south of the Copse of Trees. It was only through
skillful plugging of this gap by timely Union reinforcements and the steadfastness shown by men such as Hall's troops that the Federal line was re-
established on Cemetery Ridge. *OR*, vol. 27, pt. 1, p. 436. Pfanz, *Gettysburg
- The Second Day*, pp. 390-424 contains a fine description of this desperate
fighting near dusk on July 2.

(45) Wentworth, *Harvard Memorial Biographies*, vol. 1, pp. 236-237; *A Memorial of Paul Joseph Revere and Edward H. Revere* (Boston, Massachusetts: Wm. Parsons Lunt, 1874), p. 184; letter of Surgeon Nathan Hayward of
the 20th Massachusetts to "Father," July 8, 1863, copy courtesy GNMP; Nina
Zannien, "The Civil War Reveres: A Family Story, pp. 4-5."

There are many discrepancies as to Paul Revere being mortally wounded
on July 3, as opposed to July 2, and dying on July 4, as opposed to July 5;
however, since the 20th's regimental surgeon, Nathan Hayward, actually
treated Revere until the colonel's transfer to Westminster, and wrote home
within days of the event, the authors have chosen to use his account. Revere
was survived by his wife, Lucretia, a three-year-old son, Frank, and a one-
year-old daughter, Pauline, who collected a Federal pension of $34.00 per
month. Paul J. Revere pension file, RG 15, NARA.

Nathan Hayward was a 33-year-old physician from Roxbury, Massachusetts. *Massachusetts Soldiers, Sailors and Marines in the Civil War*, vol. 2, p.
494.

(46) *OR*, vol. 27, pt. 1, p. 445; *Massachusetts Soldiers, Sailors and Marines
in the Civil War*, vol. 2, p. 559. Charles Cowgill was shot in the upper right
thigh, with the ball severing his sciatic nerve. He was discharged for disability on March 9, 1864, and began receiving a Federal pension of $5.75 per

month. After the war, Cowgill moved to Franklin, Pennsylvania, and became an oil company superintendent. His Gettysburg wound eventually caused paralysis, which led to his death on August 9, 1911, in Oil City, Pennsylvania. Franklin, Pennsylvania, *Evening News,* August 10, 1911; Charles Cowgill pension file, RG 15, NARA.

(47) Gustave Magnitzky pension file, RG 15, NARA; Bruce, *Twentieth Regiment Massachusetts Volunteers*, p. 283; Mark De Wolfe Howe, *Oliver Wendell Holmes – the Shaping Years, 1841-1870* (Cambridge, Massachusetts: Harvard University Press, 1957), p. 86. Despite the loss of his toes, in December 1863, Gustave Magnitzky was able to return to duty with the 20th, and later attained the rank of captain. In 1867, he enlisted in the United States Regular Army, and retired as a first lieutenant in 1871. Magnitzky also began collecting a Federal pension of $4.00 per month in 1865. After leaving the Regular Army, he returned to Boston and became an attorney. Acclaimed as the last surviving member of the 20th Massachusetts, on September 18, 1910, Gustave Magnitzky died of pneumonia at his home in Jamaica Plain, Massachusetts. Gustave Magnitzky pension file, RG 15, NARA; unidentified and undated newspaper clippings found in Robert L. Brake Collection, United States Army Military History Institute, Carlisle Barracks, Pennsylvania (hereafter cited as USAMHI).

(48) George R. Stewart, *Pickett's Charge* (Dayton, Ohio: Press of Morningside Bookshop, 1983), p. 1.

Chapter 2

(1) Newly promoted to the rank of brigadier general on June 23, 1863, the 25-year-old Alexander S. Webb was a native of New York City who had graduated from West Point in 1855. Webb's brigade, of which he had just taken command on the eve of the battle, was composed of the 69th, 71st, 72nd and 106th Pennsylvania Volunteer Infantry Regiments, and was known as the "Philadelphia Brigade," since all its regiments had originally been recruited from that city. Warner, *Generals in Blue,* pp. 544-545; Stewart, *Pickett's Charge*, pp. 58-60.

(2) Coddington, *The Gettysburg Campaign*, p. 512; Raus, *A Generation on the March,* p. 86; *OR,* vol. 27, pt. 1, p. 423; inscription on 15th Massachusetts regimental marker near the Copse of Trees.

(3) Waitt, *History of the Nineteenth Massachusetts*, p. 234; Colonel Arthur F. Devereux, "Unpublished Report," p. 2, copy courtesy GNMP.

As for the 19th's losses on July 2, the unit's regimental history states that the numbers totaled over "half a hundred." However, a careful review of the compiled service and/or pension records of the 19th's casualties suffered during the entire battle indicates that the true number incurred during the fighting on July 2 was approximately 25 to 30 officers and men. Waitt, *History of the Nineteenth Massachusetts*, p. 231.

(4) Raus, *A Generation on the March,* pp. 147-148; Stewart, *Pickett's Charge,* p. 147.

As darkness was falling on July 2, the four guns of Brown's battery that had been lost in the assault by Wright's Georgians were retaken in a furious counterattack by men of General Webb's brigade. Pfanz, *Gettysburg - The Second Day*, p. 419; Rhodes, *The History of Battery B, First Rhode Island Artillery*, pp. 202-203.

(5) George N. Macy pension file, RG 15, NARA; Richard F. Miller and Robert F. Mooney, *The Civil War: The Nantucket Experience* (Nantucket, Massachusetts: Wesco Publishing, 1994), pp. 166-167.

(6) Scott, *Fallen Leaves*, p. 186; letter of Henry Abbott to John Ropes, August 1, 1863, MOLLUS- Massachusetts Commandery Collection, <u>MS Am 1084</u>. By permission of the Houghton Library, Harvard University; *OR*, vol. 27, pt. 1, p. 445; Coddington, *The Gettysburg Campaign*, pp. 511-512.

(7) Raus, *A Generation on the March,* pp. 35-36; Ford, *Fifteenth Regiment Massachusetts Volunteers,* p. 239; Waitt, *History of the Nineteenth Massachusetts*, p. 151; Colonel Arthur F. Devereux, "Unpublished Report," p. 2, copy courtesy GNMP; Miller and Mooney, *The Civil War: The Nantucket Experience*, p. 167.

(8) Correspondence of John Heiser, historian, GNMP, to authors, June 2, 2000; letter of George Ward to "My dear Wife and Children," June 19, 1863, George Ward Letters. From the Collections of Worcester Historical Museum, Worcester, MA; *A Memorial of Paul Joseph Revere and Edward H. Revere,* p. 179.

(9) Wentworth, *Harvard Memorial Biographies*, vol. 1, pp. 364-367.

After recovering from his illness, Sergeant Brown returned to duty with the regiment. At the Battle of Spotsylvania, while carrying the regimental flag, he was mortally wounded by the explosion of a shell. There is no indication that any of his relatives filed for a Federal pension after his death. Waitt, *History of the Nineteenth Massachusetts*, p. 312.

(10) Waitt, *History of the Nineteenth Massachusetts*, pp. 218, 247, states that the 19th Massachusetts began the final march to Gettysburg with 220 officers

and men and entered the battle with a total of only 160. A review of the regimental rosters of both the 15th and 19th reveals that no man deserted in June 1863, or during the battle itself.

Franklin B. Murphey was discharged for disability on November 6, 1863, but later enlisted in the Veteran Reserve Corps in September 1864 and served until November 14, 1865. After the war, he worked as a printer and received a pension of $8.00 per month for "rheumatism" of his left knee. He died in December 1920 and is buried in Nantucket.

Josiah Murphey rejoined the regiment in October 1863 and served until August 1, 1864, when he was discharged at the expiration of his service. As a result of being shot in the face on December 11, 1862, at the Battle of Fredericksburg, he gradually lost the sight in his right eye after the war, and received a pension which eventually reached the sum of $38.00 per month. He died in May 1931.

Privates Hamblin, Lane and Monaghan were never apprehended and disappeared from the rolls of the regiment forever.

On August 1, 1863, Eugene Sullivan, who, on his own volition, had returned to the 20th after a three-day absence, was charged with deserting in the face of the enemy and insubordination, found guilty and sentenced to be shot. General Meade, the commander of the Army of the Potomac, approved the sentence. A petition for clemency stated that Sullivan's father, James Sullivan, had also served as a private in Company F with his son, and was killed at his son's side at the Battle of Fredericksburg. The petition also stated, "(Sullivan) is shocked and terror-stricken at the prospect of a battle." President Lincoln himself remitted Sullivan's sentence. The young soldier returned to the ranks of the 20th, re-enlisted as a Veteran Volunteer on December 20, 1863, and was wounded in his left shoulder at the Battle of Spotsylvania on May 12, 1864. The ball shattered his humerus, which had to be resected and two inches of bone were removed. He was discharged for disability on January 15, 1865, and began receiving a Federal pension of $4.00 per month. By the time of his death in December 1903, the pension had increased to $46.00 per month.

Charles Raymond was charged with deserting his colors in the face of the enemy, court-martialed and found guilty. Sentenced to payment of a fine and imprisonment at hard labor in Dry Tortugas Prison off the Florida Keys, he was incarcerated instead at the Old Capitol Prison in Washington, D.C., until November 1863, when his sentence was commuted. Upon his release, he returned to the regiment and was taken prisoner on May 5, 1864, at the Battle of the Wilderness. On June 12, 1864, Raymond died of smallpox at the infamous Andersonville prison. His family never filed for a pension after his death.

Miller and Mooney, *The Civil War: The Nantucket Experience*, pp. 170-171, 177-178; *Massachusetts Soldiers, Sailors and Marines in the Civil War*, vol. 2, pp. 537, 548, 562; diary of Captain Herbert C. Mason, copy courtesy GNMP; Leander D. Hamblin compiled military service record, RG 94, NARA; Bruce, *Twentieth Regiment of Massachusetts Volunteer*, pp. 485, 495; Eugene Sullivan pension file, RG 15, NARA; *Boston Journal*, September 1, 1863; Eugene Sullivan and Charles Raymond file folders in RG 153, NARA, copies courtesy The Index Project, Inc.; Charles H. Raymond pension file, RG 15, NARA.

(11) Albert Everett, "Harrow's Brigade at Gettysburg," unpublished manuscript, pp. 1-2. From the Collections of Worcester Historical Museum, Worcester, MA; Ford, *Fifteenth Regiment Massachusetts Volunteer,* p. 393. No member of Corporal Butters' family ever filed for a pension from the Federal government after his death.

(12) *Massachusetts Soldiers, Sailors and Marines in the Civil War*, vol. 2, p.181; William Moore pension file, RG 15, NARA.

(13) Stewart, *Pickett's Charge*, p. 69; Hess, *Pickett's Charge*, p. 92; Frank A. Haskell, *The Battle of Gettysburg* (Boston, Massachusetts: Houghton Mifflin Company, 1957), p. 70.

(14) Further information concerning the Culp's Hill fighting during the morning of July 3 can be found in Harry W. Pfanz, *Gettysburg-Culp's Hill And Cemetery Hill* (Chapel Hill, North Carolina: the University of North Carolina Press, 1993), pp. 284-352.

(15) Captain John G. Hazard, "Report of the Artillery Brigade, Second Army Corps at Gettysburg," *OR*, vol. 27, pt. 1, p. 478.

(16) Letter of Henry Ropes to "Mother," December 20, 1862, Henry Ropes Letters, Manuscript Collection, Boston Public Library/Rare Books Department. Courtesy of the Trustees; Scott, *Fallen Leaves*, p. 184; Haskell, *The Battle of Gettysburg*, p. 75; letter of Henry Abbott to John Ropes, August 1, 1863, MOLLUS - Massachusetts Commandery Collection, <u>MS Am 1084</u>. By permission of the Houghton Library, Harvard University.

(17) A veteran of many battles, Lieutenant Colonel Macy of the 20th later estimated one in 50 Union shells exploded prematurely. Private Chester A. Leonard, a 21-year-old farmer from Northampton, Massachusetts, who was also serving in Company K of the 20th Massachusetts, had his arm fractured

by the same shell that killed Lieutenant Ropes. Leonard related the details of this tragic accident to Ropes' brother when they visited the battlefield in October 1863. The shell shattered the humerus of the young private's left arm and carried away more than half of the deltoid muscle; consequently, at a field hospital just behind the front lines, the shaft of his humerus had to be excised. Worthington Chauncey Ford, ed., *War Letters 1862-1865* (Cambridge, Massachusetts: The Riverside Press, 1927), pp. 149, 241-242; letter of Henry Abbott to John Ropes, August 1, 1863, MOLLUS - Massachusetts Commandery Collection, MS Am 1084. By permission of the Houghton Library, Harvard University; Bruce, *Twentieth Regiment of Massachusetts Volunteer*, p. 507; *OR*, vol. 27, pt. 1, p. 446; Joseph K. Barnes, ed., *The Medical and Surgical History of the Civil War,* 12 vols. (Washington, D.C.: Government Printing Office, 1870), vol. 4, p. 679; Chester A. Leonard pension file, RG 15, NARA. There is no evidence to indicate that Henry Ropes' family ever applied for a pension after his death.

(18) Thomas L. Elmore, "Torrid Heat and Blinding Rain: A Meteorological and Astonomical Chronology of the Gettysburg Campaign," *The Gettysburg Magazine*, no. 13, 1995, p. 14; Pfanz, *Gettysburg-Culp's Hill And Cemetery Hill*, pp. 351-352.

A soldier in Gibbon's division, describing this lull, later wrote: "Of that stillness you have often heard, no language of mine could cause you to imagine its reality, such a stillness I had never before experienced, nor since, and I have borne part in every engagement of the Army of the Potomac." Letter of Anthony W. McDermott to John Bachelder, June 2, 1886, in David L. Ladd and Audrey J. Ladd, eds., *The Bachelder Papers: Gettysburg in Their Own Words,* 3 vols. (Dayton, Ohio: Press of Morningside Bookshop, 1995), vol. 3, p. 1409.

(19) Haskell, *The Battle of Gettysburg*, p. 147; Bruce, *Twentieth Regiment of Massachusetts Volunteer*, p. 482; *Massachusetts Soldiers, Sailors and Marines in the Civil War*, vol. 2, p. 542.

(20) The Washington Artillery from New Orleans, Louisiana, was assigned the task of firing two signal shots to commence the grand cannonade. The friction primer failed to ignite the charge on the second piece, causing a momentary delay until a third cannon could be fired. Jennings C. Wise, *The Long Arm of Lee* (Lynchburg, Virginia: J.P. Bell Company, Inc., 1915), vol. 2, p. 677.

(21) Waitt, *History of the Nineteenth Massachusetts*, p. 234; Adams, *Reminiscences of the Nineteenth Massachusetts*, p. 68; *Massachusetts Soldiers,*

Sailors and Marines in the Civil War, vol. 2, p. 413.

In his classic account of the great Confederate assault, author George Stewart recounted three more possible results of these shots. A private in the 13th Vermont Volunteer Infantry Regiment, positioned south of the 19th Massachusetts, said that the first missile was a shell that exploded just behind his regiment. A captain in the 12th New Jersey Volunteer Infantry Regiment, stationed several hundred yards north of the Copse of Trees, said that it was a shell that hit but did not explode in the rear of his unit. The third account cited is that of a Confederate lieutenant serving in the Washington Artillery, who said that the projectile blew up a Union caisson. Stewart, *Pickett's Charge*, pp. 125-126.

(22) John W. Busey, *These Honored Dead: The Union Casualties at Gettysburg* (Hightstown, New Jersey: Longstreet House, 1988), p. 60; Waitt, *History of the Nineteenth Massachusetts*, pp. 234-235. Originally interred on Peter Frey's farm behind Cemetery Ridge, Lieutenant Robinson is now buried in Grave E-29 of the Massachusetts Plot in the National Cemetery at Gettysburg. Robinson's father, Stephen, was 69 years old when his son was killed. His only other child, a 24-year-old son named John, had also served in the ranks of the 19th Massachusetts, but died of disease on October 30, 1862. Being too infirm to work, Stephen Robinson received a Federal pension of $15.00 per month, a small recompense for losing his only two children. Sherman Robinson pension file, RG 15, NARA; Waitt, *History of the Nineteenth Massachusetts*, p. 408.

(23) Letter of Henry Abbott to John Ropes, August 1, 1863, MOLLUS - Massachusetts Commandery Collection, <u>MS Am 1084</u>. By permission of the Houghton Library, Harvard University.; Waitt, *History of the Nineteenth Massachusetts*, p. 235.

At the Battle of Gettysburg, the 15th Massachusetts was armed with Springfield rifled muskets and the 19th and the 20th with Enfield rifled muskets. Earl J. Coates and Dean S. Thomas, *An Introduction To Civil War Small Arms* (Gettysburg, Pennsylvania: Thomas Publications, 1990), pp. 88-89.

(24) Hess, *Pickett's Charge*, pp. 7-10; John Gibbon, *Personal Recollections of the Civil War* (Dayton, Ohio: Press of Morningside Bookshop, 1978), p. 147.

(25) Pension file of Carlton DeLand, RG 15, NARA; Stewart, *Pickett's Charge*, p. 138.

(26) *OR*, vol. 27, pt. 1, p. 423; pension files of Carlton DeLand, John Knight, Edwin Goulding and Thomas Brown, RG 15, NARA; *Massachusetts Soldiers, Sailors and Marines in the Civil War*, vol. 2, pp. 158, 159, 171, 198.

(27) Letter of William B. Hoitt to "Friend Mary," July 13, 1863, copy courtesy GNMP; Waitt, *History of the Nineteenth Massachusetts*, p. 235; *Massachusetts Soldiers, Sailors and Marines in the Civil War*, vol. 2, p. 476; BV Doubleday, Abner, Reports of the Battles of Gettysburg, July 1st, 2d and 3d, 1863, New York Historical Society, New York; Hunt, *Brevet Brigadier Generals In Blue*, p. 654; Scott, *Fallen Leaves*, p. 209; Ansel D. Wass pension file, RG 15, NARA.

(28) Private Goodwin, who was illiterate, survived his terrible wounds and was discharged on August 28, 1864, as an "invalid," and immediately began receiving a United States government pension of $4.00 per month. In the 1880s, an examining doctor described Goodwin as being "all shot up." Despite being blinded in a gunpowder explosion in 1892, Goodwin lived until 1923, by which time his pension had increased to $72.00 per month. *Massachusetts Soldiers, Sailors and Marines in the Civil War*, vol. 2, p. 437; Andrew Goodwin pension file, RG 15, NARA.

(29) Scott, *Fallen Leaves*, p. 186; *OR*, vol. 27, pt. 1, p. 445.

(30) Letter of Henry Abbott to John Ropes, August 1, 1863, MOLLUS - Massachusetts Commandery Collection, MS Am 1084. By permission of the Houghton Library, Harvard University; *OR*, vol. 27, pt. 1, p. 437.

(31) Statement of Oliver Oakes contained in Henry Dawson pension file, RG 15, NARA; Colonel Arthur F. Devereux, "Unpublished Report," p. 3, copy courtesy GNMP.

(32) Captain John Reynolds, "The Nineteenth Massachusetts At Gettysburg, July 2-3-4," unpublished manuscript, p. 6, copy courtesy GNMP; Captain William French, Captain William Barry and Captain Henry Hunt, *Instruction for Field Artillery* (New York, New York: D. Van Nostrand, 1864), p. 185.

Captain Reynolds himself was not present at the Battle of Gettysburg. Disabled as a result of severe wounds to his right ankle and elbow that he received at the Battle of Antietam on September 17, 1862, he never returned to active service with the regiment. However, the overall accuracy of his account indicates that Reynolds clearly spoke to or corresponded with members of the 19th who were participants in the battle. Waitt, *History of the Nineteenth Massachusetts*, p. 145; *Massachusetts Soldiers, Sailors and Marines in the Civil War*, vol. 2, p. 439.

(33) Stewart, *Pickett's Charge*, p. 138; Adams, *Reminiscences of the Nineteenth Massachusetts*, p. 68.

(34) Waitt, *History of the Nineteenth Massachusetts*, p. 410; *Massachusetts Soldiers, Sailors and Marines in the Civil War*, vol. 2, p. 427; Captain John

Reynolds, "The Nineteenth Massachusetts At Gettysburg, July 2-3-4," pp. 6-7, copy courtesy GNMP.

(35) The post-war regimental history describes these 26 officers and men being detailed to aid Lieutenant Brown's Rhode Island battery, but it is clear from reading Colonel Devereux's report that they were actually sent to the assistance of Captain Rorty's New York battery. *OR*, vol. 27, pt. 1, p. 443; Waitt, *History of the Nineteenth Massachusetts*, p. 236.

(36) Rhodes, *The History of Battery B, First Rhode Island Artillery*, p. 211; Raus, *A Generation on the March*, p. 86; *OR*, vol. 27, pt. 1, p. 480.

On July 3, 1863, Battery "B", 1st Rhode Island Artillery lost three men killed or mortally wounded, 14 men wounded and one missing. Rhodes, *The History of Battery B, First Rhode Island Artillery*, p. 214.

Unfortunately, the casualties incurred by Battery "B", 1st New York Light Artillery were not separated by date. For the entire battle, the unit lost 11 killed and 16 wounded. W. O. Beauchamp, "Dedication of Monument. Battery B-'Pettit's.' First Regiment New York Light Artillery," in New York Monuments Commission for the Battlefields of Gettysburg and Chattanooga, *Final Report on the Battlefield of Gettysburg* (Albany, New York: J. B. Lyons and Company, 1902), p. 1184. (Hereinafter cited as *New York at Gettysburg*.)

(37) The nine Confederate units were the brigades of Brigadier Generals Richard Garnett, James Kemper, Lewis Armistead, Joseph Davis, James Lane and Alfred Scales, now commanded by Colonel William Lowrance, and those of Colonels James Marshall, John Brockenbrough and Birkett Fry. Coddington, *The Gettysburg Campaign*, pp. 489-490.

(38) Coddington, *The Gettysburg Campaign*, p. 489; Kathleen R. Georg and John W. Busey, *Nothing But Glory: Pickett's Division at Gettysburg* (Highstown, New Jersey: Longstreet House, 1987), p. 9; Stewart, *Pickett's Charge*, p. 140. The exact number of Confederate casualties suffered as a result of Union counter-battery fire has never been determined, and has been a point of contention between historians, even to this day.

(39) Edmund Rice, "Repelling Lee's Last Blow at Gettysburg," in Robert U. Johnson and Clarence C. Buel, eds. *Battles and Leaders of the Civil War,* 4 vols. (New York, New York: Thomas Yoseloff, 1956), vol. 3, p. 387; Stewart, *Pickett's Charge*, pp. 183, 196-197.

(40) *OR*, vol. 27, pt. 1, p. 439; Edmund Rice to Abner Doubleday, April 19, 1887, BV Doubleday, Abner, Reports of the Battles of Gettysburg, July 1st, 2d and 3d, 1863, p. 241, New-York Historical Society, New York.

(41) Georg, *Nothing But Glory*, p. 90.

These two Vermont units were part of a brigade of five 9-month infantry regiments commanded by Brigadier General George J. Stannard, which had never before seen combat and had been assigned to the Union I Corps in June 1863, after spending their entire enlistment to that point in the defenses of Washington, D.C. Noticing a gap in the lines of the attacking Confederates, these rookie Green Mountaineers were quick to take advantage and moved forward into the gap to outflank Kemper's men. It was a source of much post-battle controversy as to whether this important movement was ordered by General Hancock or General Stannard. Stewart, *Pickett's Charge*, pp. 61-62, 232-233. Kemper's response to the advance of the Vermonters is more fully described in Georg, *Nothing But Glory*, pp. 100-103.

(42) Edmund Rice to Abner Doubleday, April 19, 1887, BV Doubleday, Abner, Reports of the Battles of Gettysburg, July 1st, 2d and 3d, 1863, p. 242, New-York Historical Society, New York; Rice, "Repelling Lee's Last Blow at Gettysburg," *Battles and Leaders*, vol. 3, p. 388.

(43) *OR*, vol. 27, pt. 1, p. 445; letter of Henry Abbott to John Ropes, August 1, 1863, MOLLUS - Massachusetts Commandery Collection, <u>MS Am 1084</u>. By permission of the Houghton Library, Harvard University; Georg, *Nothing But Glory*, pp. 66, 96; Daniel McAdams pension file, RG 15, NARA; Daniel McAdams, "A Short history of the Service of Daniel McAdams in Company I 20 Regiment Mass Vol 30 years after the War Wrote from Memory," MOLLUS - Massachusetts Commandery Collection, <u>MS Am 1084</u>. By permission of the Houghton Library, Harvard University; *OR*, vol. 27, pt. 1, p. 445.

(44) Scott, *Fallen Leaves*, p. 188; letter of Captain Henry Abbott to Charles C. Paine, July 28, 1863, copy courtesy GNMP; Georg, *Nothing But Glory*, p. 493.

(45) Stewart, *Pickett's Charge*, p. 207; Hess, *Pickett's Charge,* p. 242.

(46) R. L. Murray, *Hurrah For The Ould Flag* (Savannah, New York: Seeco Printing Services, 1998), p. 2; David Shultz, *Double Canister At Ten Yards: The Federal Artillery And The Repulse of Pickett's Charge* (Redondo Beach, California: Rank And File Publications, 1995), pp. 18, 46-47, 57.

Captain Cowan later described this movement: "[A]nother aide galloped down from the right and ordered me to report to General Webb. I was under the orders of Gen. Doubleday and hardly knew if I ought to obey Gen. Webb, whom I did not know. While doubting for an instant, I looked toward the higher grounds and at the point where you have my battery placed, saw a General waving his hat to me. I at once determined to risk disobeying orders, as I must be needed there, and at once limbered to the rear and moved by the left flank at a gallop." Letter of Andrew Cowan to John Bachelder, August

26, 1866, Ladd and Ladd, eds., *The Bachelder Papers,* vol. 1, p. 281.

(47) Letter of Andrew Cowan to John Bachelder, August 26, 1866, Ladd and Ladd, eds., *The Bachelder Papers,* vol. 1, p. 283.

Henry J. Hunt, aged 43 at the time of the battle, was a professional soldier who had graduated from West Point in 1839. Hunt had fought in the Mexican War with the artillery service and had won two promotions by brevet for gallantry. With the outbreak of the Civil War, Hunt's expertise in artillery was recognized by his being appointed to the command of the Artillery Reserve of the Army of the Potomac, winning promotion to the rank of brigadier general on September 15, 1862. At Gettysburg, he was in charge of all of the Federal artillery and received great acclaim for his handling of the guns. Warner, *Generals in Blue*, p. 242.

(48) Arthur Devereux *Testimony, Supreme Court of Pennsylvania, Appeal of the* Gettysburg Battlefield Memorial Association, *From the Decree of the Court of Common Pleas of Adams County, May Term, 1891, nos. 20 and 30.* (hereinafter cited as 72nd Penna. vs. GBMA), 292-295; Arthur F. Devereux, "Some Account of Pickett's Charge at Gettysburg," *Magazine of American History,* XVIII (1887), p. 17; Patrick Harvey pension file, RG 15, NARA; Rice, "Repelling Lee's Last Blow at Gettysburg," p. 388.

General Hancock made his way south along Cemetery Ridge to the position of the Vermont brigade. While superintending their flank attack on Kemper's men, Hancock was severely wounded in the groin. Hess, *Pickett's Charge*, pp. 281-282.

(49) Colonel Arthur F. Devereux, "Unpublished Report," p. 3, copy courtesy GNMP; Edmund Rice to Abner Doubleday, April 19, 1887, BV Doubleday, Abner, Reports of the Battles of Gettysburg, July 1st, 2d and 3d, 1863, p. 245, New York Historical Society, New York; William A. Hill *Testimony*, 72nd Penna. vs. GBMA, 348; letter of Arthur Devereux to John Bachelder, July 22, 1889, Ladd and Ladd, eds., *The Bachelder Papers,* vol. 3, p. 1610.

An oblique march, especially under fire, would certainly have been a rather complicated maneuver even for veteran troops. The movement is described as follows: "The rear rank men will preserve their distances, and march in rear of the man next on the right (or left) of their habitual file leaders." Brevet Lieut. W.J. Hardee, *Hardee's Rifle And Light Infantry Tactics* (New York, New York: J.O. Kane, 1862), p. 92.

(50) William A. Hill *Testimony*, 72nd Penna. vs. GBMA, p. 357.

(51) Ibid. p. 350-351.

(52) Edmund Rice to Abner Doubleday, April 19, 1887, BV Doubleday, Abner,

Reports of the Battles of Gettysburg, July 1st, 2d and 3d, 1863, New-York Historical Society, New York; letter of Andrew Cowan to John Bachelder, August 26, 1866, Ladd and Ladd, eds., *The Bachelder Papers,* vol. 1, p. 282; William A. Hill *Testimony*, 72nd Penna. vs. GBMA, p. 350.

(53) Ford, *Fifteenth Regiment Massachusetts Volunteer,* pp. 276, 280; Georg, *Nothing But Glory*, p. 144; Busey, *These Honored Dead*, p. 58; *Massachusetts Soldiers, Sailors and Marines in the Civil War*, vol. 2, p. 145. Murkland's widow, Sophia, received from the United States government a pension of $15.00 per month after his death. John Murkland pension file, RG 15, NARA.

(54) After an ornate ceremony, Jorgensen was buried in Leominster, Massachusetts, on July 23, 1863. There is no record of any relatives of Hans Jorgensen ever filing for a pension. Ford, *Fifteenth Regiment Massachusetts Volunteer,* p. 278; *Massachusetts Soldiers, Sailors and Marines in the Civil War,* vol. 2, p. 138.

(55) *OR*, vol. 27, pt. 1, p. 439; letter of A. C. Plaisted to John Bachelder, June 11, 1870, Ladd and Ladd, eds., *The Bachelder Papers,* vol. 1, p. 393; James Tenney pension file, RG 15, NARA; *OR*, vol. 27, pt. 1, p. 423.

(56) Haskell, *The Battle of Gettysburg*, p. 167.

(57) Georg, *Nothing But Glory*, pp. 153-154; W. O. Beauchamp, "Dedication of Monument. Battery B-'Pettit's.' First Regiment New York Light Artillery," *New York at Gettysburg*, pp. 1183-1184.

(58) The men that General Armistead led over the stone wall were from all three brigades of Pickett's division. Armistead himself was shot down at one of Cushing's guns and was taken prisoner. His wounds proved mortal and he died on July 5, 1863. Georg, *Nothing But Glory*, pp. 171-176.

(59) Letter of George N. Macy to John Bachelder, May 12, 1866, Ladd and Ladd, eds., *The Bachelder Papers,* vol. 1, pp. 252-253; *OR*, vol. 27, pt. 1, p. 439.

(60) Scott, *Fallen Leaves*, p. 188. The linear measurement of a rod is equivalent to 5.5 yards.

In his official report, written thirteen days after the battle, Abbott corrected his initial misimpression of Macy's orders: "The regiment immediately got orders to face to the right and to file to the right, with the intention of forming a line at right angles with the original one; in other words, changing front to the right." *OR*, vol. 27, pt. 1, p. 445.

(61) Letter of George N. Macy to John Bachelder, May 12, 1866, Ladd and Ladd, eds., *The Bachelder Papers,* vol. 1, p. 253; Wentworth, *Harvard Memorial Biographies*, vol. 2, p. 103; Stewart, *Pickett's Charge*, p. 228.

(62) Bruce, *Twentieth Regiment of Massachusetts Volunteer*, p. 448; *Massa-*

chusetts Soldiers, Sailors and Marines in the Civil War, vol. 2, p. 563; diary of Captain Herbert C. Mason, copy courtesy GNMP. The wound destroyed the range of motion in Mason's left hip joint, and caused his left leg to be two and a half inches shorter than his right. He was discharged for disability on March 23, 1864, and began receiving a pension of $20.00 per month. By the time of his death in September 1884, Mason's pension had been increased to $24.00 per month. Herbert C. Mason pension file, RG 15, NARA.

(63) Letter of George N. Macy to John Bachelder, May 12, 1866, Ladd and Ladd, eds., *The Bachelder Papers,* vol. 1, p. 253.

(64) Rice, "Repelling Lee's Last Blow at Gettysburg," *Battles and Leaders*, vol. 3, p. 388; Arthur F. Devereux *Testimony*, 72nd Penna. vs. GBMA, 296.

In his post-war recollections of the fighting, Major Rice asserted that he was the actual commander of the 19th Massachusetts on July 3, as Colonel Devereux was leading the demi-brigade consisting of the 19th and the 42nd New York, and Lieutenant Colonel Wass was wounded during the cannonade. However, this claim is not substantiated in any of Colonel Devereux's writings.

(65) Rice, "Repelling Lee's Last Blow at Gettysburg," *Battles and Leaders*, vol. 3, p. 389; Edmund Rice to Abner Doubleday, April 19, 1887, BV Doubleday, Abner, Reports of the Battles of Gettysburg, July 1st, 2d and 3d, 1863, New-York Historical Society, New York.

(66) Rice, "Repelling Lee's Last Blow at Gettysburg," *Battles and Leaders*, vol. 3, p. 389.

(67) Edmund Rice to Abner Doubleday, April 19, 1887, BV Doubleday, Abner, Reports of the Battles of Gettysburg, July 1st, 2d and 3d, 1863, New-York Historical Society, New York; Beyer and Keydel, *Deeds of Valor*, p. 235; letter of Edmund Rice to John Bachelder, July 27, 1867, copy courtesy GNMP; Edmund Rice pension file, RG 15, NARA; "Some Account of Pickett's Charge at Gettysburg, Brig. General Arthur F. Devereux," undated, Ladd and Ladd, eds., *The Bachelder Papers,* vol. 3, p. 1882.

Rice remained in this helpless position until the fighting ended, when he was taken to the rear for treatment of his wounds by Union surgeons. At a field hospital behind Union lines, a surgeon recorded Rice's arrival for treatment: "Major Rice came walking down with a flesh wound in the thigh, which he called a 'good joke,' and carrying three Confederate flags." Rice, "Repelling Lee's Last Blow at Gettysburg," *Battles and Leaders*, vol. 3, p. 390; J. Franklin Dyer, *The Journal of a Civil War Surgeon,* Michael B. Chesson, ed. (Lincoln, Nebraska: University of Nebraska Press, 2003), p. 223.

(68) B. T. Arrington, *The Medal of Honor At Gettysburg* (Gettysburg, Penn-

sylvania: Thomas Publications, 1996), p. 36.

The original Medal of Honor application for Edmund Rice was rejected by War Department on July 13, 1891, on the basis that "Edmund Rice was [not] distinguished above several of his comrades for bravery in battle and there seems to be lacking in the case that evidence of specific acts of bravery which would justify the granting of a medal of honor." In response, on August 28, 1891, 43 members of the 19th's Regimental Association sent a petition to the War Department asking for a reconsideration. The veterans stated that their counterattack on July 3 "was without doubt the salvation of the Union Army, and a <u>most vital step</u> in the march to a restored Union. To the daring leadership and magnificent courage of <u>Lt. Col. Rice</u> in that crisis much credit is due for the great success of the movement. . . . Without doubt, [Edmund Rice was] the leading 'man in blue' who penetrated and fell within <u>Pickett's</u> advance [emphasis in original]." On the basis of this petition, the War Department awarded Rice the Medal of Honor. Brief biography of Edmund Rice prepared by Norwich University, 1953. Norwich University Archives and Special Collections, Kreitzberg Library, Northfield, VT.

(69) Letter of Henry N. Hamilton to John Bachelder, April 22, 1864, Ladd and Ladd, eds., *The Bachelder Papers,* vol. 1, p. 179. Some modern-day historians believe that at least part of the 59th New York had fled as the Rebel infantry closed in on the stone fence. Hess, *Pickett's Charge*, p. 230.

(70) Richard F. Miller, "Brahmins Under Fire: Peer Courage and the Harvard Regiment," *Historical Journal of Massachusetts*, XXX (Winter 2002), p. 85; letter of Sumner Paine to "Fanny," May 5, 1863, Sumner Paine Papers, [micofilm], Massachusetts Historical Society.

(71) Richard F. Miller, "The Trouble with Brahmins: Class and Ethnic Tension in Massachusetts' Harvard Regiment," *The New England Quarterly* (March 2003), pp. 38-39; Rice, "Repelling Lee's Last Blow at Gettysburg," p. 389.

(72) Rice, "Repelling Lee's Last Blow at Gettysburg," *Battles and Leaders*, vol. 3, p. 389. Private Bartlett remained in this helpless position for three days, until he was finally discovered and taken to the Union II Corps hospital. He was discharged for disability on September 4, 1863, and began collecting a Federal pension of $2.00 per month. William Bartlett pension file, RG 15, NARA.

(73) Letters of Captain Henry Abbott to Charles C. Paine, July 13, 1863, and July 28, 1863, copies courtesy GNMP.

(74) Letter of Captain Henry Abbott to Charles C. Paine, July 28, 1863, copy courtesy GNMP; Busey, *These Honored Dead*, p. 62. Sumner Paine's family

never attempted to collect a pension after his death.

(75) Waitt, *History of the Nineteenth Massachusetts*, pp. 240-241; *OR*, vol. 27, pt. 1, p. 446; letter of Henry Abbott to John Ropes, August 1, 1863, MOLLUS - Massachusetts Commandery Collection, <u>MS Am 1084</u>. By permission of the Houghton Library, Harvard University; Stewart, *Pickett's Charge*, pp. 236-237.

(76) Charles Curtis pension file, RG 15, NARA; *Massachusetts Soldiers, Sailors and Marines in the Civil War*, vol. 2, p. 524; letter of Elisha Smith to "Father," July 8, 1863, contained in Elisha M. Smith pension file, RG 15, NARA; William Fuchs compiled military service record, RG 94, NARA; extract from General Orders No. 46, July 29, 1863, RG 94, NARA.

Sergeant Curtis, who had been wounded at the Battles of Glendale and Fredericksburg, and would be wounded again at the Battle of Spotsylvania, survived the war but died of heart disease in New York City on May 1, 1868. He left behind a wife and two daughters, who collected a Federal pension of $12.00 per month. Charles Curtis pension file, RG 15, NARA.

Unfortunately, on July 13, 1863, tetanus caused the death of Private Elisha Smith at the Camden Street Hospital in Baltimore, ending forever his dream of owning a commercial fishing business with his brother after the war. His parents later received a United States government pension of $12.00 per month. Elisha M. Smith pension file, RG 15, NARA.

(77) Modern scholarship has determined that between three and eight Southern battle flags were placed in and around Cushing's guns. Richard Rollins, *The Damned Red Flags of the Rebellion* (Redondo Beach, California: Rank and File Publications, 1997), p. 174; Rice, "Repelling Lee's Last Blow at Gettysburg," *Battles and Leaders*, vol. 3, p. 389.

(78) *Massachusetts Soldiers, Sailors and Marines in the Civil War*, vol. 2, p. 442; Daniel Corrigan pension file, RG 15, NARA.

(79) Georg, *Nothing But Glory*, p. 273; Captain Alphonse N. Jones, "Unpublished Report of the 7th Virginia Infantry at Gettysburg dated July 5, 1863," copy courtesy GNMP. The flag of the 7th Virginia was captured by Private Hugh Carey of the 82nd New York. Rollins, *Damned Red Flags of the Rebellion*, p. 160.

(80) Waitt, *History of the Nineteenth Massachusetts*, pp. 241, 380; *Massachusetts Soldiers, Sailors and Marines in the Civil War*, vol. 2, p. 449; Arrington, *The Medal of Honor At Gettysburg*, p. 29.

In a post-war account, Colonel Devereux wrote that Corporal DeCastro, carrying one of the 19th's flags, struck the color-bearer of the 14th Virginia with his own color staff, and then seized the Rebel banner. However, this dramatic account is not substantiated by any other participants, and Joseph DeCastro is not known to have carried either of the regiment's flags at Gettysburg. In fact, in this report, Arthur Devereux is clearly describing the actions of Sergeant Benjamin Jellison in capturing a different Confederate flag, and instead mistakenly referenced Corporal DeCastro. Undated report of Arthur Devereux to John Bachelder, Ladd and Ladd, eds., *The Bachelder Papers,* vol. 3, pp. 1879-1880.

(81) Waitt, *History of the Nineteenth Massachusetts*, pp. 246, 384; *Massachusetts Soldiers, Sailors and Marines in the Civil War*, vol. 2, p. 416; Adams, *Reminiscences of the Nineteenth Massachusetts*, p. 52; Arrington, *The Medal of Honor At Gettysburg*, p. 30; Benjamin F. Falls pension file, RG 15, NARA.

(82) Waitt, *History of the Nineteenth Massachusetts*, pp. 242, 368; *Massachusetts Soldiers, Sailors and Marines in the Civil War*, vol. 2, p. 471; Rollins, *Damned Red Flags of the Rebellion*, p. 229; Gregory A. Coco, *A Vast Sea Of Misery* (Gettysburg, Pennsylvania: Thomas Publications, 1988), p. 63. To add to the mystery, in his official report, Colonel Devereux stated that he felt this flag was "probably" carried to the rear by the wounded Edmund Rice, who then took it home. *OR*, vol. 27, pt. 1, p. 444.

(83) Arrington, *The Medal of Honor At Gettysburg*, p. 37. With five individual Medal of Honor recipients, the 19th Massachusetts had the second highest unit total of any regiment during the Gettysburg campaign. Only the 6th Pennsylvania Reserves (also known as the 35th Pennsylvania Volunteer Infantry Regiment) of the V Corps, with six, had more. Arrington, *The Medal of Honor At Gettysburg*, p. 43.

(84) *Massachusetts Soldiers, Sailors and Marines in the Civil War*, vol. 2, p. 146; letter of A. C. Plaisted to John Bachelder, June 11, 1870, Ladd and Ladd, eds., *The Bachelder Papers,* vol. 1, p. 393; information compiled from a review of numerous pension files of men in the 15th Massachusetts, RG 15, NARA.

(85) Letter of James L. Kemper to John Bachelder, February 4, 1886, Ladd and Ladd, eds., *The Bachelder Papers,* vol. 2, p. 1192; undated report of Arthur Devereux to John Bachelder, Ladd and Ladd, eds., *The Bachelder Papers,* vol. 3, p. 1879.

(86) Coco, *From Ball's Bluff to Gettysburg*, p. 164; letter of A. C. Plaisted to John Bachelder, June 11, 1870, Ladd and Ladd, eds., *The Bachelder Papers,* vol. 1, p. 393; Patrick Murphy pension file, RG 15, NARA. Sergeant Murphy had his left ear completely severed by a saber blow while on detached duty

on a gunboat in February 1862. After his Gettysburg wounding, he remained in military hospitals until his discharge in July 1864, when he began receiving a Federal pension of $8.00 per month. For the rest of his life, he never regained the use of his right arm, coughed badly and constantly spit up blood from his damaged lungs. Patrick Murphy died in the National Home for Disabled Soldiers in Danville, Illinois, in July 1910. Patrick Murphy pension file, RG 15, NARA.

(87) Waitt, *History of the Nineteenth Massachusetts*, pp. 242-243, 247, 381; *Massachusetts Soldiers, Sailors and Marines in the Civil War*, vol. 2, p. 482.

After the fighting ended, Donath was temporarily buried on Peter Frey's farm, located on the Taneytown Road. On July 24, 1863, he was reinterred in Plot 270, Section C, of the Evergreen Cemetery by Elizabeth Thorn, the cemetery superintendent's wife. Why Donath's body was moved, who moved it and who paid for the cost of the plot is unknown. Busey, *These Honored Dead*, p. 60; Brian Kennell, *Beyond the Gatehouse - Gettysburg's Evergreen Cemetery* (Gettysburg, Pennsylvania: Evergreen Cemetery Association, 2000), p. 33; Evergreen Cemetery Burial Permit Record, copy courtesy Brian Kennell. The pension records at the National Archives show no evidence that Lieutenant Donath's family ever filed for survivors' benefits from the Federal government.

(88) Beyer and Keydel, *Deeds of Valor*, p. 236. It is unclear from reading the various post-war accounts if Jellison was still carrying the 19th's United States flag that he had picked up on July 2 or if it was initially in Lieutenant Shackley's possession, and then Jellison seized the colors again after Shackley was wounded.

(89) Rollins, *Damned Red Flags of the Rebellion*, p. 176; "19 Mass Vols.," Ladd and Ladd, eds., *The Bachelder Papers,* vol. 3, p. 1991; Arrington, *The Medal of Honor At Gettysburg*, p. 30.

Arthur Devereux later stated that a fifth Confederate banner was presented to him as a trophy by a sergeant of his regiment after the fighting ended. However, Colonel Devereux then gave this flag to General Webb of the neighboring "Philadelphia Brigade," as Webb informed the colonel that his men had captured the flag, and Webb had temporarily given it to the 19th's sergeant for "safekeeping." The identity of the sergeant, and of the banner itself, is unknown. *OR*, vol. 27, pt. 1, p. 444.

(90) Arthur F. Devereux *Testimony*, 72nd Penna. vs. GBMA, 296.

(91) Johnston Acheson pension file, RG 15, NARA; *Massachusetts Soldiers, Sailors and Marines in the Civil War*, vol. 2, p. 450; William Gibbons pen-

sion file, RG 15, NARA.

(92) Arthur F. Devereux *Testimony*, 72nd Penna. vs. GBMA, 296; William A. Hill *Testimony*, 72nd Penna. vs. GBMA, 344.

William A. Hill, only 5′ 4″ tall, had enlisted in the 19th Massachusetts in February 1862. In August 1862, while on a march to Newport News, Virginia, Hill suffered such a severe sunstroke that he could hardly speak for several days. Colonel Devereux then made him adjutant of the regiment, so that he could ride a horse rather than march and thus remain with the unit. Adams, *Reminiscences of the Nineteenth Massachusetts*, p. 40; William A. Hill pension file, RG 15, NARA.

(93) Letter of A. C. Plaisted to John Bachelder, June 11, 1870, Ladd and Ladd, eds., *The Bachelder Papers,* vol. 1, p. 393.

(94) Arthur F. Devereux, "Some Account of Pickett's Charge at Gettysburg," *Magazine of American History*, XVIII (1887), p. 19.

(95) Waitt, *History of the Nineteenth Massachusetts*, p. 244; Hess, *Pickett's Charge*, pp. 276, 280.

(96) Waitt, *History of the Nineteenth Massachusetts*, p. 250; *Massachusetts Soldiers, Sailors and Marines in the Civil War*, vol. 2, p. 484.

The ball was removed some nine inches from its point of entrance. Sergeant McGinnis survived his wound and later returned to duty with the regiment. He was discharged in May 1865 and began receiving a United States government pension of $6.00 per month. William McGinnis died in Boston in December 1896, still suffering from the effects of his wound. William A. McGinnis pension file, RG 15, NARA.

(97) Letter of A. C. Plaisted to John Bachelder, June 11, 1870, Ladd and Ladd, eds., *The Bachelder Papers,* vol. 1, p. 393.

(98) Waitt, *History of the Nineteenth Massachusetts*, p. 250; Busey, *These Honored Dead*, p. 60. Sergeant Hervey's mother, Jane, collected a Federal pension of $8.00 per month, in compensation for losing her only son. Joseph H. Hervey pension file, RG 15, NARA.

(99) Letter of Andrew Cowan to John Bachelder, December 2, 1885, Ladd and Ladd, eds., *The Bachelder Papers,* vol. 2, p. 1156.

(100) Stewart, *Pickett's Charge*, p. 235; William A. Hill *Testimony*, 72nd Penna. vs. GBMA, 345-346.

(101) Waitt, *History of the Nineteenth Massachusetts*, p. 243.

(102) Albert Everett, "Harrow's Brigade at Gettysburg," unpublished manuscript, p. 7. From the Collections of Worcester Historical Museum, Worcester, MA; Ford, *Fifteenth Regiment Massachusetts Volunteers*, pp. 366, 393.

There is no evidence that any member of Corporal Fletcher's family ever filed for a pension after his death.

(103) Miller and Mooney, *The Civil War: The Nantucket Experience*, pp. 186-187.

According to an item in an 1863 Nantucket newspaper, the sword that Summerhayes picked up was being displayed in his father's photography shop in Nantucket, and was advertised as belonging to General Garnett. Many years after the war, Garnett's sword turned up in a "second-hand shop" in Baltimore, Maryland, where it was purchased by former Confederate General George H. Steuart, who had also fought with the Army of Northern Virginia at Gettysburg. When General Steuart died in 1903, his nephew returned the sword to Garnett's relatives in Richmond, Virginia. The sword is now held in the collections of the Museum of the Confederacy.

Also of note is the fact that on June 1, 1862, John Summerhayes, then with the rank of sergeant, was credited with the capture of Confederate General J. Johnston Pettigrew during the Battle of Seven Pines. Pettigrew's pistols were also sent by Summerhayes for display in his father's shop. Correspondence of Richard F. Miller to authors, April 5, 2002; Winfield Peters, "The Lost Sword of Gen. Richard B. Garnett, Who Fell at Gettysburg," in *Southern Historical Society Papers*, 52 vols. and 2 vol. index, ed. J. William Jones and others (1876-1959; reprint, Wilmington, North Carolina: Broadfoot Publishing, 1990-92), 33: 26-27; Robert K. Krick, "Armistead and Garnett: The Parallel Lives of Two Virginia Soldiers," in Gary W. Gallagher, ed., *The Third Day at Gettysburg & Beyond* (Chapel Hill, North Carolina: University of North Carolina Press, 1994), p. 123; Miller and Mooney, *The Civil War: The Nantucket Experience*, p. 187.

(104) Arthur F. Devereux *Testimony*, 72nd Penna. vs. GBMA, 301; Colonel Arthur F. Devereux, "Unpublished Report," p. 4, copy courtesy GNMP.

(105) Waitt, *History of the Nineteenth Massachusetts*, p. 245; *OR*, vol. 27, pt. 1, p. 423.

Chapter 3

(1) Rhodes, *History of Battery B, First Rhode Island Artillery*, p. 213.

(2) Scott, *Fallen Leaves*, p. 188.

(3) George A. Bowen, "The Diary of Captain George A. Bowen 12th Regiment New Jersey Volunteers," *The Valley Forge Journal*, vol. II, no. 2 (December 1984), p. 134.

(4) James I. Sale, "Pickett's Charge," *The Philadelphia Weekly Press* (4 July 1887), p. 1.

(5) *OR*, vol. 27, pt. 1, p. 176; Busey, These *Honored Dead*, pp. 57-59; Elisha G. Buss pension file, RG 15, NARA.

(6) Waitt, *History of the Nineteenth Massachusetts*, pp. 245, 247; letter of William B. Hoitt to "Friend Mary," July 13, 1863, copy courtesy GNMP.

(7) *OR*, vol. 27, pt. 1, p. 176.

(8) Busey, *These Honored Dead*, p. 60; Waitt, *History of the Nineteenth Massachusetts*, p. 249. In 1890, 71-year-old John Johnson, father of Charles Johnson, began receiving a Federal pension of $12.00 per month. However, there is no indication that any relatives of Daniel Reardon ever filed for a pension. Charles A. Johnson pension file, RG 15, NARA; Daniel F. Reardon compiled military service record, RG 94, NARA.

(9) *OR*, vol. 27, pt. 1, p. 444. Nichols, who was 5' 4" tall, was a pre-war sailor who had been born in Brunswick, Maine. He remained absent from the 19th until August 22, 1863. However, the regimental records show that after his return to the unit, the youthful Corporal Nichols redeemed himself by his soldierly conduct for the remainder of the war. He reenlisted as a Veteran Volunteer on December 21, 1863, was subsequently promoted to the rank of sergeant and fought in all the battles the regiment was engaged in for the balance of the war. Sergeant Nichols suffered a wound to his left wrist at the Battle of Spotsylvania on May 10, 1864, and was later taken prisoner on October 27, 1864, during the Petersburg Campaign. He escaped in February 1865 and made his way back to Union lines. Nichols was mustered out on June 30, 1865. On November 16, 1869, he died of consumption at the National Asylum for Disabled Volunteer Soldiers in Augusta, Maine. Waitt, *History of the Nineteenth Massachusetts*, pp. 323, 403; *Massachusetts Soldiers, Sailors and Marines in the Civil War*, vol. 2, p. 433; E. Augustus Nichols pension file, RG 15, NARA.

(10) *OR*, vol. 27, pt 1, p. 176.

A review of the pension records at the National Archives reveals that one man listed as missing in the regiment, 19-year-old Private William Barrett of Company I, a Nantucket farmer, was wounded and captured in the fighting on July 3. After a three-month stay in Confederate prisons, Barrett was paroled on September 29, 1863, and returned to duty. *Massachusetts Soldiers, Sailors and Marines in the Civil War*, vol. 2, p. 568; William Barrett pension file, RG 15, NARA.

(11) Bruce, *Twentieth Regiment of Massachusetts Volunteers*, pp. 297-298;

Busey, *These Honored Dead*, pp. 61-63; George Cate pension file, RG 15, NARA; Leonard Harrington pension file, RG 15, NARA; Regimental Papers of the 20th Massachusetts Infantry Regiment, RG 94, NARA; *Massachusetts Soldiers, Sailors and Marines in the Civil War*, vol. 2, pp. 497, 499.

Sergeant Cate, who was single, left behind a widowed mother to collect an $8.00 per month Federal pension. Private Harrington died in a hospital in Washington on March 2, 1864. He was survived by a wife and four minor children. It took until December 1864 for his family to finally learn Harrington's fate and begin collecting a $16.00 per month United States government pension. George Cate pension file, RG 15, NARA; Leonard Harrington pension file, RG 15, NARA.

(12) Letter of Surgeon Nathan Hayward of the 20th Massachusetts to "Father," July 8, 1863, copy courtesy GNMP; *Massachusetts Soldiers, Sailors and Marines in the Civil War*, vol. 2, p. 501; Scott, *Fallen Leaves*, p. 184.

(13) Ford, *Fifteenth Regiment Massachusetts Volunteers*, p. 355; Coco, *From Ball's Bluff to Gettysburg*, p. 200; John Marsh, Jr., pension file, RG 15, NARA; Busey, *These Honored Dead*, p. 58.

(14) Busey, *These Honored Dead*, p. 57; Ford, *Fifteenth Regiment Massachusetts Volunteers*, p. 379; *Massachusetts Soldiers, Sailors and Marines in the Civil War*, vol. 2, p. 170; Henry C. Ball pension file, RG 15, NARA.

(15) Ford, *Fifteenth Regiment Massachusetts Volunteers*, p. 363; Alexander Lord pension file, RG 15, NARA.

(16) Waitt, *History of the Nineteenth Massachusetts*, p. 382; *Massachusetts Soldiers, Sailors and Marines in the Civil War*, vol. 2, p. 442; Thomas Doyle pension file, RG 15, NARA.

(17) Busey, *These Honored Dead*, p. 60; Thomas Tuttle Jr, pension file, RG 15, NARA; *Massachusetts Soldiers, Sailors and Marines in the Civil War*, vol. 2, p. 480.

(18) Bruce, *Twentieth Massachusetts Volunteers*, p. 465; Busey, *These Honored Dead*, p. 61; *Massachusetts Soldiers, Sailors and Marines in the Civil War*, vol. 2, p. 515; August Duttling pension file, RG 15, NARA; *Report of the Select Committee Relative to the Soldiers' National Cemetery* (Commonwealth of Pennsylvania, 1865), p. 49.

(19) Busey, *These Honored Dead*, p. 63; Michael Kennarick pension file, RG 15, NARA.

(20) Bruce, *Twentieth Regiment Massachusetts Volunteers*, p. 484; Patrick Quinlan pension file, RG 15, NARA; Busey, *These Honored Dead*, p. 62.

(21) Sergeant George Joeckel now lies in Grave A-12 of the Massachusetts

plot. Busey, *These Honored Dead*, p. 61; *Massachusetts Soldiers, Sailors and Marines in the Civil War*, vol. 2, p. 507; George Joeckel pension file, RG 15, NARA.

(22) Charles Murray pension file, RG 15, NARA; Barnes, *The Medical and Surgical History of the Civil War,* vol. 4, p. 533.

(23) David Welch pension file, RG 15, NARA.

(24) William Moore pension file, RG 15, NARA.

(25) Joseph Matthews pension file, RG 15, NARA; statement contained in James Tenney pension file, RG 15, NARA.

(26) *Massachusetts Soldiers, Sailors and Marines in the Civil War*, vol. 2, p. 192; Thomas Henry pension file, RG 15, NARA.

(27) Adams, *Reminiscences of the Nineteenth Massachusetts*, pp. 69-72.

Despite being captured on June 22, 1864, and held for several months in terrible conditions in Confederate prisons, Adams survived the rest of the war and returned to civilian life.

On December 16, 1896, he was awarded a Congressional Medal of Honor for his gallantry at the Battle of Fredericksburg. Adams did file for and receive a Federal disability pension, but unfortunately, his file at the National Archives has been lost. Waitt, *History of the Nineteenth Massachusetts*, p. 334; Beyer and Keydel, *Deeds of Valor*, pp. 110-111; George Lang, Raymond Collins and Gerard F. White, comps., *Medal of Honor Recipients, 1863 - 1994*, 2 vols. (New York, New York: Facts on File, Inc., 1995), vol. 1, p. 1.

(28) Waitt, *History of the Nineteenth Massachusetts*, p. 388; *Massachusetts Soldiers, Sailors and Marines in the Civil War*, vol. 2, p. 476; George P. Ham pension file, RG 15, NARA.

(29) Stephen Armitage pension file, RG 15, NARA.

(30) William Edwards pension file, RG 15, NARA.

(31) William B. Parker pension file, RG 15, NARA; Barnes, *The Medical and Surgical History of the Civil War,* vol. 4, p. 627.

(32) James F. Goulding pension file, RG 15, NARA.

(33) Lusher White pension file, RG 15, NARA; Anna M. E. Holstein, *Three Years in Field Hospitals of the Army of the Potomac* (Philadelphia, Pennsylvania: J. B. Lippincott & Co., 1867), pp. 41-42.

(34) Patrick Manning pension file, RG 15, NARA; Barnes, *Medical and Surgical History of the Civil War,* vol. 4, p. 970; Busey, *These Honored Dead,* p. 62.

(35) *Massachusetts Soldiers, Sailors and Marines in the Civil War*, vol. 2, p. 503; Thomas Tiernan pension file, RG 15, NARA.

(36) Arthur Hughes pension file, RG 15, NARA.

(37) *Massachusetts Soldiers, Sailors and Marines in the Civil War*, vol. 2, p. 584; Edward Murphy pension file, RG 15, NARA.

(38) Georg, *Nothing But Glory*, pp. 512-513.

(39) A full discussion of how far Pickett himself advanced in the attack is found in Georg, *Nothing But Glory*, pp. 194-205.

(40) Brigadier General Richard Garnett was shot off his horse and killed just west of the Union battle line behind the stone wall on Cemetery Ridge, near the Copse of Trees. His body was never found and he was probably buried in a mass grave with many others from his division. As stated above, Brigadier General Lewis Armistead led a charge over the Union breastworks. He was mortally wounded near one of Cushing's guns and died in Federal hands on July 5,1863. Brigadier General James Kemper was shot in the groin near the Union line, so close that Kemper later wrote, ". . . I was then near enough to the enemy's line to observe the features and expressions on the faces of the men in front of me, and I thought I observed and could identify the soldier who shot me." Left behind in the retreat of Lee's army and captured, Kemper survived his wound, which was originally thought to be mortal; after his exchange, he was never again fit for active field service. Georg, *Nothing But Glory*, pp. 120-121, 171-176, 186; letter of James L. Kemper to John Bachelder, February 4, 1886, Ladd and Ladd, eds., *The Bachelder Papers,* vol. 2, p. 1192.

(41) Jeffry D. Wert, *Gettysburg Day Three* (New York, New York: Simon & Schuster, 2001), pp. 291-292.

(42) Georg, *Nothing But Glory*, pp. 529-533.

(43) Waitt, *History of the Nineteenth Massachusetts*, pp. 249, 381; *Massachusetts Soldiers, Sailors and Marines in the Civil War*, vol. 2, p. 442; letter of Cornelius Linehan to "Father," July 17, 1863, copy courtesy GNMP.

Doherty's widow, Anastasia, who was illiterate, and 9-year-old daughter, Ann, collected a pension of $10.00 per month from the Federal government. Doherty himself rests in an unknown grave, most probably at the Richmond National Cemetery. John Doherty pension file, RG 15, NARA; correspondence of Robert E. L. Krick, historian, Richmond National Battlefield, to authors May 15, 2004.

One man of the 15th Massachusetts, 21-year-old Corporal Warren H. Alger of Company D, a machinist from Worcester, was captured on July 2, in the fighting near the Emmitsburg Road. The regimental records show that Alger was released from Confederate captivity sometime prior to February 1864, when he reenlisted as a Veteran Volunteer. On June 22, 1864, in combat outside Petersburg, Virginia, Corporal Alger was again taken prisoner. This time he was not so fortunate, as he later died in Andersonville on August 14, 1864. His widow, Emma, received a Federal pension of $8.00 per month until her death in 1871. *Massachusetts Soldiers, Sailors and Marines in the Civil War*, vol. 2, p. 145; Warren Alger pension file, RG 15, NARA.

(44) Charles Brown pension file, RG 15, NARA.

(45) Bruce, *Twentieth Regiment of Massachusetts Volunteers*, p. 482.

Chapter 4

(1) Major General George G. Meade "Report from Headquarters Army of the Potomac," *OR*, vol. 27, pt. 1, p. 118.

(2) *OR*, vol. 29, pt. 1, pp. 280, 679.

(3) Ford, *Fifteenth Regiment Massachusetts Volunteers,* pp. 306, 311.

(4) *OR*, vol. 29, pt. 1, pp. 249, 680.

(5) Bruce, *Twentieth Regiment of Massachusetts Volunteers*, p. 315; *OR*, vol. 29, pt. 1, p. 680.

(6) Waitt, *History of the Nineteenth Massachusetts*, p. 283.

(7) James M. McPherson, *Battle Cry Of Freedom: The Civil War Era* (New York, New York: Ballantine Books, 1988), pp. 719-720.

(8) Ford, *Fifteenth Regiment Massachusetts Volunteers,* pp. 318-319. The actual final tally of veterans who reenlisted from the ranks of the 15th Massachusetts was 64. James L. Bowen, *Massachusetts in the War* (Springfield, Massachusetts: Bowen & Son, 1893), p. 261.

(9) Waitt, *History of the Nineteenth Massachusetts*, pp. 282, 284; Adams, *Reminiscences of the Nineteenth Massachusetts*, p. 80.

(10) According to a post-war calculation, 173 men of the 20th Massachusetts reenlisted as Veteran Volunteers prior to May 1864. Bowen, *Massachusetts in the War,* p. 321; Bruce, *Twentieth Regiment of Massachusetts Volunteers*, pp. 329-330.

(11) Ford, *Fifteenth Regiment Massachusetts Volunteers,* p. 317; Waitt, *History of the Nineteenth Massachusetts*, p. 302; Bruce, *Twentieth Regiment of Massachusetts Volunteers*, pp. 329-330; Scott, *Fallen Leaves*, p. 244.

(12) The records indicate that on January 14, 1864, Shackley enlisted in the 59th Massachusetts Volunteer Infantry Regiment with the rank of sergeant. Unfortunately, he was mortally wounded in the abdomen during the Battle of Spotsylvania and died on May 13. No relatives of Moses Shackley ever filed

for a Federal pension after his death. Moses Shackley compiled military service record, RG 94, NARA; Moses Shackley file folder in RG 153, NARA,
copy courtesy The Index Project, Inc.

(13) Waitt, *History of the Nineteenth Massachusetts*, p. 300.

(14) *Battles and Leaders of the Civil War,* vol. 4, p. 179; *Massachusetts Sol-
diers, Sailors and Marines in the Civil War*, p. 199; Ford, *Fifteenth Regiment
Massachusetts Volunteers*, p. 38; Waitt, *History of the Nineteenth Massachu-
setts*, p. 300; Arthur F. Devereux pension file, RG 15, NARA; Bruce, *Twentieth
Regiment of Massachusetts Volunteers*, p. 353; Miller and Mooney, *The Civil
War: The Nantucket Experience*, p. 167.

(15) Ford, *Fifteenth Regiment Massachusetts Volunteers*, p. 325; Waitt, *History of the Nineteenth Massachusetts*, p. 300.

(16) See Bruce, *Twentieth Regiment of Massachusetts Volunteers*, pp. 379-
382 for a listing of the regimental casualties incurred from May 5, 1864, to
May 17, 1864; John M. Priest, *Victory Without Triumph* (Shippensburg, Pennsylvania: The White Mane Publishing Company, Inc., 1996), p. 233.

(17) William F. Perkins pension file, RG 15, NARA.

After the war, William Perkins moved to New Orleans, where he worked
in a law firm. He never fully recovered from his severe wound and wore his
partially paralyzed left arm in a sling. He was also plagued by a chronic
cough, had difficulty swallowing, and had "the appearance generally of a
nervous, broken-down man." William Perkins died of consumption in New
Orleans in January 1876, leaving behind his widow, Anna, and two young
children, who collected a Federal pension of $24.00 per month. William
Perkins pension file, RG 15, NARA.

(18) Miller and Mooney, *The Civil War: The Nantucket Experience*, p. 99.

(19) Miller and Mooney, *The Civil War: The Nantucket Experience*, p. 168;
Scott, *Fallen Leaves*, pp. 250-254; *OR*, vol. 36, pt. 2, pp. 438-439; Henry L.
Abbott compiled military service record, RG 94, NARA; Martha A. Perry,
comp., *Letters from a Surgeon of the Civil War* (Cambridge, Massachusetts:
Little, Brown and Company, 1906), pp. 171-172. Abbott's family never ap-
plied for a Federal pension.

(20) Fox, *Regimental Losses*, pp. 161, 164.

(21) Waitt, *History of the Nineteenth Massachusetts*, pp. 308, 322-324.

Falls' company commander later wrote, "No man in the ranks of the Union
army rendered better service than Benj. F. Falls. Always ready for duty, ever
cheerful, his influence for good extended through the regiment." His body
was returned home and buried in the Pine Grove Cemetery in Lynn. After his

death, Falls' wife and two children received a pension of $12.00 per month. Adams, *Reminiscences of the Nineteenth Massachusetts*, p. 89; Lang, Collins and White, comps., *Medal of Honor Recipients, 1863 - 1994*, vol. 1, p. 407; Benjamin F. Falls pension file, RG 15, NARA.

Lieutenant Colonel Rice escaped Rebel captivity and was back in command of the 19th by early August 1864. Waitt, *History of the Nineteenth Massachusetts*, p. 344.

(22) Ford, *Fifteenth Regiment Massachusetts Volunteers*, p. 331; Waitt, *History of the Nineteenth Massachusetts*, pp. 322, 324-325; Fox, *Regimental Losses*, p. 164.

(23) Ford, *Fifteenth Regiment Massachusetts Volunteers*, p. 332; Fox, *Regimental Losses*, p. 161; Waitt, *History of the Nineteenth Massachusetts*, pp. 322, 324-325; Benjamin H. Jellison pension file, RG 15, NARA.

(24) Bruce, *Twentieth Regiment of Massachusetts Volunteers*, pp. 400-401; Fox, *Regimental Losses*, p. 164; Miller and Mooney, *The Civil War: The Nantucket Experience*, p. 187.

John Summerhayes was discharged on June 5, 1865. In 1867, he enlisted as a second lieutenant in the 33rd United States Infantry Regiment and remained in the regular army for 33 years. Summerhayes resigned in 1900, after having a "general nervous breakdown." He died of heart failure in March 1911, and was buried in Arlington National Cemetery. Miller and Mooney, *The Civil War: The Nantucket Experience*, pp. 187-188; John Summerhayes pension file, RG 15, NARA.

(25) *Massachusetts Soldiers, Sailors and Marines in the Civil War*, vol. 2, p. 321; Waitt, *History of the Nineteenth Massachusetts*, pp. 320, 326.

(26) Noah Andre Trudeau, *The Last Citadel: Petersburg, Virginia, June 1864-April 1865* (Boston, Massachusetts: Little, Brown and Company, 1991), pp. 64-79.

(27) Ford, *Fifteenth Regiment Massachusetts Volunteers*, pp. 334-335; Trudeau, *The Last Citadel*, p. 72.

(28) Waitt, *History of the Nineteenth Massachusetts*, pp. 326-328; John Robinson pension file, RG 15, NARA.

(29) Bruce, *Twentieth Regiment of Massachusetts Volunteers*, pp. 408-409.

(30) Ford, *Fifteenth Regiment Massachusetts Volunteers*, pp. 340-341; Waitt, *History of the Nineteenth Massachusetts*, pp. 328-332.

(31) John Talbott, "Combat Trauma in the American Civil War," *History Today*, vol. 46, no. 13, (March 1996), p. 44.

(32) Wentworth, *Harvard Memorial Biographies*, vol. 1, pp. 462-463.

(33) Ford, *Fifteenth Regiment Massachusetts Volunteers*, pp. 341-343.

(34) Waitt, *History of the Nineteenth Massachusetts*, pp. 363-365; Bruce, *Twentieth Regiment of Massachusetts Volunteers*, pp. 440-441.

(35) Waitt, *History of the Nineteenth Massachusetts*, p. 367.

(36) Waitt, *History of the Nineteenth Massachusetts*, p. 367; Bruce, *Twentieth Regiment of Massachusetts Volunteers*, p. 441.

Chapter 5

(1) Leonard Harrington pension file, RG 15, NARA.

(2) Ford, *War Letters 1862-1865*, p. 240; *Massachusetts Soldiers, Sailors and Marines in the Civil War*, vol. 2, p. 573.

(3) Ford, *War Letters 1862- 1865*, p. 240.

(4) Captain Herbert Mason of the 20th's Company C had taken the shell fragment that killed Henry Ropes. It was already in the possession of his bereaved brother within two weeks of his death. Ford, *War Letters 1862-1865*, pp. 149, 240-241.

John Ropes was born in Russia in 1836 while his father, a prominent businessman, was pursuing financial interests in St. Petersburg. As a youth, he was stricken with a spinal defect which evolved into a chronic condition. However, he graduated from Harvard University in 1857 and became a successful lawyer. During the war, he grew close to the members of the 20th Massachusetts through their association with his brother. Although he gathered much information about the unit, he never wrote its regimental history. After the Civil War, Ropes established the Military Historical Society of Massachusetts. John Ropes passed away in 1899, leaving undone his partially written history of the Civil War. http://1911encyclopedia.org/index.htm, the 1911 Edition Encyclopedia.

(5) *Report of the Select Committee Relative to the Soldiers' National Cemetery*, p. iii. During the Gettysburg campaign, David McConaughy organized a group of local residents who helped keep the Federal forces apprised of Confederate activities prior to the battle. Stephen W. Sears, *Gettysburg* (New York, New York: Houghton Mifflin Company, 2003), pp. 118, 141, 511.

(6) Kathleen R. Georg, *"This Grand National Enterprise,"* The Origins of Gettysburg's Soldiers' National Cemetery & Gettysburg Battlefield, Battlefield Memorial Association. May 1982, p. 8, copy courtesy GNMP.

(7) *Report of the Select Committee Relative to the Soldiers' National Cemetery*, p. iii; Kathleen R. Georg, *"A Fitting And Expressive Memorial,"* The Develop-

ment of Gettysburg National Military Park. January 1988, p. 1, copy courtesy GNMP.

(8) Vanderslice, *Gettysburg Then And Now*, p. 19.

(9) Richard A. Sauers, "John B. Bachelder: Government Historian of the Battle of Gettysburg," *The Gettysburg Magazine*, no. 3, July 1990, pp. 116-117.

(10) Barbara L. Platt, *"This is holy ground," A history of the Gettysburg Battlefield* (Harrisburg, Pennsylvania: Barbara L. Platt, 2001), p. 5.

(11) Vanderslice, *Gettysburg Then And Now*, pp. 360-361.

(12) Frederick W. Hawthorne, *Gettysburg: Stories of Men And Monuments As Told By Battlefield Guides* (Gettysburg, Pennsylvania: the Association of Licensed Battlefield Guides, 1988), p. 7.

(13) Platt, *"This is holy ground,"* p. 6.

(14) William A. Frassanito, *Early Photography at Gettysburg* (Gettysburg, Pennsylvania: Thomas Publications, 1995), pp. 234, 239-240; William A. Frassanito, *Gettysburg: Then & Now, Touring The Battlefield With Old Photographs, 1863-1889* (Gettysburg, Pennsylvania: Thomas Publications, 1996), p. 43.

For more information about the photographic history of the Copse of Trees, Bachelder's role in recognizing its importance and an analysis of its early neglect, see Frassanito, *Early Photography at Gettysburg,* pp. 234-240.

(15) Patricia L. Faust, *Historical Times Illustrated Encyclopedia of the Civil War* (New York, New York: Harper & Row, 1986), pp. 317-318.

(16) Vanderslice, *Gettysburg Then And Now*, p. 368; *Star and Sentinel*, Gettysburg, Pennsylvania, August 15, 1883.

(17) Vanderslice, *Gettysburg Then And Now*, pp. 367-368; *Star and Sentinel*, August 15, 1883.

(18) Minute Book Gettysburg Battlefield Memorial Association, 1872-1895, transcribed by Kathleen R. Georg, September 1982, minutes of June 21, 1880 and June 26, 1882, copy courtesy GNMP.

(19) Henry Harrison Bingham was born in Philadelphia in 1841. He enlisted in the Union army on August 22, 1862, with the rank of first lieutenant in the 140th Pennsylvania Volunteer Infantry Regiment. At the Battle of Gettysburg, he served as a captain on General Hancock's staff. He later received the Congressional Medal of Honor for actions that took place during the Battle of the Wilderness. After the war, Bingham was first elected to the United States Congress in 1879, and served 17 terms until his death in 1912. Henry Bingham is best remembered for aiding Confederate General Lewis Armistead after he had been mortally wounded leading his men over the stone wall on

July 3, 1863. Captain Bingham is preserved for immortality with General Armistead on the "Friend to Friend" monument in the National Cemetery Annex. Wert, *Gettysburg Day Three*, pp. 246-247; Henry Harrison Bingham biographical information, http://bioguide.congress.gov, The Biographical Directory of the United States Congress 1774-Present.

(20) *Compiler*, Gettysburg, Pennsylvania, March 11, 1880.

(21) *Compiler*, July 13, 1881.

(22) Platt, *"This is holy ground,"* p. 6; *Compiler*, July 12, 1882; Minute Book Gettysburg Battlefield Memorial Association, 1872-1895, minutes of November 4, 1887.

(23) Even by 1899, the Gettysburg National Park Commission only owned a narrow piece of land 100 feet wide, which encompassed Hancock Avenue itself and approximately 40 feet of ground on each side. Large portions of the battlefield were still privately owned and it was necessary to obtain the owners' consent before touring this land. Benjamin Y. Dixon, *The Gettysburg Battlefield, One Century Ago* (Gettysburg, Pennsylvania: Adams County History, Adams County Historical Society, 2000), p. 22.

(24) *Compiler*, July 12, 1882.

(25) Gettysburg and Harrisburg Railroad Company, *To Gettysburg By Train* (Gettysburg, Pennsylvania: Thomas Publications, 1988), unpaginated introduction; *Star and Sentinel*, September 19, 1883, September 26, 1883, and November 7, 1883.

(26) *Star and Sentinel*, February 5, 1884, and April 1, 1884; Gettysburg and Harrisburg Railroad Company, *To Gettysburg By Train*, unpaginated.

(27) Gettysburg and Harrisburg Railroad Company, *To Gettysburg By Train*, unpaginated.

(28) Gettysburg and Harrisburg Railroad Company, *To Gettysburg By Train*, unpaginated; *Star and Sentinel*, September 20, 1882, April 22, 1884 and May 6, 1884.

(29) Gettysburg and Harrisburg Railroad Company, *To Gettysburg By Train*, unpaginated.

(30) Vanderslice, *Gettysburg Then And Now*, pp. 371-372; *Star and Sentinel*, July 11, 1883, August 15, 1883 and October 24, 1883.

(31) *Star and Sentinel*, May 2, 1883, August 22, 1883 and August 27, 1883.

(32) *Compiler*, October 24, 1883; *Star and Sentinel*, October 24, 1883, and October 31, 1883; David M. Earle, *History of the Excursion of the Fifteenth Massachusetts Regiment and its Friends to the Battle-fields of Gettysburg, PA., Antietam, MD., Balls Bluff, Virginia, and Washington, D.C. May 31 -*

June 12, 1886, p. 4

(33) Ford, *Fifteenth Regiment Massachusetts Volunteers*, pp. 280, 365; Patrick Murphy pension file, RG 15, NARA.

Henry T. Dudley was a 20-year-old machinist from Sutton, Massachusetts, when he enlisted in Company G of the 15th on July 12, 1861. Promoted to sergeant in December 1862, he was quickly advanced in rank to lieutenant in January 1863, and was subsequently assigned to Company A in April of that year. Dudley was wounded in the leg at Antietam, side at Gettysburg, knee during the Battle of the Wilderness and leg at Second Deep Bottom. He was taken prisoner on August 25, 1864, at the Battle of Reams' Station while serving with the 20th Massachusetts. After his release from captivity, Dudley left the army with the rank of captain on March 25, 1865. Ford, *Fifteenth Regiment Massachusetts Volunteers*, pp. 345, 386.

David Earle was an integral part of the 15th's entire history from the time of his enlistment on July 12, 1861, and on into the twentieth century. During his service with the regiment, he suffered two gunshot wounds at the Battle of Antietam, and returned to duty on November 20, 1862. He remained with the unit, except for a period of recruiting duty, until his discharge on July 28, 1864. After the war, he wrote the history of the 1886 regimental battlefield excursion, organized the 1898 excursion and worked on the organizing committee for the 1900 excursion. Earle also served the regimental association in various capacities, including as its president. He lived until 1917, by which time he was receiving a monthly pension of $30.00 per month. David Earle pension file, RG 15, NARA; 15th Regiment Association Record Book. From the Collections of Worcester Historical Museum, Worcester, MA.

Enlisting as a sergeant in Company D on July 12, 1861, Thomas Hastings was subsequently captured at the Battle of Ball's Bluff, and spent some time in Confederate prison. Hastings was again taken prisoner, with most of the regiment, before Petersburg on June 22, 1864. He was not paroled until March 1, 1865. After the war, Hastings' initial pension of $8.50 per month began almost immediately, as he suffered from malarial poisoning and general debility. His pension had increased to $17.00 per month by August 1881. Thomas Hastings pension file, RG 15, NARA.

(34) *Compiler*, October 24, 1883; Earle, *History of the Excursion of the Fifteenth Massachusetts Regiment and its Friends*, p. 4; Ford, *Fifteenth Regiment Massachusetts Volunteers*, pp. 361, 366-367.

(35) Ford, *Fifteenth Regiment Massachusetts Volunteers* , p. 367.

(36) *Star and Sentinel*, October 31, 1883.

John Krauth was born in Gettysburg on March 3, 1846. During the war, he served in Company A of the 26th Regiment of Pennsylvania Militia from June 9 to June 30, 1863, and then in the United States Signal Corps from March 28, 1864, to August 28, 1865. After the war, he became a lawyer after studying under local attorney David McConaughy. Krauth served as secretary of the Gettysburg Battlefield Memorial Association from 1872 until his death on May 10, 1890. *Star and Sentinel*, May 13, 1890; Vanderslice, *Gettysburg Then And Now*, p. 392; Minute Book, Gettysburg Battlefield Memorial Association, 1872-1895, minutes of September 3, 1890.

(37) *Star and Sentinel*, October 31, 1883.

Colonel Charles H. Buehler was born in 1825 and became associated with the Gettysburg Battlefield Memorial Association in 1880. He served as vice president from 1887 until his death in 1896. During the Civil War, he held the rank of captain in the three-month 2nd Pennsylvania Volunteer Infantry Regiment in 1861, became a major in the 87th Pennsylvania Volunteer Infantry Regiment in 1862 and was promoted to the rank of colonel in the nine-month 165th Pennsylvania Volunteer Infantry Regiment in December 1862. At the time of the Gettysburg campaign, Buehler led the unit in the area of Suffolk, Virginia. He mustered out of the army on July 28, 1863. Correspondence of John Heiser, historian, GNMP, to authors, September 9, 2003; Vanderslice, *Gettysburg Then And Now*, p. 395; Samuel P. Bates, *History of Pennsylvania Volunteers, 1861-5, Prepared In Compliance With Acts Of The Legislature*. 5 vols. (Harrisburg, Pennsylvania. 1869-1871), vol. 4, pp. 1084-1086.

(38) *Star and Sentinel*, November 14, 1883.

Charles Coffin was a 37-year-old journalist when he covered the First Battle of Bull Run in July 1861. Taking the pseudonym "Carleton," he continued reporting the war, traveling to all areas of combat, until its conclusion in 1865. In the post-war period, he parlayed his war record into a career as an author, frequent lecturer and Massachusetts politician. Coffin died in Boston at the age of 72 in 1896. Faust, *Historical Times Illustrated Encyclopedia of the Civil War,* p. 149.

(39) *Star and Sentinel*, February 5, 1884.

(40) Minute Book Gettysburg Battlefield Memorial Association, 1872-1895, minutes of March 25, 1884; *Star and Sentinel*, April 1, 1884.

(41) *Star and Sentinel*, September 23, 1884, and October 7, 1884.

(42) Earle, *History of the Excursion of the Fifteenth Massachusetts Regiment and its Friends*, p. 5; *Star and Sentinel*, April 8, 1884.

(43) Earle, *History of the Excursion of the Fifteenth Massachusetts Regiment*

and its Friends, p. 5.

(44) Undated and unidentified newspaper article contained in Cornelius Linehan letter collection, Western Michigan University, Kalamazoo, Michigan.

William R. Driver, at age 23, had enlisted as a private in Company H in November 1861. Wounded in June 1862, he was promoted to second lieutenant for gallant conduct at the Battle of Nelson's Farm. He went on detached service in March 1864, and was promoted to the rank of captain in June. Consequently, Driver was not with the regiment when most of the unit was captured on June 22, 1864. Waitt, *History of the Nineteenth Massachusetts*, pp. 111, 299, 382, 448.

At the age of only 17, Medford resident George E. Teele enlisted in the 19th Massachusetts on August 28, 1861, after previously serving in the 90-day 5th Massachusetts Volunteer Infantry Regiment. During the 1863 Chancellorsville campaign, he was among the volunteers who crossed the Rappahannock River in small boats. This was nerve-wracking duty, as the memory of the deadly passage on December 11, 1862, was still fresh in the men's minds. Although the landing went without incident, Colonel Devereux was so moved by the bravery involved that he "marked each man for promotion." Teele was discharged on August 28, 1864, when his term of enlistment expired, with the rank of corporal. The former carriage painter was receiving $50.00 per month as a Federal pension when he died in October 1923, just weeks shy of his 80th birthday. George E. Teele pension file, RG 15, NARA; Waitt, *History of the Nineteenth Massachusetts*, pp. 202-203.

John C. Chadwick was a 27-year-old insurance agent when he enlisted in the 19th from Salem, Massachusetts, on August 22, 1861. He was wounded on June 25, 1862, during the Peninsula Campaign. As captain of Company C, he was the first man off the boats during the dangerous Rappahannock River crossing at the Battle of Fredericksburg on December 11, 1862. Chadwick and another man later rushed from a place of safety and braved Confederate rifle fire in order to bring off a mortally wounded comrade from the field. After the combat ended, he discovered that an unread letter placed in his pocket prior to engaging the enemy had been shot in two, "as if by a knife, by a minie ball which had passed through his knapsack." *Massachusetts Soldiers, Sailors and Marines in the Civil War*, vol. 2, p. 411; Waitt, *History of the Nineteenth Massachusetts*, pp. 168, 183.

(45) Earle, *History of the Excursion of the Fifteenth Massachusetts Regiment and its Friends,* p. 5.

(46) 15th Regiment Association Record Book, minutes of September 17, 1885.

From the Collections of Worcester Historical Museum, Worcester, MA; Earle, *History of the Excursion of the Fifteenth Massachusetts Regiment and its Friends*, p. 6.

(47) 15th Regiment Association Record Book, minutes of September 17, 1885. From the Collections of Worcester Historical Museum, Worcester, MA.

(48) 15th Regiment Association Record Book, minutes of September 17, 1885. From the Collections of Worcester Historical Museum, Worcester, MA.

Amos C. Plaisted entered the Soldiers' Home at Chelsea, Massachusetts, on January 29, 1883, and was discharged on October 29, 1886. He was receiving a Federal pension of $12.00 per month when he died in Boston on February 10, 1902. Master Patient Index Card, The Commonwealth of Massachusetts Executive Office of Health and Human Services Soldiers' Home, Chelsea, Massachusetts; Amos C. Plaisted pension file, RG 15, NARA.

(49) *Massachusetts Soldiers, Sailors and Marines in the Civil War*, vol. 2, p. 145; Earle, *History of the Excursion of the Fifteenth Massachusetts Regiment and its Friends*, p. 6; 15th Regiment Association Record Book, minutes of September 17, 1885. From the Collections of Worcester Historical Museum, Worcester, MA. Mrs. Alger was receiving survivor's benefits from the Federal government, since Corporal Alger's wife, Emma, had died in 1871. Warren Alger pension file, RG 15, NARA.

(50) Earle, *History of the Excursion of the Fifteenth Massachusetts Regiment and its Friends,* p. 6; *Star and Sentinel*, September 29, 1885, and October 6, 1885.

(51) Kathleen R. Georg, Compiler, *The Location of the Monuments, Markers, and Tablets on Gettysburg Battlefield* (Gettysburg, Pennsylvania: Eastern National Park and Monument Association In Cooperation With Gettysburg National Military Park, 1984), pp. 4-5; *Star and Sentinel*, September 22, 1885, and October 6, 1885.

(52) *Star and Sentinel*, October 6, 1885, and October 13, 1885.

(53) *Star and Sentinel*, October 6, 1885. The newspaper reported that Joseph Smith's son found the skull protruding from the dirt on East Cemetery Hill

(54) Russell was discharged for disability from the 15th on September 8, 1863, but in May 1864 joined the 3rd Massachusetts Heavy Artillery Regiment. On September 18, 1865, he was mustered out of that unit with the rank of captain. In the post-war years, he was active in the association of the 15th's veterans, serving in various capacities. Edward Russell was over 82 years of age when he passed away in Worcester on December 16, 1915, at which time he was receiving a Federal pension of $30.00 per month. 15th

Regiment Association Record Book, minutes of September 17, 1885. From the Collections of Worcester Historical Museum, Worcester, MA; Edward Russell pension file, RG 15, NARA; *Star and Sentinel*, October 6, 1885, and October 13, 1885.

(55) *Star and Sentinel*, October 13, 1885.

(56) *Star and Sentinel*, October 13, 1885.

(57) Photograph entitled "'High Water Mark' showing the monuments of the 15th, 19th, and 20th Massachusetts at Gettysburg numbered SF-2B-123 #2B-MOLLUS #2FR#14," copy courtesy GNMP; Georg, Compiler, *The Location of the Monuments, Markers, and Tablets on Gettysburg Battlefield*, p. 4; J. Howard Wert, *A Complete Hand-Book of the Monuments And Indications and Guide To The Positions of the Gettysburg Battle-Field* (Harrisburg, Pennsylvania: R.M Sturgeon & Co., 1886), p. 46; *Star and Sentinel*, September 22, 1885, and October 13, 1885.

(58) Wert, *A Complete Hand-Book of the Monuments*, p. 46.

(59) J. Howard Wert, *Newspaper Scrapbooks*, Wert Collection, Adams County Historical Society, Gettysburg, PA, vol. 1, p. 85.

Joseph W. Sawyer was listed as missing in action near Glendale, Virginia, on June 30, 1862, and later discharged for disability on February 16, 1863. George M. Barry resigned from the army on February 8, 1862. *Massachusetts Soldiers, Sailors and Marines in the Civil War*, vol. 2, pp. 441, 479; Wert, *A Complete Hand-Book of the Monuments*, p. 48.

Coffin stated that the other two seminal events were the Battles of Bunker Hill and Bennington during the Revolutionary War. *Star and Sentinel*, October 13, 1885.

(60) Wert, *Newspaper Scrapbooks*, Wert Collection, Adams County Historical Society, Gettysburg, PA, vol. 1, p. 85.

Archibald Higgins completed his term of service on August 28, 1864. Charles Tibbetts was captured at the Battle of Antietam. He re-enlisted on December 20, 1863, and was promoted to hospital steward on March 1, 1865. Tibbetts was mustered out of the army on June 30, 1865. *Massachusetts Soldiers, Sailors and Marines in the Civil War*, vol. 2, pp. 417, 434; *Star and Sentinel*, October 13, 1885.

(61) *Star and Sentinel*, October 13, 1885.

(62) *Star and Sentinel*, October 13, 1885.

D. A. Buehler was born in 1821 and was the brother of Charles Buehler. He served as vice president of the Gettysburg Battlefield Memorial Association from 1883 until his death in 1887. He was also an attorney and the editor and business agent of the *Star and Sentinel*. Correspondence of John Heiser, historian, GNMP, to authors, September 9, 2003; Vanderslice, *Gettysburg Then And Now*, p. 395; *Star and Sentinel,* July 4, 1883.

(63) *Star and Sentinel*, October 13, 1885, and October 20, 1885.

(64) *Star and Sentinel*, October 13, 1885, and October 20, 1885.

At the age of 16, George Patch had enlisted in the 19th's Company F on August 28, 1861. He survived his military service unscathed, and on August 28, 1864 was discharged from the unit. After the war, Patch earned a solid reputation as a speaker at various G.A.R. functions, regimental reunions and monument dedications. He died of bronchitis on July 26, 1887, at his home in South Framingham, Massachusetts. George Patch pension file, RG 15, NARA; *National Tribune,* October 7, 1886; *Star and Sentinel,* October 12, 1886.

(65) *Star and Sentinel*, October 13, 1885, and October 20, 1885.

(66) Earle, *History of the Excursion of the Fifteenth Massachusetts Regiment and its Friends,* p. 10.

(67) Earle, *History of the Excursion of the Fifteenth Massachusetts Regiment and its Friends*, pp. 6, 12.

Charles F. May was a 19-year-old farmer when he mustered into the 15th on July 16, 1861. He reenlisted as a Veteran Volunteer on December 22, 1863, was wounded on June 9, 1864, and was absent, wounded, when he transferred to the 20th Massachusetts, since the 15th had mustered out of the army. May was discharged on July 13, 1865. Ford, *Fifteenth Regiment Massachusetts Volunteers*, p. 350.

An article in the *Compiler* may have caused some confusion in town, as the paper announced on the very evening the excursion arrived that "The 15th Connecticut [sic] will dedicate their monument at the "clump of trees" on Round-Top Avenue and the Gen. Ward monument on the Round-Top Branch Railroad, to-morrow." Wert, *Newspaper Scrapbooks*, Wert Collection, Adams County Historical Society, Gettysburg, PA, vol. 1, p. 150.

(68) Earle, *History of the Excursion of the Fifteenth Massachusetts Regiment and its Friends*, pp. 12-13.

William D. Holtzworth enlisted on September 25, 1861, in Company E of the 87th Pennsylvania Volunteer Infantry Regiment, which was raised in Adams County. He was discharged on a surgeon's certificate on May 12, 1865, with the rank of sergeant. Samuel P. Bates, *History of Pennsylvania Volunteers, 1861-5*, vol. 3, p. 47; *Star and Sentinel*, June 1, 1886.

(69) Earle, *History of the Excursion of the Fifteenth Massachusetts Regiment*

and its Friends, p. 13; *Star and Sentinel*, June 8,1886.

(70) Earle, *History of the Excursion of the Fifteenth Massachusetts Regiment and its Friends*, p. 13; *Report of the Select Committee Relative to the Soldiers' National Cemetery*, pp. 53-55.

George Boss of Fitchburg was a 21-year-old private in Company B who was mortally wounded in the right thigh by a piece of shell on July 2. He died on July 5 and was initially buried on the Schwartz farm near Rock Creek. James Tenney, another member of Company B, was wounded on July 3 at the height of the fighting at the Copse of Trees. Upon reaching a Union hospital on July 4, he found other wounded comrades from his company, including George Boss. Tenney later wrote that Boss had lain with his injuries untended until the evening of July 4 when, with a blanket draped over him for protection from the rain, he crawled to the comfort of a fire, where he died. Buried under the name George Bass in the National Cemetery, his stone has since been corrected. George Boss pension file, RG 15, NARA; James H. Tenney pension file, RG 15, NARA; John W. Busey, *The Last Full Measure - Burials in the Soldiers' National Cemetery at Gettysburg* (Hightstown, New Jersey: Longstreet House, 1988), pp. 30-31, 33.

(71) Dixon, *The Gettysburg Battlefield, One Century Ago,* p. 20. Only a few monuments had been dedicated along the entire length of Cemetery Ridge prior to the October 8, 1885, dedication of 19th's monument. Georg, Compiler, *The Location of the Monuments, Markers, and Tablets on the Gettysburg Battlefield*, pp. 1-43.

A photograph entitled "15th Mass Party at Monument" clearly shows the sign nailed to one of the trees behind the Massachusetts excursion party, with the yet unnamed "Hancock Avenue" immediately in the front of the group. From the Collections of Worcester Historical Museum, Worcester, MA.

John Bachelder was so concerned about this type of vandalism that he unsuccessfully pressed the Gettysburg Battlefield Memorial Association in 1885 and 1886 to install an iron fence around the Copse of Trees. It was not until February 27, 1887, that the Association moved to protect the area by instructing its Executive Committee to place a fence around the trees. Frassanito, *Early Photography at Gettysburg*, p. 240; Minute Book, Gettysburg Battlefield Memorial Association, 1872-1895, minutes of February 27, 1887.

(72) WilliamTipton photograph. From the Collections of Worcester Historical Museum, Worcester, MA.

Gettysburg-born William Tipton began his career in photography with a local firm as a 12-year-old apprentice in 1863. By the 1880s, he was a well established and respected businessman in his own right. His firm had taken well over 30,000 photographs by the time he passed away in 1929. Frassanito, *Early Photography at Gettysburg*, p. 37; Garry E. Adelman and Timothy H. Smith, *Devil's Den: A History and Guide* (Gettysburg, Pennsylvania: Thomas Publications, 1997), p. 95.

(73) Earle, *History of the Excursion of the Fifteenth Massachusetts Regiment and its Friends*, pp. 14-26; *Star and Sentinel*, June 8, 1886.

(74) Earle, *History of the Excursion of the Fifteenth Massachusetts Regiment and its Friends*, pp. 27-28, 32-35; *Star and Sentinel*, June 8, 1886.

Chase Philbrick was born in Sanbornton, New Hampshire, in 1823. He left his profession of stone-cutting and joined the 15th's Company H as its captain when the unit was organized on May 27, 1861. Promoted first to the rank of major on April 29, 1862, and then to lieutenant colonel on November 13, 1862, he commanded the regiment at the Battle of Fredericksburg, where he was wounded in the ankle. Subsequently, Philbrick was frequently absent from the regiment, not only because of his injury, but also due to sickness. At a result of his continuing ill health, Chase Philbrick resigned and was discharged from the army on April 16, 1863. Ford, *Fifteenth Regiment Massachusetts Volunteers*, pp. 7, 29, 239-240.

George Frisbie Hoar was born on August 29, 1826, in Concord, Massachusetts. Hoar's relationship with the regiment went back to the very beginning of the war. He had been a pre-war law partner of Charles Devens and was the brother-in-law of the 15th's Lieutenant Thomas Spurr, who was mortally wounded at the Battle of Antietam. While serving as a state senator, he represented the ladies of Worcester in presenting the regiment with its first flag on August 7, 1861. After the war, Hoar served four terms in the United States House of Representatives and from 1877 until his death in 1904 in the United States Senate. Ford, *Fifteenth Regiment Massachusetts Volunteers*, pp. 43, 206; http://bioguide.congress.gov, The Biographical Directory of the United States Congress 1774 - Present.

(75) Earle, *History of the Excursion of the Fifteenth Massachusetts Regiment and its Friends*, p. 35.

Ward was lauded in a local newspaper as an "exceptionally gallant" leader who had rejoined his regiment over the objections of worried friends despite a "defective operation" endured when he lost his leg as a result of the wounds suffered at the Battle of Ball's Bluff. *Star and Sentinel*, June 8, 1886.

(76) Earle, *History of the Excursion of the Fifteenth Massachusetts Regiment and its Friends*, pp. 35-47; *Star and Sentinel*, June 8, 1886.

(77) Ibid., pp. 47-48.

(78) Ibid., p. 48.

(79) Ibid., pp. 50-51. The photographer's effort was ruined by the reflection of the bright afternoon sunshine.

(80) Ibid., pp. 51-55, 57.

(81) George Rockwood pension file, RG 15, NARA; Faust, *Historical Times Illustrated Encyclopedia of the Civil War,* pp. 243, 604; Ford, *Fifteenth Regiment Massachusetts Volunteers,* pp. 116-118, 124.

Henry Bowman was a 26-year-old bookkeeper from Lancaster, Massachusetts, who enlisted in the 15th as Company C's initial captain. Due to an inability to secure an exchange after his capture at Ball's Bluff, Bowman resigned his commission on August 6, 1862. He later became colonel of the 36th Massachusetts Volunteer Infantry Regiment and in mid-1863 commanded a brigade in the Trans-Mississippi Theater. In early 1864, he became an assistant quartermaster and served as such until mustering out of the army on August 15, 1866. Ford, *Fifteenth Regiment Massachusetts Volunteers*, pp. 37, 124, 357-358.

William Raymond Lee was a 54-year-old pre-war civil engineer from Roxbury when he became the first colonel of the 20th Massachusetts in July 1861. He had been a West Point classmate of Confederate President Jefferson Davis and later participated in the Indian War in Florida. After his capture at Ball's Bluff, imprisonment and subsequent parole, he returned to duty with the regiment and was wounded during the 1862 Peninsula Campaign. Lee resigned from the army due to disability in December 1862. Bruce, *Twentieth Regiment of Massachusetts Volunteers*, pp. 136, 446, ii.

(82) Ford, *Fifteenth Regiment Massachusetts Volunteers*, p. 117. Rockwood resigned in January 1863. On August 29, 1864, he enlisted in the 4th Massachusetts Heavy Artillery Regiment and was discharged on June 17, 1865. George Rockwood pension file, RG 15, NARA.

Former Colonel W. Raymond Lee of the 20th Massachusetts, in a letter dated April 3, 1882, wrote, "After many days of this terrible experience Capt. Godwin of North Carolina, the Confederate Officer in command of the prison guards, a gentleman of honor and humanity overstretching all the forms of military etiquette, disregarding the medical officers and even the Commanding General John H Winder appealed directly and personally to the Confederate Secty of War for the removal of Rockwood to the military hospital in Richmond . . . ." George Rockwood pension file, RG 15, NARA.

Archibald Campbell Godwin, the Confederate officer who intervened to help George Rockwood, was born in 1831 in Virginia. He served as provost marshal in Richmond with the rank of major early in the war. He later commanded the 57th North Carolina Infantry Regiment at the Battles of Fredericksburg and Chancellorsville and a brigade during the Gettysburg campaign. In November 1863, Godwin was captured at the Battle of Rappahannock Station and subsequently exchanged. He was killed on September 19, 1864, at the Third Battle of Winchester. Faust, *Historical Times Illustrated Encyclopedia of the Civil War,* p. 313.

(83) George Rockwood pension file, RG 15, NARA.

(84) Only a month after the last of the group returned home, David Earle was selected by the directors of the Regimental Association to write a history of the excursion and the events leading up to it. Earle performed this task admirably. Earle, *History of the Excursion of the Fifteenth Massachusetts Regiment and its Friends,* pp. 3, 56-57.

(85) Georg, compiler, *The Location of the Monuments, Markers, and Tablets on Gettysburg Battlefield,* p. 4; Wert, *A Complete Hand-Book of the Monuments,* pp. 49-50.

An article in the *Compiler* dated June 22, 1886, describing the arrival and placement of the monument, misidentified the 20th as the 28th Massachusetts. The 20th's monument committee consisted of Gustave Magnitzky, James Holland and Charles Rost. Wert, *Newspaper Scrapbooks,* Wert Collection, Adams County Historical Society, Gettysburg, PA, vol. 1, pp. 87, 157.

James Holland was a 22-year-old from Mansfield, Massachusetts, who enlisted in Company D as a sergeant in July 1861. He was wounded during the bloody fighting in May 1864 and was discharged due to his wounds on July 26, 1864. *Massachusetts Soldiers, Sailors and Marines in the Civil War,* vol. 2, p. 526.

Charles Rost, a pre-war carpenter, was born in Prussia on December 11, 1841. He enlisted from Worcester in the 20th's Company B on July 14, 1861. He received a gunshot wound in the left leg on May 5, 1864, during the Battle of the Wilderness.

Rost was promoted to the rank of lieutenant in June and discharged on August 19, 1864. Later that year, he reenlisted in the 20th, mustering out of the army on July 16, 1865. In 1867, Rost served in the Regular Army for a short period of time. He began receiving a Federal pension of $6.00 per month in 1871. Charles Rost died on October 2, 1918. Charles Rost pension file, RG 15, NARA; Bruce, *Twentieth Regiment of Massachusetts Volunteers,* p. 447.

(86) Vanderslice, *Gettysburg Then And Now,* p. 411; Wert, *Newspaper Scrap-*

books, Wert Collection, Adams County Historical Society, Gettysburg, PA, vol. 1, p. 87; Bruce, *Twentieth Regiment of Massachusetts Volunteers*, p. 3; Henry T. Secrist, "The Pudding-Stone," *The Roxbury Magazine*, 1899, unpaginated.

(87) *The Boston Daily Globe*, July 4, 1886; Georg, compiler, *The Location of the Monuments, Markers, and Tablets on Gettysburg Battlefield*, p. 11.

(88) This event was reported in the July 13, 1886, edition of the *Compiler*. Wert, *Newspaper Scrapbooks*, Wert Collection, Adams County Historical Society, Gettysburg, PA, vol. 1, p. 187.

During the years of the Gettysburg Battlefield Memorial Association's stewardship of the battlefield, other monuments were also moved for a variety of reasons. For example, this same newspaper article reported the changing of position of Knap's Pennsylvania battery monument on Culp's Hill.

(89) Joshua L. Chamberlain, *Dedication of the Maine Monuments at Gettysburg*, http://www.curtislibrary.com/pejepscot/joshme.htm, Pejepscot Historical Society, Chamberlain's Gettysburg Speeches. For example, men from 15 military organizations that did not fight at Gettysburg, including one navy veteran, accompanied the 15th Massachusetts excursion in 1886.

Chapter 6

(1) Vanderslice, *Gettysburg Then And Now*, p. 376; Minute Book Gettysburg Battlefield Memorial Association, 1872-1895, minutes of May 5, 1887.

A brigade line of battle was the standard combat formation used by units in the Civil War. Its width depended upon the number of regiments in the brigade and the numerical strength of those units. This "line of battle" philosophy was subsequently formalized at the December 1887 meeting of the Gettysburg Battlefield Memorial Association. Among a number of rules and regulations submitted concerning monuments was number VI: "The monument must be on the line of battle held by the brigade unless the regiment was detached, and if possible the right and left flanks of the regiment or battery must be marked with stones not less than two feet in height. If the same line was held by other troops, the monuments must be placed in the order in which the several commands occupied the grounds, the first being on the first line, the second at least twenty feet in the rear of it and so on, the inscriptions explaining the movements." Minute Book Gettysburg Battlefield Memorial Association, 1872-1895, minutes of December 16, 1887.

(2) Vanderslice, *Gettysburg Then And Now*, p. 376; Minute Book Gettysburg

Battlefield Memorial Association, 1872-1895, minutes of May 5, 1887.

(3) Minute Book Gettysburg Battlefield Memorial Association, 1872-1895, minutes of February 27, May 5 and July 12, 1887.

(4) Georg, compiler, *The Location of the Monuments, Markers, and Tablets on Gettysburg Battlefield*, p. 11.

(5) Minute Book Gettysburg Battlefield Memorial Association, 1872-1895, minutes of December 16, 1887.

(6) Ibid.

(7) Acts and Resolves of the Commonwealth of Massachusetts, Resolve Chapter 58, approved April 19, 1888, copy courtesy GNMP.

(8) *Compiler*, May 8, 1888; David M. McGlaughlin, "Monumental Litigation," *The Gettysburg Magazine*, no. 20, p. 123.

(9). Minute Book Gettysburg Battlefield Memorial Association, 1872-1895, minutes of July 3, 1888; McGlaughlin, "Monumental Litigation," p. 123; *Compiler*, July 10, 1888.

(10) Minute Book Gettysburg Battlefield Memorial Association, 1872-1895, minutes of September 25, 1888.

(11) Letter of Charles Devens to "The President & Directors of the Gettysburg Battle Field Association," October 22, 1888, 15th Regiment Association Record Book. From the Collections of Worcester Historical Museum, Worcester, MA.

(12) *Compiler*, October 2, 1888.

(13) *Star and Sentinel*, October 2, 1888.

(14) Letter of Charles Devens to "The President & Directors of the Gettysburg Battle Field Association," October 22, 1888, 15th Regiment Association Record Book. From the Collections of Worcester Historical Museum, Worcester, MA.

(15) Ibid.

(16) Ibid.

(17) Ibid.

(18) Ibid.

(19) Ibid.

(20) Letter of Charles Devens to "The President & Directors of the Gettysburg Battle Field Association," October 22, 1888, 15th Regiment Association Record Book. From the Collections of Worcester Historical Museum, Worcester, MA.

Samuel Fletcher was a 30-year-old farmer from Whitinsville, Massachusetts, when he enlisted as a sergeant in the 15th's Company H on July 12, 1861. He received a gunshot wound at Gettysburg on July 2, 1863. The ball entered his head in front of his right ear, passed through his jaw and exited near his left eye. He was left for dead on the battlefield but, fortunately, was found alive when his comrades later were burying the dead. After his return to duty, during the 1864 Overland Campaign, Fletcher was shot in his left wrist and lost his left thumb. He was mustered out of the regiment on June 28, 1864, and suffered from headaches and diarrhea during the rest of his long life. Fletcher was the vice president of the 15th Regimental Association when he signed Devens' letter. When Samuel Fletcher died on July 11, 1924, he was receiving a Federal pension of $40.00 per month. Samuel Fletcher pension file, RG 15, NARA; 15th Regiment Association Record Book. From the Collections of Worcester Historical Museum, Worcester, MA, minutes of October 21, 1896.

Edward Rice was born in Boston and was a 27-year-old clerk when he entered the army on July 12, 1861, as a private in Company D. During his time in the 15th, he attained the rank of quartermaster sergeant and mustered out of the regiment on July 28, 1864. Rice was serving as the secretary of the 15th's association in October 1888. Edward Rice died on January 30, 1909. *Massachusetts Soldiers, Sailors and Marines in the Civil War*, vol. 2, p. 160.

Luther Goddard was 34 years of age and working as a merchant when he enlisted in the 15th's Company D on July 12, 1861. He was captured at the Battle of Ball's Bluff on October 21, 1861, and released the following February. Due to disability, he was discharged from the army on June 20, 1862. After the war he lived in Worcester and was chaplain of the 15th Regimental Association at the time of Devens' letter. He died on August 8, 1906. *Massachusetts Soldiers, Sailors and Marines in the Civil War*, vol. 2, p. 158.

Henry Smith was a 20-year-old shoemaker from North Brookfield, Massachusetts, when he enlisted as a corporal in Company E on July 12, 1861. He was wounded in the Battles of Antietam and the Wilderness. In July 1864, Smith was transferred to the ranks of the 20th Massachusetts. In February 1865, he joined the Veteran Reserve Corps. Henry Smith was again transferred in April 1865 and ended his military career as a member of the 193rd New York Volunteer Infantry Regiment. He mustered out of the army on January 18, 1866, with the rank of second lieutenant. Smith signed the October 22, 1888, letter as a director of the regimental association. He died on June 7, 1902. *Massachusetts Soldiers, Sailors and Marines in the Civil War*, vol. 2, p. 175.

William Andrews was born in 1839 in Antrim, New Hampshire, and was working as a pattern maker when he joined the 15th in July 12, 1861. As a member of Company D, he was among those captured at Ball's Bluff and was released from captivity on February 22, 1862. Almost one year later, he was discharged from the army for reasons of disability. Andrews was also a director of the 15th veterans' organization. He lived until April 20, 1913. *Massachusetts Soldiers, Sailors and Marines in the Civil War*, vol. 2, p. 155.

Amos Bartlett, a native of Webster, Massachusetts, was a 25-year-old teacher in civilian life before joining the 15th as one of the regiment's first enlistees on April 20, 1861. He was commissioned on July 12, 1861, into Company I with the rank of first lieutenant. Promoted to captain in May 1862, he was wounded later that year at Antietam and subsequently was discharged for disability on January 7, 1863. After the war, he returned to Webster and remained active in the affairs of the unit's association. He was also a director when Charles Devens wrote his letter of complaint about the regiment's Gettysburg monument. Bartlett died on November 30, 1912. *Massachusetts Soldiers, Sailors and Marines in the Civil War*, vol. 2, p.190.

(21) Letter of C. H. Buehler to "Genl Devens Presdt," November 5, 1888, 15th Regiment Association Record Book. From the Collections of Worcester Historical Museum, Worcester, MA.

(22) Ibid.

(23) Ibid. Buehler was referring to the actions taken by the Memorial Association at its May 7 and December 16, 1887 meetings, hardly "several years ago."

(24) Ibid.

(25) Ibid.

(26) Ibid.

(27) Board Of Commissioners, *Pennsylvania At Gettysburg - Ceremonies At The Dedication Of The Monuments Erected By The Commonwealth Of Pennsylvania To Mark The Positions Of The Pennsylvania Commands Engaged In The Battle*. 2 vols. (Harrisburg, Pennsylvania,1893), vol. 1, p. 387; McGlaughlin, "Monumental Litigation," p.124; *Compiler*, December 18, 1888.

(28) Letter of C. H. Buehler to "E. A. Rice Esq.," December 7, 1888, 15th Regiment Association Record Book. From the Collections of Worcester Historical Museum, Worcester, MA.

(29) *Compiler*, November 27, 1888.

(30) *Compiler*, December 11, 1888.

(31) *Star and Sentinel*, October 20, 1891.

(32) Entry after letter of C. H. Buehler to "E. A. Rice Esq.," December 7, 1888, 15th Regiment Association Record Book. From the Collections of Worcester Historical Museum, Worcester, MA.

(33) Letter of C. H. Buehler to "My dear Col.," November 30, 1888, Ladd and Ladd, eds., *The Bachelder Papers,* vol. 3, p. 1562.

(34) Letter of Arthur F. Devereux to "My dear Col.," December 10, 1890, Ladd and Ladd, eds., *The Bachelder Papers,* vol. 3, p. 1779.

(35) Entry after letter of C. H. Buehler to "E. A. Rice Esq.," December 7, 1888, 15th Regiment Association Record Book. From the Collections of Worcester Historical Museum, Worcester, MA.

(36) McGlaughlin, "Monumental Litigation," p. 124.

(37) Entry of March 7, 1889, 15th Regiment Association Record Book. From the Collections of Worcester Historical Museum, Worcester, MA.

(38) McGlaughlin, "Monumental Litigation," pp. 124-125.

(39) For example, see William H. Good *Testimony*, 63; Frank Weible *Testimony*, 112; Henry Russell *Testimony*, 163; 72nd Penna. vs. GBMA.

(40) Arthur F. Devereux *Testimony*, 72nd Penna. vs. GBMA, 289; William A. Hill *Testimony*, 72nd Penna. vs. GBMA, 340.

(41) Arthur F. Devereux *Testimony*, 72nd Penna. vs. GBMA, 299, 303-340; William A. Hill *Testimony*, 72nd Penna. vs. GBMA, 342- 343, 347-359.

(42) Arthur F. Devereux *Testimony*, 72nd Penna. vs. GBMA, 316-317.

(43) Alexander S. Webb *Testimony*, 72nd Penna. vs. GBMA, 248, 250, 258; Charles H. Banes *Testimony*, 72nd Penna. vs. GBMA, 212-213, 221; *Star and Sentinel*, August 29, 1883. The "military crest" is the term applied to the portion of a ridge or hill facing the enemy, rather than the rear slope.

(44) Anthony McDermott *Testimony*, 72nd Penna. vs. GBMA, 368; William Stockton *Testimony*, 72nd Penna. vs. GBMA, 410; Joseph Garrett *Testimony*, 72nd Penna. vs. GBMA, 423.

(45) John Bachelder *Testimony*, 72nd Penna. vs. GBMA, 246-253.

(46) Ibid.

(47) Ibid.

(48) Ibid.

(49) McGlaughlin, "Monumental Litigation," pp. 125-126; report of William McClean, Master in Equity, 72nd Penna. vs. GBMA, 88.

(50) Letter of Arthur F. Devereux to "My dear Col.," December 10, 1890, Ladd and Ladd, eds., *The Bachelder Papers,* vol. 3, p. 1779.

(51) Minute Book Gettysburg Battlefield Memorial Association, 1872-1895, minutes of May 18, 1891.

(52) McGlaughlin, "Monumental Litigation," pp. 125-126; report of William McClean, Master in Equity, 72nd Penna. vs. GBMA, 88.

(53) A Gettysburg newspaper article reporting the dedication of the 72nd

Pennsylvania's monument criticized the actions of the regiment and also stated that some of the unit's veterans admitted that the memorial had been placed incorrectly. *Star and Sentinel*, July 7, 1891.

(54) *Boston Daily Globe*, October 16, 1891; *Star and Sentinel*, October 20, 1891.

(55) *Boston Daily Globe*, October 16, 1891.

(56) *Star and Sentinel*, October 6, 1891; *Compiler*, October 13, 1891, and October 27, 1891.

(57) *Star and Sentinel*, October 20, 1891.

(58) Letter of Edward Rice to "My dear Colonel," October 21, 1891, Ladd and Ladd, eds., *The Bachelder Papers,* vol. 3, p. 1824.

(59) Letter of Arthur F. Devereux to "Col. J. B. Bachelder," November 15, 1890, Ladd and Ladd, eds., *The Bachelder Papers,* vol. 3, p. 1825.

(60) *Star and Sentinel*, June 7, 1892.

(61) *Star and Sentinel*, June 7, 1892; Frassanito, *Early Photography at Gettysburg,* pp. 239-240.

(62) The other commissioners were John P. Nicholson, who had served with the 28th Pennsylvania Volunteer Infantry Regiment during the Civil War, and William H. Forney, a Confederate veteran from Alabama. Forney commanded the 10th Alabama Infantry Regiment at Gettysburg where he received six wounds, which left him crippled. After the battle, he was captured and not exchanged for over a year. Dixon, *The Gettysburg Battlefield,One Century Ago,* p. 9; Gettysburg National Military Park Commission. *Annual Reports To The Secretary Of War 1893-1901* (Washington, D.C.: Government Printing Office, 1902), p. 5; Uzal W. Ent, "The world's most famous Civil War site became a tourist attraction as soon as the guns fell silent." *America's Civil War,* July 2002, p. 72; Kathleen Georg, "'Patriotic and Enduring Efforts': An Introduction to the Gettysburg Battlefield Commission," contained in *The Fourth Annual Gettysburg Seminar: Gettysburg 1895-1995: The Shaping of an American Shrine,* March 4, 1995, p. 63.

(63) Letter of Gustave Magnitzky to "Hon. Commisioners Battlefield of Gettysburg," January 20, 1895, Records of the Gettysburg Nat'l Park Comm, Monuments and Markers, US Commission, vol. 1, GNMP Archives.

Emmor B. Cope had served in the Federal Topographical Engineer Corps during the Gettysburg Campaign. Harrison, "'Patriotic and Enduring Efforts': An Introduction to the Gettysburg Battlefield Commission," contained in *The Fourth Annual Gettysburg Seminar: Gettysburg 1895-1995: The Shaping of an American Shrine*, March 4, 1995, p. 67.

(64) Letter of E.B. Cope to Col. John P. Nicholson, September 17, 1895, copy courtesy GNMP.

(65) Letter of David M. Earle to the National Park Commission of Gettysburg. November 21, 1896, Records of the Gettysburg Nat'l Park Comm, Monuments and Markers, U.S. Commission, vol. 1, GNMP Archives; entry in Gettysburg National Park Commission Journal, November 25, 1896, p. 147, copy courtesy GNMP; letter of David M. Earle to the National Park Commission of Gettysburg, December 4, 1896, copy courtesy GNMP; letter of William. M. Robbins to "My dear Col. Nicholson," August 10, 1897, copy courtesy GNMP.

Robbins replaced William Forney on the Gettysburg National Park Commission after Forney's death in January 1894. During the Civil War, Robbins was the major of the 4th Alabama Infantry Regiment, and fought at the Battle of Gettysburg. Ent, "The world's most famous Civil War site became a tourist attraction as soon as the guns fell silent." *America's Civil War,* July 2002, p. 72; letter of D. M. Earle to the Gettysburg National Park Commission, August 23, 1897, copy courtesy GNMP; letter of W. F. Miller to the National Park Commission, October 30, 1897, Records of the Gettysburg Nat'l Park Comm, Monuments and Markers, US Commission, vol.1, GNMP Archives; Alfred S. Roe, *Monuments, Tablets and Other Memorials Erected in Massachusetts to Commemorate the Services of Her Sons in the War of the Rebellion 1861-1865* (Boston, Massachusetts: Wright and Potter Printing Company), 1910, p. 132.

(66) Gettysburg National Military Park Tour Roads, HAER No. PA-485, p. 169, courtesy GNMP Archives; Gettysburg National Military Park Commission, *Annual Reports,* p. 15.

(67) Ibid.

(68) Letter of E.B. Cope to the Gettysburg National Park Commission, February 11, 1896, Records of the Gettysburg Nat'l Park Comm, Monuments and Markers, US Commission, vol.1, GNMP Archives.

(69) Letter of C.A. Richardson to "Col. J.P. Nicholson," May 1, 1896, Records of the Gettysburg Nat'l Park Comm, Monuments and Markers, US Commission, vol.1, GNMP Archives.

Richardson was appointed to the Gettysburg National Park Commission to replace John Bachelder, who had passed away the previous December. Richardson served in the 126th New York Volunteer Infantry Regiment during the Civil War and was present at the Battle of Gettysburg. Ent, "The world's most famous Civil War site became a tourist attraction as soon as the guns fell silent." *America's Civil War,* July 2002, p. 72.

(70) 15th Regiment Association Record Book, minutes of October 21, 1897. From the Collections of Worcester Historical Museum, Worcester, Massachusetts; William Tipton photograph. From the Collections of Worcester Historical Museum, Worcester, MA.

(71) George W. Ward, *History of the Excursion of the Fifteenth Massachusetts Regiment and its Friends to the Battlefields of Gettysburg, Antietam, Balls Bluff and the City of Washington, D.C., September 14-20, 1900.* (Worcester, Massachusetts: Press of O.B. Wood, 1901), unpaginated introduction.

(72) Ward, *History of the Excursion of the Fifteenth Massachusetts Regiment and its Friends to the Battlefield,* pp. 6-13.

(73) Ibid., pp. 14-18.

(74) Ibid., p. 51. Andrew O'Connor was the sculptor of the Antietam Lion, as well as the Ward medallion and the soldier bas-relief on the Gettysburg regimental monument.

(75) Ibid., pp. 24, 36, 57-61.

(76) Letter of William M. Robbins to "My dear Col. N.," October 9, 1900, copy courtesy GNMP.

Calvin Hamilton lived with his family just north of Gettysburg before the war. In 1858, he enrolled in the preparatory department of Pennsylvania College, located in the town of Gettysburg. While still a student, he enlisted in Company K of the 1st Pennsylvania Reserve Infantry Regiment. In the fighting on July 2, 1863, Hamilton, then 20 years old, suffered a serious wound to his right leg. November 19, 1863, the day of the dedication of the National Cemetery, found the still-recovering Hamilton, together with several other wounded soldiers, on the same platform as President Abraham Lincoln as he gave his immortal address. Hamilton later transferred to the Veteran Reserve Corps. After the war, in addition to his job as a teacher, he served as a director of the Gettysburg Battlefield Memorial Association from 1887 to 1890. After the death of the association's secretary, John Krauth, in 1890, Hamilton held that position until 1896. In 1889, he also became the superintendent of the Soldiers' National Cemetery in Gettysburg. Frassanito, *Early Photography at Gettysburg,* p. 248; William C. Storrick, "When I Saw and Heard Mr. Lincoln," *American History Magazine,* August 2003, p. 86; Vanderslice, *Gettysburg Then And Now,* p. 395.

(77) Letter of George F. Hoar to "Col. John P. Nicholson," December 14, 1900, copy courtesy GNMP.

(78) Ibid.

(79) Ibid.

(80) Ibid.

(81) Ibid.

(82) Letter of George F. Hoar to "Col. John P. Nicholson," December 14, 1900, copy courtesy GNMP; *Journal of William McKenna Robbins, Commissioner, Gettysburg National Park, 1898 to 1905*, p. 98, copy courtesy GNMP.

(83) Letter of George F. Hoar to "Col. John P. Nicholson," December 14, 1900, copy courtesy GNMP.

(84) Letter of John P. Nicholson to "Hon. George F. Hoar," December 29, 1900, copy courtesy GNMP.

(85) Letter of Charles L. Peirson to "Dear Colonel," February 20, 1903, Records of the Gettysburg Nat'l Park Commission, Monuments and Markers, US Commission, vol.1, GNMP Archives.

Charles Peirson was born on January 15, 1834, in Salem, Massachusetts. He joined the 20th Massachusetts from his civilian occupation of farming on July 1, 1861, with the rank of first lieutenant. On August 31, 1862, he was promoted to the rank of lieutenant colonel of the 39th Massachusetts Volunteer Infantry Regiment. Peirson was wounded on May 10, 1864, during the Overland Campaign. After being promoted to the rank of colonel in July 1864, he was again wounded on August 17, 1864, just prior to the Battle of Weldon Railroad during the Petersburg Campaign. Charles Peirson was discharged on January 5, 1865, as a result of his wounds suffered the previous year. He attained the rank of brigadier general by brevet in March 1865. Charles Peirson died on January 23, 1920, in Boston, at the age of 86. *Massachusetts Soldiers, Sailors and Marines in the Civil War*, vol. 2, p. 494.

(86) Letter of Charles L. Peirson to "Colonel John P. Nicholson," March 3, 1903, Records of the Gettysburg Nat'l Park Commission, Monuments and Markers, US Commission, vol.1, GNMP Archives; letter of John P. Nicholson to "Hon. Secretary of War," March 4, 1903, Records of the Gettysburg Nat'l Park Commission, Monuments and Markers, US Commission, vol.1, GNMP Archives; entry Gettysburg National Park Commission Journal, March 16, 1903, p. 16, copy courtesy GNMP Archives.

(87) *Star and Sentinel*, July 8, 1903.

(88) Entries Gettysburg National Park Commission Journal, January 17, 1906, p. 7, May 4, 1906, p. 45, May 9, 1906, pp. 45-46, GNMP Archives; letter of Edward J. Russell to the Commissioners of the Gettysburg Battlefield Asso-

ciation, November 2, 1906, Records of the Gettysburg Nat'l Park Commission, Monuments and Markers, US Commission, vol. 1, GNMP Archives; 15th Regiment Association Record Book, undated entry. From the Collections of Worcester Historical Museum, Worcester, MA.

(89) 15th Massachusetts Papers. From the Collections of the Worcester Historical Museum, Worcester, MA; Oliver Wendell Holmes 1884 Memorial Day Speech, http://www.harvardregiment.org, The Harvard Regiment.

Josiah Converse was an 18-year-old farmer when he joined Company F. He was wounded in the thigh at Antietam and was captured, along with most of the regiment, on June 22, 1864, during the Petersburg Campaign. Ford, *Fifteenth Regiment Massachusetts Volunteers*, p. 381.

(90) Letter of Kathleen Georg to Edwin Root, April 15, 1993, Edwin Root Collection.

(91) Gettysburg National Military Park Tour Roads, HAER No. PA-485, pp. 169-170, courtesy GNMP Archives

(92) Letter of Brad Bean to Edwin Root, February 27, 1993, Edwin Root Collection.

(93) Memorandum of Regional Director to Superintendent, October 4, 1985, copy courtesy GNMP Archives; letter of Kathleen Georg to Edwin Root, April 15, 1993, Edwin Root Collection; letter of Jose A. Cisneros to Edwin Root, April 15, 1993, Edwin Root Collection.

(94) Letter of Edwin Root to Kathleen Georg, April 8, 1993, Edwin Root Collection; letter of Jose A. Cisneros to Edwin Root, April 15, 1993, Edwin Root Collection; letter of Jose A. Cisneros to Edwin Root, April 15, 1993, Edwin Root Collection.

(95) *Compiler*, December 18, 1888.

Chapter 7

(1) *Massachusetts Soldiers, Sailors and Marines in the Civil War*, vol. 2, p. 193.

(2) George Joslin pension file, RG 15, NARA.

(3) *Boston Globe*, November 22, 1916.

(4) George Joslin pension file, RG 15, NARA; *Boston Globe*, November 22, 1916.

(5) David Earle obituary dated January 30, 1917, unidentified newspaper clipping. From the Collections of Worcester Historical Museum, Worcester, MA.

(6) David Earle obituary dated January 17, 1917, unidentified newspaper clipping. From the Collections of Worcester Historical Museum, Worcester, MA.

(7) David Earle pension file, RG 15, NARA; David Earle obituaries dated January 29 and 30, 1917, unidentified newspaper clippings. From the Collections of Worcester Historical Museum, Worcester, MA.

(8) David Earle obituaries dated January 29 and 30, 1917, unidentified newspaper clippings. From the Collections of Worcester Historical Museum, Worcester, MA.

(9) Earle's first wife, Emily, preceded him in death in 1908. David Earle obituary dated January 17, 1917, unidentified newspaper clipping. From the Collections of Worcester Historical Museum, Worcester, MA.

(10) Arthur Devereux pension file, RG 15, NARA; Hunt, *Brevet Brigadier Generals in Blue*, p. 159; *Boston Globe*, February 14, 1906.

(11) *Boston Globe*, February 14, 1906.

(12) Arthur Devereux pension file, RG 15, NARA.

(13) Arthur Devereux pension file, RG 15, NARA; *Boston Globe*, February 14, 1906.

(14) Ansel Wass pension file, RG 15, NARA; Waitt, *History of the Nineteenth Massachusetts,* pp. 261, 271, 300.

(15) Waitt, *History of the Nineteenth Massachusetts*, pp. 327, 344; Ansel Wass pension file, RG 15, NARA; Dyer, *The Journal of a Civil War Surgeon*, p. 166.

(16) Roger D. Hunt, *Colonels in Blue: Union Army Colonels of the Civil War* (Atglen, Pennsylvania: Schiffer Military History, 2001), p. 66; Hunt, *Brevet Brigadier Generals in Blue*, p. 654; Ansel Wass pension file, RG 15, NARA.

(17) Ansel Wass pension file, RG 15, NARA; inscription on tombstone of Ansel Wass, Evergreen Cemetery, Portland, Maine.

(18) Waitt, *History of the Nineteenth Massachusetts*, pp. 367, 407. Brief biography of Edmund Rice prepared by Norwich University, 1953. Norwich University Archives and Special Collections, Kreitzberg Library, Northfield, VT.

(19) Privately printed, *History of Edward W. Kinsley Post No. 113, G.A.R.* (Norwich, Massachusetts: The Norwood Press, 1913), pp. 277-281; Brief biography of Edmund Rice prepared by Norwich University, 1953. Norwich University Archives and Special Collections, Kreitzberg Library, Northfield, VT.

(20) Edmund Rice pension file, RG 15, NARA; *History of Edward W. Kinsley Post No. 113, G.A.R.,* pp. 277-279.

(21) Waitt, *History of the Nineteenth Massachusetts*, p. 392; Benjamin Jellison pension file, RG 15, NARA.

(22) Waitt, *History of the Nineteenth Massachusetts*, p. 380; Joseph DeCastro pension file, RG 15, NARA.

(23) Waitt, *History of the Nineteenth Massachusetts*, p. 408; John Robinson pension file, RG 15, NARA.

(24) Miller and Mooney, *The Civil War: The Nantucket Experience*, pp. 167-168.

(25) Miller and Mooney, *The Civil War: The Nantucket Experience*, pp. 168-169; Joshua L. Chamberlain, *The Passing of the Armies* (Dayton, Ohio: Press of Morningside Bookshop, 1982), p. 334.

(26) Hunt, *Brevet Brigadier Generals in Blue*, p. 375.

(27) George Macy pension file, RG 15, NARA; *Boston Evening Transcript*, February 15, 1875.

(28) *Boston Evening Transcript*, February 15, 1875; George Macy pension file, RG 15, NARA; Miller and Mooney, *The Civil War: The Nantucket Experience*, p. 169.

(29) Ford, *War Letters 1862- 1865*, pp. 241-242.

(30) Chester Leonard pension file, RG 15, NARA.

(31) Ibid.

Appendix I

(1) Major Francis Le Baron Monroe, a 27-year-old physician from Boston, served as a surgeon with the 15th Massachusetts during the Battle of Gettysburg. He was mustered out with the regiment on July 29, 1864. Ford, *Fifteenth Regiment Massachusetts Volunteers*, p. 8.

(2) On July 12, 1861, at the age of 21, George A. Harwood left his home in Fitchburg, Massachusetts, and his job as an "ornamenter," to serve in the 15th as a musician. Harwood remained with the regiment until he was discharged on July 28, 1864. Twenty-eight-year-old Daniel R. Pierce also enlisted in the 15th on July 12, 1861, from his home town of Fitchburg, where he worked as a rattan worker. Pierce was named Principal Musician of the unit on June 16, 1864, and remained in this position until his discharge on July 29, 1864. Musicians were frequently used as litter-bearers and hospital attendants during the Civil War. *Massachusetts Soldiers, Sailors and Marines in the Civil War*, vol. 2, pp. 144, 146.

(3) Joseph B. Matthews and George L. Boss have already been discussed in detail in the main body of the work. Henry M. Carpenter was a 24-year-old harness maker from Southbridge, Massachusetts, who enlisted as a private in the 15th's Company B on August 6, 1861. In the fighting on July 2, 1863, Carpenter sustained a gunshot wound to his right thigh and was struck on the head by a piece of shell. He received treatment in various hospitals for almost a year, until he was transferred to the Veteran Reserve Corps. Carpenter was discharged from the army on August 4, 1864, and began receiving a pension from the Federal government in the amount of $4.00 per month. He

died on October 7, 1933; by that time, his pension had increased to the sum of $90.00 per month. Henry Carpenter pension file, RG 15, NARA.

(4) The only Howard listed as a member of the 15th's Company B was N. Porter Howard, a 30-year-old lumberman from Westminster, Massachusetts, who enlisted as a private in the company on July 12, 1861. Howard remained on duty with the regiment until he was mustered out on July 28, 1864. *Massachusetts Soldiers, Sailors and Marines in the Civil War*, vol. 2, p. 144.

(5) A 27-year-old baker from Fulton, New York, Private Daniel Kearn was serving in Company A of the 111th New York Volunteer Infantry Regiment when he suffered a gunshot wound to his left thigh in the fighting on July 2, 1863. He remained in various army hospitals for six months and was then transferred to a unit of the Veteran Reserve Corps. After his discharge, Kearn returned to his pre-war occupation and began collecting a Federal pension of $4.00 per month. Daniel Kearn pension file, RG 15, NARA.

(6) James Tenney pension file, RG 15, NARA.

BIBLIOGRAPHY

Archival Sources

Adams County Historical Society. Gettysburg, Pennsylvania.
  J. Howard Wert Newspaper Scrapbooks, No. 32, vol. 1 and No. 33, vol. 2, Wert Collection.

Boston Public Library. Boston, Massachusetts.
  Henry Ropes Letters.
  John C. Ropes Papers.

Civil War and Underground Railroad Museum of Philadelphia. Philadelphia, Pennsylvania.
  August Sessler Collection
  John Bachelder Letter of November 13, 1885.
  Winfield Scott Hancock Letter of December 12, 1885.

Commonwealth of Massachusetts Executive Office of Health and Human Services Soldiers' Home. Chelsea, Massachusetts.
  Master Patient Index Cards.

Evergreen Cemetery. Gettysburg, Pennsylvania.
  Burial Permit Record.

Gettysburg National Military Park. Gettysburg, Pennsylvania.
  E. B. Cope Letter of September 17, 1895.
  E. B. Cope Letter of February 11, 1896.
  E. B. Cope Notebook.
  David M. Earle Letter of November 21, 1896.
  David M. Earle Letter of December 4, 1896.
  David M. Earle Letter of August 7, 1897.
  David M. Earle Letter of August 23, 1897.
  Kathleen R. Georg. "This Grand National Enterprise," The Origins of Gettysburg's Soldiers' National Cemetery and Gettysburg Battlefield, Battlefield Memorial Association. May, 1982.
  Kathleen R. Georg. "A Fitting And Expressive Memorial," The Development of Gettysburg National Military Park.
  Gettysburg National Military Park Tour Roads.
  Nathan Hayward Letter of July 8, 1863.
  George Hoar Letter of December 14, 1900.
  William B. Hoitt Letter of July 13, 1863.
  Captain Alphonse N. Jones. "Unpublished Report of the 7th Virginia Infantry at Gettysburg dated July 5, 1863."

Cornelius Linehan Letter of July 17, 1863.

Gustave Magnitzky Letter of January 20, 1895.

Herbert Mason Diary.

W. F. Miller Letter of October 30, 1897.

Minute Book Gettysburg Battlefield Memorial Association, 1872-1895.

John Nicholson Letter of November 3, 1897.

John Nicholson Letter of December 29, 1900.

John Nicholson Letter of March 4, 1903.

Charles Peirson Letter of February 20, 1903.

Charles Peirson Letter of March 3, 1903.

John Reynolds. "The Nineteenth Massachusetts At Gettysburg, July 2-3-4."

Edmund Rice Letter of July 27, 1867.

Charles Richardson Letter of May 1, 1896.

William Robbins Letter of December 5, 1896.

William Robbins Memorandum of August 9, 1897.

William Robbins Letter of August 10, 1897.

William Robbins Letter of October 9, 1900.

William McKenna Robbins Journal.

Edward Russell Letter of November 2, 1906.

Historical Society of Pennsylvania. Philadelphia, Pennsylvania.

Henry Mason Letters.

Howard Gotlieb Archival Research Center. Boston University, Boston, Massachusetts.

Index Project Inc. Woodbridge, Virginia.

Massachusetts Historical Society. Boston, Massachusetts.

Sumner Paine Papers.

MOLLUS (Military Order of the Loyal Legion of the United States) -

Massachusetts Commandery Collection, MS Am 1084. Houghton Library, Harvard University, Cambridge, Massachusetts.

Henry Abbott Letter of August 1, 1863.

Daniel McAdams. "A Short history of the Service of Daniel McAdams in Company I 20 Regiment Mass Vol 30 years after the War Wrote from Memory."

National Archives and Records Administration, Washington, D.C.

Record Group 15 (Various Pension Records).

Record Group 94 (Various Compiled Military Service Records; Morning Reports, Regimental and Company Papers of the 15th, 19th and 20th Massachusetts Volunteer Infantry Regiments).

Charles Raymond File Folder in National Archives-Record Group 153.

Moses Shackley File Folder in National Archives-Record Group 153.

Eugene Sullivan File Folder in National Archives-Record Group 153.

New-York Historical Society. New York, New York.

Edmund Rice Letter of April 19, 1887.

Norwich University. Northfield, Vermont Archives and Special Collections, Kreitzburg Library, Brief biography of Edmund Rice prepared by Norwich University.

Paul Revere Memorial Association. Boston, Massachusetts.

Nina Zannien. "The Civil War Reveres: A Family Story."

Edwin Root Collection. Coopersburg, Pennsylvania.

Brad Bean Letter of February 27, 1993.

Jose A. Cisneros Letter of April 15, 1993.

Jose A. Cisneros Letter of June 24, 1993.

Kathleen Georg Harrison Letter of April 15, 1993.

United States Army Military History Institute, Carlisle Barracks, Pennsylvania.

Robert L. Brake Collection.

Gustave Magnitzky Newspaper Obituaries.

Western Michigan University, Kalamazoo, Michigan.

Cornelius Linehan Papers.

Worcester Historical Museum, Worcester, Massachusetts.

"Address Commemorative of Fifteenth Regiment Massachusetts Volunteers, Delivered at Dedication of Monument to the Regiment at Gettysburg, June 2, 1886, by BR. Maj-Gen. Devens, and Remarks at Dedication of Monument to Col. Geo. H. Ward."

Albert Everett. "Harrow's Brigade at Gettysburg."

15th Regiment Association Record Book.

George Ward Letters.

Newspapers

Boston Daily Globe.

Boston Evening Transcript.

Boston Globe.

Boston Herald.

Boston Journal.

Boston Morning Journal.

Cambridge Chronicle, Cambridge, Massachusetts.

Franklin, Pennsylvania, Evening News.

Gettysburg Compiler.
Gettysburg Star and Sentinel.
National Tribune.
Philadelphia Weekly Press.
West Philadelphia Hospital Register.

Electronic Sources: Internet
http://www.1911encyclopedia.org
http://bioguide.congress.gov
http://www.curtislibrary.com/pejepscot/joshme.htm
http://www.eh.net/hmit/ppowerusd
http://www.harvardregiment.org
http://www.nps.gov/
http://politicalgraveyard.com

Official Compilations
Bates, Samuel P.
> *History of Pennsylvania Volunteers, 1861-5; Prepared In Compliance With Acts Of The Legislature.* 5 Volumes. Harrisburg, Pennsylvania. 1869-1871.

Board Of Commissioners.
> *Pennsylvania At Gettysburg - Ceremonies At The Dedication Of The Monuments Erected By The Commonwealth Of Pennsylvania To Mark The Positions Of The Pennsylvania Commands Engaged In The Battle.* 2 Volumes. Harrisburg, Pennsylvania. 1893.

Gettysburg National Military Park Commission.
> *Annual Reports To The Secretary Of War 1893-1901.* Washington D.C.: Government Printing Office, 1902.

New York Monuments Commission for the Battlefields of Gettysburg and Chattanooga. *Final Report on the Battlefield of Gettysburg.* Albany, New York: J. B. Lyons and Company, 1902.

Office of the Adjutant General of Massachusetts.
> *Massachusetts Soldiers, Sailors and Marines in the Civil War.* Brookline, Massachusetts: Riverdale Press, 1935.

Reed, John, Sylvester Byrne, Frederick Middleton, et al, representing the survivors of the Seventy-second Regiment of Pennsylvania Volunteers, Plaintiffs vs. Gettysburg Battlefield Memorial Association, and John P. Taylor, J. P. S. Gobin, John P. Nicholson, and R. B. Ricketts, Commissioners appointed by the Governor of the State of Pennsylvania, Defendants.

Testimony in the Court of Common Pleas of Adams County. In Equity,
No.1. January Term, 1889.

Report of the Select Committee Relative to the Soldiers' National Cemetery.
Commonwealth of Pennsylvania, 1865.

U.S. War Department.
*The War of the Rebellion: A Compilation of the Official Records of the Union
and Confederate Armies.* 128 volumes. Washington D.C.: U.S. Government
Printing Office, 1880-1901.

Books and Articles

Adams, John G. B. *Reminiscences of the Nineteenth Massachusetts Regiment.*
Boston, Massachusetts, Wright & Potter Printing Company, 1899.

Adelman, Garry E., and Timothy H. Smith. *Devil's Den: A History and Guide.*
Gettysburg, Pennsylvania, Thomas Publications, 1997.

Arrington, B.T. *The Medal of Honor at Gettysburg.* Gettysburg, Pennsylvania:
Thomas Publications, 1996.

Bachelder, John B. *Gettysburg: What To See, And How To See It.* Boston,
Massachusetts: John B. Bachelder, Publisher, 1873.

Barnes, Joseph K., ed. *The Medical and Surgical History of the Civil War.*
12 vols. Washington, D.C.: Government Printing Office, 1870.

Beyer, W. F., and O. F. Keydel. *Deeds of Valor.* Stamford, Connecticut:
Longmeadow Press, 1992.

Boatner, Mark M., III, *The Civil War Dictionary.* New York, New York: David
McKay Company, Inc., 1959.

Bowen, George A., ed. "The Diary of Captain George D. Bowen, 12th New
Jersey Volunteers." *Valley Forge Journal 2* (1984).

Bowen, James L. *Massachusetts in the War 1861-1865.* Springfield,
Massachusetts: Bowen & Son, 1893.

Bruce, George A. *The Twentieth Regiment of Massachusetts Infantry.* Baltimore,
Maryland: Butternut and Blue, 1988.

Busey, John W. *The Last Full Measure - Burials in the Soldiers' National Cemetery
at Gettysburg.* Hightstown, New Jersey: Longstreet House, 1988.

———. *These Honored Dead.* Hightstown, New Jersey: Longstreet House, 1988.

Chamberlain, Joshua L. *The Passing of the Armies.* Dayton, Ohio: Press of
Morningside Bookshop, 1982.

Chesson, Michael B., ed. *J. Franklin Dyer - The Journal of a Civil War Surgeon.*
Lincoln, Nebraska. University of Nebraska Press, 2003.

Coates, Earl J., and Dean S. Thomas. *An Introduction To Civil War Small Arms.*

Gettysburg, Pennsylvania: Thomas Publications, 1990.

Coco, Gregory A. *A Vast Sea of Misery: A History and Guide to the Union and Confederate Field Hospitals at Gettsyburg, July 1 - November 20, 1863.* Gettysburg, Pennsylvania: Thomas Publications, 1988.

——. *From Ball's Bluff to Gettysburg…and Beyond.* Gettysburg, Pennsylvania: Thomas Publications, 1994.

Coddington, Edwin B. *The Gettysburg Campaign: A Study In Command.* Dayton, Ohio: Press Of Morningside Bookshop, 1979.

Devereux, Arthur F. "Some Account of Pickett's Charge at Gettysburg." *Magazine of American History 18* (July - December 1887):13-19.

Dixon, Benjamin Y. *"The Gettysburg Battlefield, One Century Ago."* Gettysburg, Pennsylvania: Adams County History, Adams County Historical Society, 2000.

Ducharme, Robert R. *"A Journey Into Hell." The story of Co. "E" Fifteenth Massachusetts Regiment in the War of the Rebellion 1861 - 1864.* Privately Printed. No date.

Earle, David M. *History of the Excursion of the Fifteenth Massachusetts Regiment and its Friends to the Battle-fields of Gettysburg, Pa., Antietam, Md., Balls Bluff, Virginia, and Washington, D.C. May 31 - June 12, 1886.* Worcester, Massachusetts: Press of Charles Hamilton, 1886.

Elmore, Thomas L. "Torrid Heat and Blinding Rain: A Meteorological and Astronomical Chronology of the Gettysburg Campaign," *The Gettysburg Magazine*, no. 13, 1995.

Ent, Uzal W. "The world's most famous Civil War site became a tourist attraction as soon as the guns fell silent." *America's Civil War,* July, 2002.

Faust, Patricia L., ed. *The Historical Times Illustrated Encyclopedia of the Civil War.* New York, New York: Harper and Row, 1986.

Fay, Eli. *Discourse at the Funeral of Hans P. Jorgensen.* Fitchburg, Massachusetts: Caleb C. Curtis, 1863.

Ford, Andrew E. *The Story of the Fifteenth Regiment Massachusetts Volunteer Infantry in the Civil War, 1861 - 1864.* Clinton, Massachusetts: Press of W.J. Coulter, 1898.

Fox, William L. *Regimental Losses In The American Civil War 1861 - 1865.* Dayton, Ohio: Press of Morningside Bookshop, 1985.

Frassanito, William A. *Early Photography at Gettysburg.* Gettysburg, Pennsylvania: Thomas Publications, 1995.

——. *Gettysburg: A Journey In Time.* New York, New York: Charles Scribner's Sons, 1975.

———. *Gettysburg Then and Now: Touring The Battlefield With Old Photographs, 1863-1889*. Gettysburg, Pennsylvania: Thomas Publications, 1996.

French, William, William Barry and Henry Hunt, Captains. *Instruction in Field Artillery*. New York, New York: D. Van Nostrand, 1864.

Gallagher, Gary W., ed. *The Third Day at Gettysburg and Beyond*. Chapel Hill, North Carolina: University of North Carolina Press, 1994.

Georg, Kathleen R., comp. *The Location of the Monuments, Markers, and Tablets on Gettysburg Battlefield*. Eastern National Park and Monument Association in cooperation with Gettysburg National Military Park, 1984.

———. "Patriotic and Enduring Efforts: An Introduction to the Gettysburg Battlefield Commision." Gettysburg 1895-1995: *The Shaping of an American Shrine*, March 4, 1995.

Georg, Kathleen R., and John W. Busey. *Nothing But Glory: Pickett's Division at Gettysburg*. Hightstown, New Jersey: Longstreet House, 1987.

Gettysburg and Harrisburg Railroad Company. *To Gettysburg By Train*. Gettysburg, Pennsylvania: Thomas Publications, 1988.

Gibbon, John. *Personal Recollections of the Civil War*. Dayton, Ohio: Press of Morningside Bookshop, 1978.

Gottfried, Bradley M. "Wright's Charge on July 2, 1863: Piercing the Union Line or Inflated Glory?," *The Gettysburg Magazine*, no. 20, July 1997.

Gray, John C., and John C. Ropes. *War Letters 1862-1865 of John Chipman Gray and John Codman Ropes*, ed. Worthington Chauncey Ford. Cambridge, Massachusetts: The Riverside Press, 1927.

Hardee, W. J. *Hardee's Rifle and Light Infantry Tactics*. New York, New York: J.O. Kane, 1862.

Haskell, Frank A. *The Battle of Gettysburg*. Boston, Massachusetts: Houghton Mifflin Company, 1957.

Hawthorne, Frederick W. *Gettysburg: Stories of Men and Monuments as Told by Battlefield Guides*. Gettysburg, Pennsylvania: The Association of Licensed Battlefield Guides, 1988.

Hess, Earl J. *Pickett's Charge-The Last Attack at Gettysburg*. Chapel Hill, North Carolina: The University of North Carolina Press, 2001.

History of Edward W. Kinsley Post No. 113, G. A. R. Norwood, Massachusetts: The Norwood Press, 1913. Privately Printed.

History of Essex County, Massachusetts. Boston, Massachusetts: C.F. Jewett & Co., 1878. Privately Printed.

Holstein, Anna M. E. *Three Years in Field Hospitals of the Army of the Potomac*. Philadelphia, Pennsylvania: J. B. Lippincott & Co., 1867.

Howe, Mark De Wolfe. *Oliver Wendell Holmes - The Shaping Years, 1841-1870.* Cambridge, Massachusetts: Harvard University Press, 1957.

Hunt, Roger D. *Colonels In Blue: Union Army Colonels of the Civil War.* Atglen, Pennsylvania: Schiffer Military History, 2001.

Hunt, Roger D., and Roger R. Brown. *Brevet Brigadier Generals In Blue.* Gaithersburg, Maryland: Olde Soldier Books Inc., 1990.

Jamison, Jocelyn P., comp. *They Died at Fort Delaware 1861 - 1865.* Delaware City, Delaware: The Fort Delaware Society, 1997.

Kennell, Brian A. *Beyond the Gatehouse: Gettysburg's Evergreen Cemetery.* Gettysburg, Pennsylvania: Evergreen Cemetery Association, 2000.

Ladd, David L. and Audrey J. Ladd, eds. *The Bachelder Papers: Gettysburg in Their Own Words.* 3 vols. Dayton, Ohio: Press of Morningside Bookshop, 1994-1995.

Lang, George, Raymond Collins and Gerard White, comps. *Medal of Honor Recipients,1863-1994.* New York, New York: Facts on File Inc., 1995.

McGlaughlin, David M. "Monumental Litigation." *The Gettysburg Magazine,* no. 20, January 1999.

McPherson, James M. *Battle Cry Of Freedom: The Civil War Era.* New York, New York: Ballantine Books, 1988.

Marvin, Abijah P. *History of Worcester in the War of the Rebellion.* Worcester, Massachusetts: Privately printed, 1870.

A Memorial of Paul Joseph Revere and Edward H. Revere. Boston, Massachusetts: Wm. Parsons Lunt, 1874. Privately Printed.

Miller, Richard F. "Brahmins Under Fire: Peer Courage and the Harvard Regiment," *Historical Journal of Massachusetts,* XXX (Winter 2002).

——. "The Trouble with Brahmins: Class and Ethnic Tensions in Massachusetts' Harvard Regiment," *New England Quarterly,* (March 2003).

Miller, Richard F., and Robert F. Mooney. *The Civil War: The Nantucket Experience.* Nantucket, Massachusetts: Wesco Publishing, 1994.

Murray, R. L. *Hurrah for the Ould Flag.* Savannah, New York: Seeco Printing Services, 1998.

Perry, Martha A., comp. *Letters from a Surgeon of the Civil War.* Cambridge, Massachusetts: Little, Brown and Company, 1906.

Pfanz, Harry W. *Gettysburg - The Second Day.* Chapel Hill, North Carolina: The University of North Carolina Press, 1987.

——. *Gettysburg - Culp's Hill and Cemetery Hill.* Chapel Hill, North Carolina: The University of North Carolina Press, 1993.

Platt, Barbara L. *"This is holy ground": A history of the Gettysburg Battlefield.*

Harrisburg, Pennsylvania: Barbara L. Platt, 2001.

Priest, John M. *Victory Without Triumph.* Shippensburg, Pennsylvania: The White Mane Publishing Company, Inc., 1996.

Purcell, Hugh Devereux. *The Nineteenth Massachusetts Regiment At Gettysburg.* Essex Institute Historical Collections, Salem, Massachusetts, October 1963.

Raus, Edmund J., Jr. *A Generation on the March - The Union Army at Gettysburg.* Lynchburg, Virginia: H.E. Howard, Inc., 1987

Reardon, Carol. *Pickett's Charge in History and Memory.* Chapel Hill, North Carolina: The University of North Carolina Press, 1997.

Rhea, Gordon C. *The Battle of the Wilderness May 5-6, 1864.* Baton Rouge, Louisiana: Louisiana State University Press, 1994.

———. *The Battles for Spotsylvania Court House and the Road to Yellow Tavern May 7-12, 1864.* Baton Rouge, Louisiana: Louisiana State University Press, 1997.

Rhodes, J. H. *The History of Battery B, First Rhode Island Artillery in the War to Preserve the Union, 1861 - 1865.* Providence, Rhode Island: Snow and Farnham, 1894.

Rice, Edmund. "Repelling Lee's Last Blow at Gettysburg." *Battles and Leaders of the Civil War.* vol. 3. New York, New York: Thomas Yoseloff, 1956.

Roe, Alfred S. *Monuments, Tablets and Other Memorials Erected in Massachusetts to Commemorate the Services of Her Sons in the War of the Rebellion 1861-1865.* Boston, Massachusetts: Wright & Potter Printing Company, 1910.

Richard, Rollins. *The Damned Red Flags of the Rebellion.* Redondo Beach, California: Rank and File Publications, 1997.

Sale, James I. *"Pickett's Charge," The Philadelphia Weekly Press* (4 July 1887).

Sauers, Richard A. "John B. Bachelder: Government Historian of the Battle of Gettysburg," *The Gettysburg Magazine*, no. 3, July 1990.

Sears, Stephen W. *Gettysburg.* New York, New York: Houghton Mifflin Company, 2003.

Schultz, David. *"Double Canister at Ten Yards": The Federal Artillery and the Repulse of Pickett's Charge.* Redondo Beach, California: Rank and File Publications, 1995.

Scott, Robert Garth, ed. *Fallen Leaves: The Civil War Letters of Major Henry Livermore Abbott.* Kent, Ohio: The Kent State University Press, 1991.

Secrist, Henry T. "The Pudding-Stone," *The Roxbury Magazine*, 1899.

Stewart, George R. *Pickett's Charge: A Microhistory of the Final Attack at Gettysburg, July 3, 1863.* Boston, Massachusetts: Houghton Mifflin

Company, 1959.

Storrick, William C. "When I Saw and Heard Mr. Lincoln," *American History Magazine*, August, 2003.

Talbott, John. "Combat Trauma in the American Civil War," *History Today*, vol. 46, no.13 (March 1996).

Trudeau, Noah Andre. *Gettysburg: A Testing of Courage*. New York, New York: Harper Collins Publishers Inc., 2002.

——. *The Last Citadel: Petersburg, Virginia, June 1864-April 1865*. Boston, Massachusetts: Little, Brown and Company, 1991.

Tucker, Glenn. *High Tide At Gettysburg*. Dayton, Ohio: Press of Morningside Bookshop, 1973.

Vanderslice, John M. *Gettysburg, Then and Now*. Dayton, Ohio: Press of Morningside Bookshop, 1983.

Ward, George W. *History of the Excursion of the Fifteenth Massachusetts Regiment and its Friends to the Battlefields of Gettysburg, Antietam, Balls Bluff and the City of Washington, D.C. September 14-20, 1900*. Worcester, Massachusetts: Press of O.B. Wood, 1901.

Warner, Ezra J. *Generals in Blue*. Baton Rouge, Louisiana: Louisiana State University Press, 1964.

Wentworth, Thomas, ed. *Harvard Memorial Biographies*. 2 vols. Cambridge, Massachusetts: Sever and Francis, 1866.

Wert, J. Howard. *A Complete Hand-Book of the Monuments and Indications and Guide to the Positions of the Gettysburg Battle-Field*. Harrisburg, Pennsylvania: R. M. Sturgeon & Co., 1886.

Wert, Jeffery D. *Gettysburg Day Three*. New York, New York: Simon & Schuster, 2001.

Wiley, Bell Irwin. *The Life of Billy Yank*. Baton Rouge, Louisiana: Louisiana State University Press, 1971.

Wise, Jennings C. *The Long Arm of Lee*. Lynchburg, Virginia: J. P. Bell Company, Inc., 1915.

INDEX

ABOUT THE AUTHORS

Edwin R. Root is a retired systems business analyst. Mr. Root is a two-time past president of the Civil War Round Table of Eastern Pennsylvania, Inc. in Allentown, Pennsylvania. A long-time advocate of historic preservation, he has also served on the Board of Directors of the Civil War Library and Museum (now the Underground Railroad and Civil War Museum of Philadelphia) and the Gettysburg Battlefield Preservation Association. He is currently a member of the Board of Families of Flight 93, Inc., serving in memory of his cousin, Lorraine G. Bay. He was a member of the jury which selected the recommended design for the new National Park Service Flight 93 Memorial in Somerset County, Pennsylvania. This will honor the heroic actions of the plane's forty crew members and passengers on September 11, 2001. Mr. Root resides in Coopersburg, Pennsylvania with his wife, Nancy, and numerous cats.

Jeffrey D. Stocker is a practicing attorney in Allentown, Pennsylvania. He is a 1980 graduate of Muhlenberg College with a Bachelor of Arts degree in History; in 1983 he graduated from Temple University School of Law. Mr. Stocker is the editor of *From Huntsville to Appomattox,* Robert T. Coles' History of the 4th Alabama Infantry Regiment, which was published by the University of Tennessee Press in 1996, as part of their Voices of the Civil War Series. A past president of the Civil War Round Table of Eastern Pennsylvania, Inc., Mr. Stocker resides in Center Valley, Pennsylvania with his wife, Marliese Walter, and several cats.

OCT   2007